PREPARE FOR THE LANDINGS!

Part One of the Divine Blueprint Series

By

Michael Ellegion

&

Aurora Light

Edited by:
Marcia L. Walker, Ph.D.

Cover & Illustrations by:
Rebecca Sherwood

PREPARE FOR THE LANDINGS!

Vortex Network

6929 N. Hayden Rd., Suite 408

Scottsdale, Arizona 85250

TABLE OF CONTENTS

ABOUT THE FRONT COVER SCENE & ARTIST

This very prophetic image, created by Visionary Artist Rebecca Sherwood, spontaneously manifested one day after experiencing a private transformational channeling session with Michael Ellegion. During her session, she experienced a very personal and powerful "Creative Cosmic Activation" which shifted her artistic career from a traditional design to a completely different expressive style. Her present work now reflects a creative style that is attuned to the Higher Cosmic Energies that are sweeping the planet as Mother Earth's Ascension begins to speed up.

This cover scene is a very realistic one that exhibits what is Destined to occur very soon when mass Divine Intervention takes place. It represents thousands of Merkabah Lightships of the Intergalactic Confederation that descend toward Earth to begin what is called "First Contact" which is the start of the waves of Worldwide Evacuation.

Rebecca has "Cosmically Subliminally Encoded" specific Higher energetic words, symbols, and frequencies within this historical image. Although the conscious mind does not see these images, the subconscious mind will detect them and this will help "Cosmically Trigger" the lifting of the "Cosmic Amnesia Veils" that most Light Workers had placed over their minds before taking Earth embodiment. The lifting of these veils will help them remember their Cosmic origins and beautiful memories that they have of Higher realms. These Volunteer Souls of Light will experience a wonderful Awakening of their Missions on the planet. At the same time, this scene is designed to help draw the dark "denial spirits" back to the Light and to disempower them from any more sabotaging of the Sacred Laws of Creation.

Rebecca warmly welcomes personal requests for similar and unique Cosmic and planetary scenes. She may be emailed at: sherwooddesign@comcast.net. You may also call her at: 248-363-5129.

DEDICATION

We dedicate this book:

To God, our Divine Creator, the I Am That I Am, our Radiant One; Who's Divine Blueprint Plan and Sacred Promise of Divine Intervention is about to be Fulfilled.

To all members of all Commands and Fleets of the Intergalactic Confederation of Worlds/Universal Federation of Light who orbit this planet in Guardian Action and who Monitor, Protect, and Overshadow all Volunteers and Light Workers presently in Earth embodiment.

To all those who are fulfilling their Missions of helping heal Mother Earth and assisting with her Ascension experience.

To those involved in exposing and transmuting all imbalanced forces of the "cabal" and, thus, ushering in the long overdue Golden Age of Peace.

To all the early '50's contactees who were the authentic Pioneers of the original "Flying Saucer Movement," including George Adamski, Howard Menger, George Van Tassel, Aleo Angelucci, and all the other equally well-known initiates from that Era.

To Tuella, and to the other very clear Channels, who have helped Prepare humanity by providing details of the Plan for the upcoming Divine Intervention.

And to all our fellow Volunteers (Souls of Light) who are also known as Star People, Wanderers, Walk-ins, Indigos, and Crystal Children. We salute you as you lift your "Cosmic Amnesia Veils" and we honor your courage and "Unbearable Compassion" for having Volunteered to leave the more-advanced worlds and take Earth embodiment at this time, as we now Prepare to complete our Missions and fulfill the **SACRED PROMISE**!

Michael Ellegion & Aurora Light

ABOUT THE AUTHORS...

MICHAEL ELLEGION

Michael Ellegion has had a fascinating and unique background, having been trained in the Edgar Cayce method of Channeling at a very young age. While growing up in southern California, he experienced a life-threatening emergency. During this life-changing event, Michael was physically beamed aboard a Higher Dimensional "Merka-bah" Lightship where he encountered very spiritually-evolved angelic ETs. These benevolent human-appearing beings rescued him and helped release his trauma from the experience. Throughout the years, he has had numerous "etheric" visitations from these same Cosmic Beings of Light who have shared extensive information with him about numerous topics.

In 1979, he experienced another life-threatening emergency and was once again physically beamed aboard a Merkabah Lightship. During this encounter, his DNA/RNA was vibrationally altered by these Space Brothers, so that he would be able to do Trans-formational Channeling. Since then, Michael has become well-known for these Channeling sessions that help fellow Volunteers awaken to their individual Missions. These "Star People" who have taken Earth embodiment at this time are from more advanced worlds.

Unlike most Volunteers, he was born without the Veils or "Cosmic Amnesia" being in place. Therefore, he has had conscious memory of his Galactic past and recalls being a member of the Higher Councils of Light. These Councils are a part of the Universal Federation of which the benevolent human-appearing beings also belong.

One of the memories that Michael refers to herein is the "SACRED PROMISE" that was specifically discussed in these Higher Councils by these "Guardians of Light." He explains that this is a DEFINITE PLAN to manifest planetary Divine Intervention and a Worldwide Evacuation, which includes mass landings.

In addition to Michael's physical encounters aboard the Lightships, he has also had the wonderful experience of having an ET (who was incognito and looked like any other Earthling) walk right up to him on Earth and telepathically communicate very critical information. Michael has had numerous other communications with these same Higher Forces in which the information about the DEFINITE PLAN was VERIFIED and RECONFIRMED. At the present time, it is critical to understand that we, on the planet, are getting very close to this awesome historical moment when at long-last this planet will officially become a member of the Intergalactic Confederation, as we join our Cosmic Extended Family throughout the Intergalactic Realms of Light. Yes, this book truly does help one *"Prepare for the Landings!"*

AURORA LIGHT
(a.k.a. Aurora Ellegion)

Since her early years growing up, Aurora has had first-hand knowledge of human-appearing extraterrestrials. Her experiences consist of more than one life-saving intervention, visitations, telepathic communications, and having been aboard their craft. It seems that Aurora was destined to speak out on the controversial subject of UFOs and ET contact.

Aurora has had a colorful and interesting background, having appeared on hundreds of television and radio shows over the past two decades, including the BBC and Armed Forces Radio. She has produced, directed, hosted, and been a guest on programs that have dealt with many cutting-edge subjects. Two of the many topics that she has spoken out about are: human-appearing extraterrestrials and the nature of the extraterrestrial cover-up.

Throughout the years, she has lectured to standing-room-only-crowds at Universities from Hawaii to Florida. Since having met with many ex-undercover agents and ex-military personal, Aurora has learned that the truth is out there and that a concerted effort by our government has kept it from us. She feels at last the veils are lifting and the tie-in between science, religion, global politics, economics, and social engineering can now be addressed in a cohesive way. Aurora believes that it is time for the final showdown on Earth between good and evil, freedom and control-enslavement, and openness and secrecy to come to the awareness of all, and, specifically, it is time for a spiritual activation to take place within us to save mankind and planet Earth from destruction.

Aurora has worked privately with individuals as a Muse and a health intuitive helping thousands of people realize and tap into their Higher natures, and to discover greater health and rejuvenation for themselves. She is a trained hypnotherapist who works with past-life regressions and teaches an ancient technique called "tresspasso" that allows people to see their own (and others) past lives. With a strong background in metaphysics, Aurora has had many "Signs" and insights that she will share with you, the reader, in this book and throughout the Divine Blueprint Series.

INTRODUCTION

This is the first book of "The Divine Blueprint Series" which is the compilation of many years of our (Michael & Aurora's) first-hand experiences and communications with benevolent, angelic-type human-appearing ETs, as well as information from numerous other contactees and channels with similar experiences. Until recently, the theme of this book would have been considered extremely "controversial" by many within the "UFO community" and probably would have been rejected by them due to their lack of understanding, their bias, and their "hidden agendas."

Now, since there has been a recent consciousness shift on the planet, many individuals are more open to considering the "possibility" that this planet will, in fact, be experiencing what is referred to as a mass planetary "Divine Intervention." This Divine Intervention will include mass landings of starships at some point in the very near future.

The fact is that over the years, there have been many reports by the mass media about the negative "grey aliens" who have come to Earth to abduct humans for experimentations. At the same time, there has been major suppression and denial in regard to positive encounters with benevolent human-appearing beings. The truth is that the majority of those coming to this planet are these angelic Beings.

There was a surge of information during the "flying saucer movement" ('50's and early '60's), when the original and sincere Pioneers, the contactees of that era, were having encounters and communications, as we have had, with these very beautiful and benevolent human-appearing ETs. Unfortunately, there has been a major "cover-up" during the last few decades, where "agents of disinformation" (with secret ties to the cabal) have attempted to mislead the public about these Beings. These "spin doctors," who refer to themselves as "professional" UFO investigators are well-known names within the UFO community.

This book will start you on a journey toward understanding the truth about these wonderful Beings and their Mission to help us on planet Earth, particularly during the present times of extreme upheaval that is occurring, as well as what we will be encountering in the very near future. Readers will also gain an understanding of the Divine Intervention and the Worldwide Evacuation that has been planned from on-High and what should be done to Prepare for this imminent Event. Recent messages from these Beings through numerous sources (personal contacts and channelings) suggest that humanity on Earth will very soon be receiving more direct help which will guarantee our survival as a species. They will also be assisting us on Earth in spiritually uplifting this planet. This book verifies the DEFINITE PLAN AND SACRED PROMISE of this occurring and will help the reader *"Prepare for the Landings!"*

CHAPTER 1

MICHAEL'S FIRST EXPERIENCES

Memory at Birth

Realization, or rather firsthand knowledge of the reality of existing benevolent extraterrestrials, was something I have always had. I clearly remember my ET connection prior to and even at birth during this present earth incarnation. When my first experience as a contactee occurred, during my early childhood, it was merely a physical confirmation to me of what I already knew for certain to be true. In fact, these unusual experiences that I had were all destined to occur as I had written them into my "life script" prior to my taking earth embodiment.

These extraterrestrials that I had physical contact with were actually very familiar to me. I clearly remember saying goodbye to them when I prepared to leave my other body before coming to earth. That much more evolved human-appearing, "Higher density," immortal physical body was left in a type of Higher energy storage. Approximately 20 minutes before I was born, my soul and spirit was literally projected down from the Merkabah Lightship I was on into my Earth mother's womb.

I do not remember much concerning the moment of my being propelled into the womb. However, I do clearly recall that on the Higher worlds of the Confederation, the more advanced human-appearing ETs are not physically born through the womb, but are instead "energy-birthed." These highly advanced Cosmic parents, as I refer to them, literally materialize the body as a beautiful infant child. The infant is not a cloned being; rather, the child's spirit, body energy, and personality are always "Divinely Unique."

Just as the millions of my fellow volunteer extraterrestrial souls did, I recall that I volunteered for a particular mission and chose my parents specifically to help me fulfill that mission. In fact, on the Higher dimensional worlds of the Confederation there is actually a type of "Cosmic referral service." The Volunteers are allowed to choose from the best possible choices concerning what one needs to help them to fulfill their earthly missions and to hopefully be examples to others on how to overcome the many obstacles they have to face.

Unfortunately in regard to Earth parents, there is a limited selection from which the Volunteers can choose. This is not meant to be critical of Earth parents, considering what they have to put up with when we more evolved and intellectually challenging individuals are born through them. In reality, there are many challenges that both the Earth parents and the incoming soul have to deal with, some quite humorous. This is indeed quite a learning and eye-opening experience for both parties!

My particular parents were specifically chosen because they were attuned to a metaphysical philosophy and because of their holistic natural health interests. Metaphysically, they were both very interested in the famous American psychic-channel, Edgar Cayce. This turned out to be of great importance to my future work as a channel. Also, I knew with their more natural lifestyle, that I would be allowed to grow up healthy and that my immune system would not be jeopardized and weakened. As a child, I ate only healthy, natural foods, rather than the sensitivity numbing, refined, and processed "garbage" diet that most people tend to eat.

As a matter of fact, one of the worst forms of child abuse that so many of today's Earth parents are guilty of, is all the chemically grown, refined, processed unwholesome food that they feed their children, rather than real quality, healthy foods that are meant to truly nourish their physical bodies. Then, they wonder why they have birth defects, behavioral and learning problems, sickness, and disease - it's all such a huge mystery!

Before coming into Earth embodiment, I was also aware of information that would threaten the billion dollar profits of certain money interests connected with the dental, medical, and powerful pharmaceutical cartel. I knew that my parents were enlightened about the dangers of fluoride and vaccinations and that I would not be forced to take either of these dangerous, insight-numbing, poisonous substances into my pure temple of the Holy Spirit. In my opinion, the fact that I did not have the free fluoride treatments given to me at my school or the many vaccinations is why today both my consciousness, as well as my immune system, is much stronger and healthier. I realize this is contrary to what the mass-publicized and accepted version is and what the medical sources of news and the information establishment wants to brainwash us into believing

I must share this particular health information with the readers, because this is one of the most important factors that helped me choose who I would incarnate through in this my final Earth life. This was very important for my particular mission and for being here in Earth embodiment. The health aspect would definitely influence my being as attuned as I wanted and needed to be in order to be the very clear "Cosmic telephone line" or direct-voice and telepathic channel that I was to become.

This prepared me to channel the Higher knowledge and Cosmic-harmonic energy-frequencies that would help awaken or trigger the many other fellow

Volunteers. These important Volunteers must have their extraterrestrial DNA activated, so that their Cosmic amnesia can now be removed. Most Volunteers are born with amnesia that has been placed over their minds and consciousness as a protection. Once their extraterrestrial DNA is activated, they can then get on with their individual missions, their reasons for being here.

It was this consciousness knowledge and memory of who I was prior to this Earth life, and the fact that I literally had "Friends in High Places" off this planet on Higher dimensions, that helped give me strength and inspiration. Not too many of the mundane and everyday childhood problems or challenges got me down or bothered me as much as other children may have experienced, because I naturally had a much deeper and more philosophical Cosmic insight into this third dimensional level of existence.

Often I could see and hear what went on in these Higher dimensions or realms of consciousness, so I tended not to "sweat the small stuff" or get very attached to it. I had the "this too shall pass" attitude, knowing that when I matured I would begin to fulfill my life's true mission and purpose. My "individual prime directive" is part of the "collective prime directive" of all the volunteers here in Earth embodiment from the Higher worlds of the Intergalactic Confederation.

Volunteer Souls

The Volunteer souls have been termed "Star People" by authors Brad and Francie Stieger, who are well known for their interviews with NASA scientists and engineers. A list of Star People Characteristics can be found in a following chapter.

Some of these Volunteers come into the earthly realm as incarnates at the time of birth. Others come into the earthly realm years later as "Walk-ins," as author Ruth Montgomery first coined the phrase in her famous books titled Strangers Among Us and Aliens Among Us. Research shows that there are two types of "Walk-ins." One type is a complete soul transfer and the other is known as a "soul-mergence."

The process known as "soul transfer" takes place as a "Walk-in" occurs. An entirely different soul of Higher extraterrestrial origin, often with a very different and more powerful personality, suddenly comes down in place of the other less advanced soul of Earth origin. This most often occurs because the soul that has chosen to leave is ready to move on and is crying out for Higher help. These replaced souls are asking for immediate relief from a situation that they do not feel capable of handling. So, these souls are then released from this embodiment and replaced by a "Walk-in" soul, a Volunteer.

In the case of a "soul-mergence," the original soul remains in the body and allows the other soul to assist with their Mission. This also strengthens the person and helps them in fulfilling their Destiny.

An aspect that the Volunteers may confront is that they may have created some karma for themselves in their past lives on earth, which necessitates in their having to again connect with certain individuals to balance things out. As an example, upon looking into the background of the saints throughout the ages, many of them had really rough childhoods, which were probably connected to their karma from earlier lives. However, they were able to move beyond this and by their loving and forgiving examples, they have lessened the suffering, hatred, and karma of this planet.

All Volunteers have been forewarned and prepared as best as they could be, prior to taking Earth embodiment, to be aware of the imbalanced or dark forces and the military-industrial complex. These dark astral forces are often utilized by the cabal or illuminati. The Volunteers are aware that these forces will attempt to attack and destroy them through various forms of deadly force, both physical and psychic in nature.

My Fall from the Oceanside Pier

I grew up in the small town of Vista, California. Psychologically, I tended to be somewhat withdrawn and silent as a child, because of the conscious memory of my beautiful and joyous past on the Higher worlds. I realized that most people would not be open to my sharing what I knew concerning these Higher Worlds and would just assume that I must have quite an overactive imagination.

I believe I literally went unconscious during my very early years on the planet, because my next conscious memory is when I was six years of age. Few experiences of my childhood have struck in my mind as clearly as that which took place during the summer of 1959.

On a warm sunny day, my parents, my older brother, and I were walking along the pier in Oceanside, California. Out of more than normal curiosity and without realization or fear of the possible consequences, I decided to climb up onto the railing alongside the pier where I proceeded to precariously stand. It is still very clear in my mind that it was not enough for me to climb up to the top of the railing, but I also had a strong compulsion to lean far over the perilous ledge. It is my perception that under the subtle disguise of curiosity and showing off, that my Higher Self allowed me to be in that dangerous position which permitted a subtle attempt by the dark astral forces to emotionally-psychologically traumatize me. On a conscious level, I assumed in my innocence that I was just showing off, as many young children will tend to do. I was just being like so many other kids who have unknowingly climbed into dangerous places.

My next recollection was the sudden terror when I realized I had foolishly leaned too far forward, uncontrollably slipping over the side. The moment was filled with sickening fear. I had the realization that I could not at that instant do anything except fall into the turbulent ocean, which seemed at that young age much further than the forty feet below me. On the Higher Worlds, I recall having the ability to naturally levitate, teleport, and having use of other Higher Powers, unfortunately I clearly realized at that terrifying childhood moment, I did not possess these Higher Powers of levitation.

For those who do not believe in such a reality, what happened next may seem inconceivable. Just as the ocean came crashing up to engulf me, I found myself instantaneously in an entirely different environment. I was physically back in, what to me, had always been my real home environment; an environment that I consciously remembered since birth on this third dimensional planet. I have recalled being aboard these incredibly beautiful and magnificent Lightships (often sighted as UFOs here on earth) which are also known as "Merkabahs" within the Confederation.

Initially in shock, I was overwhelmed by all the incredible joy and excitement. The beautiful chamber that I suddenly found myself physically transported into was a type of medical or examination room that was illuminated by glowing white walls. I want to stress here that this was not an astral, out-of-body, or etheric experience; my body was most certainly physically there.

It took a moment for my eyes to fully adjust to the beautiful, soft glowing light that was emanating from the actual walls of the ship itself. Then I saw very human-appearing, beautiful beings standing around me. Of course, because of the suddenness of my physical reappearance into an entirely different environment, it was somewhat disconcerting to my Earthly-human conscious self for the first few moments. To be truthful, most humans would have called this an "alien" environment.

Instinctively, I reached out to touch the nearby glowing white wall of the chamber. There was an unusual sensation - a warm feeling and loving response to my touch - as if the wall itself was alive. Actually, this was reassuring to me as I experienced incredible feelings of love, as if the very walls of the ship telepathically were comforting me and I remembered this Higher consciousness technology that the ships of the Confederation utilized.

Feelings of exaltation coursed through me with the incredible beauty, joy, and wonderment of the ship's miraculous surroundings. These feelings conflicted drastically with the horrifying terror I had experienced only a few moments earlier. I was initially expecting to slam into the cold turbulent ocean and instead here I was standing in this lovely, peaceful, wonderful environment.

I have attempted to find suitable earthly terms to describe this joyous celebration and wonderful love that I was experiencing aboard this Lightship. To accurately describe these feelings, the closest I have come (and this is a rough analogy) is to ask others to think back to a time when they had felt the greatest joy or other wonderful feelings that they can remember and then imagine multiplying this feeling a thousand times. This analogy can only partially explain what I was experiencing, being physically back amongst my wonderful Cosmic relatives.

The Merkabah Beings

The attractive beings standing near me were all dressed in metallic blue and silver colored jumpsuits. If they had been dressed in Earth clothes, they could have easily have passed as very good-looking humans. Eight of them were in the immediate chamber, four men and four women. They were all approximately six to seven feet tall and all of them had magnificent body structures – youthful, muscular, and well-proportioned. Their skin had a golden copper hue, rather like how a good suntan looks, yet somewhat translucent in quality. Most of them had beautiful golden-colored hair, although some had golden-brown. Their eyes were shaped like ours here on Earth with either bright-blue, violet, green, or golden pupils. Through their eyes and through the energy around them, they exhibited a feeling that radiated love and compassion that was directed towards me. They appeared to be between thirty and forty years old (in Earth ages), though with faces that expressed great wisdom for their apparent ages.

I immediately recognized two of the beings as my Higher Cosmic parents and I knew their names were Lord Orion and Lady Angelica. Orion, who is written about in many metaphysical teachings, has been referred to as an Elohim and is also titled the "Protector of the Christ Energies." He is directly under the command of our great Commander-In-Chief, Sananda (Lord Jesus the Christ). Lord Orion is a most handsome and regally magnificent appearing being, with golden hair and strong chiseled features. Lady Angelica is a very beautiful goddess, with a classic Grecian appearance.

I knew, in fact, that Lord Orion was in charge of a very powerful group or Command within the Intergalactic Confederation. This Command is known collectively as the Universal Federation of Light and the division that I recall being a part of is called the Jerusalem Command. I clearly remember that the Jerusalem Command was from the Higher 6th to 12th and 13th dimensional levels of the Universe and is also working closely with the Ashtar Command.

Years later growing up, I began to come across literature generated from other contactees and channels. These individuals also knew firsthand about these two Commands from either their own personal physical experience or from telepathic contacts with these Higher human-appearing extraterrestrial beings. My feelings and reactions to this contact were great joy, which is usually the case with those of us termed "contactees." It is quite the opposite for those termed "abductees."

There have been many books published on the topic of these renegade beings well known as the "grays" and the negative abductions that have been going on for numerous years. It is my opinion, as well as that of other contactees and the sincere unbiased UFO researchers in the field, that the majority of the well known UFO lecturers and writers on the subject of abductions are agents of disinformation or "spin-doctors" within the UFO community. In the next book of The Divine Blueprint Series, I will clearly explain and compare the differences between those who experience beautiful, uplifting encounters or reunions with human-appearing ETs and the abductions with the "grays." There is a definite reason why both types of UFO encounters are happening. There is also a reason why most UFO investigators have rarely talked about the human-appearing ETs and the more positive aspects of the UFO field, unless it has been to ridicule it. But, for now let's get back to my experience.

At that moment, all the many memories I had of who I had been prior to this present Earth life were totally confirmed by my being physically present in this Higher dimensional ship hovering above earth. As I was there in the Lightship examination room, both Lord Orion and Lady Angelica projected their strong love and understanding to me. In fact, I started to cry just like a child would who was reunited with his parents after a long separation. I began to express all the pain and loneliness that I was suddenly aware of. As my human emotions were overflowing, I expressed the fear and pain experienced on Earth since my birth six years before. I found myself literally pleading with them not to send me back again to Earth, even though I knew deep down I would have to go back.

I was aware that prior to taking Earth embodiment, I had written into my "life script" this encounter that I was now experiencing. These beings had physically intervened for a specific reason as they were fulfilling their personal promises to me. This experience was a physical reassurance to me that in extreme times of danger these Higher beings would, have, and will, divinely intervene, not only for me, but also for all my fellow Volunteers, until our Earthly missions are complete.

Realigning My Chakras

I stood by the glowing wall of the "medical chamber" taking in what were familiar surroundings. A sudden movement out of the corner of my eye attracted my attention, as an instrument merged out of the wall. The instrument resembled a large paddle, approximately a square foot in size and one inch in thickness that was attached to a flexible cable. One of the beings held it, passing it up and down around my body a few times, as bright rainbow colored rays shot out of the instrument into my body. I suddenly felt even greater inner peace and contentment.

Later, I realized they were realigning the seven main chakras or energy vortex points in my body. Oftentimes when an individual experiences trauma, the person's chakras can be weakened, unless one has learned how to quickly balance, align, and strengthen him or herself, through the use of powerful centering techniques. (Many years later, I have taught strengthening techniques in my workshops to specifically accomplish this very powerful alignment.)

The different colored harmonic frequencies that were being projected were the same as those of the seven main chakras as they appear clairvoyantly. These chakras are now scientifically proven to exist through advanced forms of Kirlian photography.

A shock or trauma that dramatically weakens the aura can cause one's immune system to become weakened on the physical level. That sudden and horrifying fall off the pier had definitely been enough to shock me out of balance. For that reason, these loving beings were helping realign my energy and bringing it back into balance and vitality.

During all this, there was an intense flow of telepathic communication from them to me. Some of it was comforting me from the trauma of falling off the pier and some of it was reminding me of why I was experiencing all of this. A lot of the communication was specific reconfirmation and verification, as I have stated, of what I had consciously remembered prior to taking Earth embodiment and was now experiencing while once again being aboard the Merkabah Lightship of the Confederation.

There was also a flow of important information that a normal child of six years is not usually allowed to know. Years later when watching the Superman movie, some of the scenes of Clark Kent as an infant in his little escape ship traveling thru the universe and eventually crashing on Earth, showed the scenes of knowledge very quickly flowing into his brain. These scenes were very similar to my real life telepathic experience aboard the Merkabah Lightship. Although the information I received was not from a machine, as in a fictional story, but instead it was from very real and compassionate, benevolent beings.

Much of this advanced knowledge and awareness, that included "Higher energy-harmonics," was stored deep within my consciousness for a future time when I needed access to it. I knew it was important that I grew up as a normal Earth child, except, of course, for my ability to be a clear channel for the Spiritual Hierarchy. This mission I had volunteered for was to inspire my fellow Volunteers and all truth seekers who will read this book. It was also to help trigger and awaken many precious souls to their true Cosmic heritage and to assist the activation of their Higher extraterrestrial DNA/RNA.

It is hard to say how long I was actually physically aboard the Lightship, because the Earthly concept of "time" does not exist on these Higher vibrational dimensions. I can only say that there was a "timelessness" aspect to this experience. As Earth beings know, "time" seems to go by much faster when we are enjoying ourselves, rather than if what we are experiencing is something boring or painful.

Lord Orion and Lady Angelica came over and were standing near me. Orion reached over with a firm, but gentle grasp, placing his hand upon my shoulder for a few moments. As I stared up at him, his intense compassionate eyes peered deep into my soul as he telepathically made a very significant statement: "You must go back now, my son, for the human race depends upon it." After his heart-felt statement, intense emotions again welled up very deep within me.

What he was stating was not that my mission was necessarily anymore important or of a higher priority than other Volunteers here in Earth embodiment, but it was more a reminder of how important it really was for me to stay on course and not get sidetracked, as has happened to so many of my fellow Volunteers. Unfortunately, some Volunteers have become casualties in this spiritual war against the dark forces who have tried to take over mankind on Earth and elsewhere in the cosmos. Never-the-less, each of these Volunteer missions are still individually, as well as collectively, very important for the whole process of Preparing this planet for the ultimate Divine Intervention.

What Orion next communicated to me, in those last brief moments of being physically onboard the Merkabah before they physically beamed me back to Earth, was actually blocked from my conscious mind until recently. Then, suddenly this whole interaction with Orion came flooding back into my conscious mind with great lucid clarity and the accompanying emotions of joy and revela-

12

tion. As the veil of Cosmic Amnesia parted, I became aware of the incredible significance of what he had shared with me and I knew I could now share this with others. I also sensed that this final telepathic message to me had been temporarily hidden for some reason, perhaps because when this very important memory surfaced it would be a CONFIRMATION of my experience many years before. And, maybe also, I would have been unable to retain the information at that time and it would have been too overwhelming for my six year-old self. And, quite possibly, the final message has more significance at the present time when I am closer to fulfilling my Mission on the planet and since the information pertains to what the benevolent forces of the Federation of Light have always been planning to do one day when the time was right. Regardless of the reasons why this information was not revealed to me earlier, when Orion did relay this message to me he did so with great intensity which I am sure was done so that it would be strongly positioned forever within my mind and consciousness until it was destined to be unveiled.

The key point that Orion revealed to me at that time was that one day I was destined to publish a book that would powerfully help Prepare humanity on Earth for the Divine Intervention and Worldwide Evacuation that is to take place. "This is most important for you," Orion stated, "to ultimately share with others this plan that we of the Federation have for the coming time on Earth. As your physical Earth body matures and you grow up, one of your main Missions will be to help Prepare (on a mass level) the inhabitants of Earth for this Divine Intervention which will require a Worldwide Evacuation that will include mass appearances and landings of our Lightships when the time is right."

He continued, "In fact, one of my close friends and a fellow Space Brother, who is a key member of the Higher Galactic Councils of Light, is Lord Ashtar. He has his own Command, the Ashtar Command. Ashtar will be playing a major role in fulfilling this ultimate plan for Earth's Ascension which will end the control of the imbalanced forces who have controlled this planet for many ages. You too, my son, have been very connected with the Ashtar Command, as well as a member of my own Command, the Jerusalem Command."

"Ashtar is also very spiritually connected with you, as you will discover and remember and he will be communicating with and through you quite extensively after you physically mature. He is, in fact, very much in charge of fulfilling this plan of what many others of the Federation have termed **Operation Deliverance**. This plan is one that you will share with others who will know deep within their hearts and souls that it is true. This is the plan of our Divine Creator we of the Federation would not do it. This plan will occur many decades in the (Earth time) when the time is right and it will definitely be fulfilled."

I was reminded that I had quite an important task ahead of me, to assist in the awakening and activation of many other Volunteers. My mission is to help individuals to consciously remember what I have been allowed to remember ever since I was born. It is also to help "Prepare everyone for the ultimate Graduation Party, Divine Intervention, and Worldwide Evacuation," when it is deemed (from above) to occur. This mission was to be accomplished through conducting workshops and personal Channeled Transformational Readings and, now, by bringing critical information to other Volunteers through the books of The Divine Blueprint Series.

Orion then said, "Now, go back to Earth, my son, with greater peace and comfort from having been in the presence of your Cosmic family, as you, of course, remember before your present Earth life. And, do not forget this most important message of our plan for future Divine Intervention. Prepare now for us to beam you back down to Earth. Peace and love to your spirit and entire being."

After receiving the information from my Cosmic parents, I began to cry again. I felt a new hopelessness, partly because of my having to go back once more to the third dimensional Earth level and partly because of a feeling of homesickness. I was very sad knowing that I had to leave these very beautiful and familiar beings and their lovely surroundings. The last I remember of this experience was saying a tearful goodbye to my space friends. Then, in the next moment, I was back on Earth (in the third dimension) falling through the air and just about to hit the ocean below.

Most of what happened right after that is somewhat confusing and I feel the reason for the confusion is because of the intervention by my radiant "Friends Upstairs." My very brief memories at this point consisted of me suddenly hitting the ocean and going under and, then, an impression of someone else jumping off the pier after me. I was made to feel quite detached from the rest of the experience. Next, I remember sitting in the back of my Earth parent's car with a towel wrapped around me as we drove away from the pier towards home.

Immediately after the incident, I was put into a slightly aloof state, so that most of my initial terror of falling off the pier was removed, but I did suffer some fear from this and it took many years for me to be able to get into deep water. In other words, I still had to deal with some of the responsibility or karma, concerning my decision that got me into that dangerous position.

Understanding the Experience

Sometimes our experiences can be fatal or the result can be an extreme psychological and emotional scaring for the rest of a person's life. This can cause one to shutdown, withdraw, and be afraid to be oneself. It is my opinion that the spiritual explanation for this event is that it was an attempt by the negative forces to traumatize me. Under the disguise of just one more dangerous childhood experience, I would then have intense fear and always know the terror from accidentally having slipped off the edge of the railing. I would then be forever traumatized from this horrible fall into the ocean.

Looking back on it, perhaps these demonic forces knew or suspected my true Higher spiritual identity. On the Higher galactic-spiritual realms, I remember being a spiritual warrior in the "Cosmic-Line" of Archangel Michael. I am openly admitting to the fact that I am specifically here on this planet as a "Secret Agent of God." With the help of God, the other Volunteers, and the Higher spiritual forces of Light and love, our "Cosmic Spiritual Espionage Mission of Light" is to expose and eliminate, once and for all, the hold the imbalanced forces have had on earth.

My conscious memory, intense feelings, and knowledge were acting as a specific energy target, a focal point that usually was not allowed by the Spiritual Hierarchy and Confederation, for this very reason. Volunteers from these Higher realms, who have conscious memory and knowledge and who specifically understand their missions to eliminate and transmute these dark forces, can be targeted by these forces since they can read minds. The dark forces knew who I was and, of course, they were determined to destroy and ultimately kill me, if at all possible.

Having been fully warned before I was born, I also realized that I would get plenty of Cosmic back-up and support from my "Friends Upstairs." They would be personally monitoring me and protecting me as they do all fellow Volunteers. There have been many incidences where life-threatening attempts have been made on Volunteers who should have been killed or severely injured, but there were "Divine Interventions." For me, miraculously, the Divine Forces have stopped many imminent dangers, some of which I have been aware of and have accepted as a matter of fact.

Like all Volunteers, I not only have survived these incidences, but also have grown spiritually, gained insight, and have become psychologically stronger. These dark forces are able to manipulate people into dangerous situations, without most of them ever being aware that such manipulations are actually taking place. One factor that has contributed greatly to the lack of awareness of many people is that most people ingest many horrible pollutants that specifically affect the shutting down of their Higher spiritual links. Without this contamination, people would be more insightful and effective against these imbalanced forces that have controlled this planet for vast ages.

Never have I considered myself paranoid about these forces. Rather, I believe I am just a realist who is very aware and attuned concerning what I have gone through. I also consider myself an optimist in regard to the future. I recall the "Great Promise" that was made to me when I signed up for this Cosmic assignment. I read the small print in that agreement. One of the promises given to all the volunteers was that eventually, at some point in the later part of our lives, "Divine Intervention" will collectively occur for this planet. This "Divine Intervention" is destined to happen on a mass, planetary scale, when the "Worldwide Evacuation" and "Graduation" ultimately takes place. This means that all the Volunteers (including myself) will be physically lifted up during the early stages of the "Shift." "Worldwide Evacuation" is definitely part of this Cosmic scenario being played out in coming Earthly events.

This big Earth changing event is traditionally and Biblically referred to as the "Rapture." It is also a description of mass spiritual ascension for all souls who are "Graduating off the wheel of karma." This event results in Earth (terra) being cleansed and making her "planetary ascension" into a Higher dimension, as well. Much more on this scenario will be shared in a later chapter.

This specific memory and "promise" has helped give me inspiration and strength to continue on at times when things seemed bleak or hopeless. It has also been a comfort to me when I have been psychically attacked on the spiritual front lines by the dark forces, who from behind the scenes have attempted to make my life as miserable as they could. Volunteers learn quite quickly to put up their "light shields" (deflectors) and to spiritually-psychically brush themselves off, so that they are not overwhelmed. Otherwise, they can most certainly become very depressed about the present state of affairs on this planet. It is a comfort to know deep down that "Divine Intervention" and "Worldwide Evacuation," followed by a "Golden Age" is imminent for this planet and that soon all evil acts in this world will at long last be over.

Later On

As a child I tended to be somewhat introverted and for many years, until I was much older, I was not very talkative. I never spoke about this experience, either to my family or to anyone else, until I was in my late teens. I rather suddenly became much more extraverted in my late teens and I asked my parents if they remembered the time when I had fallen off the pier. Curiously, neither one were able to remember anything concerning the incident. I was surprised that they could not recall me falling off the pier and being rescued and I never brought it up to them again. Later, I discovered that sometimes even the people who are indirectly connected with an ET or UFO experience have partial or total memory loss concerning the actual events that transpired. This has been brought out in other UFO cases.

Interestingly, years later at one of the many hundreds of ET/UFO lecturers that I have given, I connected with the man who had jumped off the Oceanside Pier to rescue me. What he and no one else understood at the time was what went on behind the scenes. So, I explained to him that I went through what can only be described as a "time-space warp" and how I had been physically beamed aboard the Lightship. I conveyed to him about my experience on this Higher dimension with the beautiful beings and how I was then beamed back down to this third dimensional level at the exact moment that they had first beamed me up. I expressed that this was a very smooth operation and no one else suspected at the time that I had been physically removed, taken to a beautiful Higher dimensional realm, and then returned.

A few years later I connected with two other fellow Volunteers, who told me that they remember being on board the very ship that I had been taken aboard and that they remembered seeing me there. I do not specifically remember them, but they each individually claimed that they definitely saw me there in that particular chamber.

Ashtar and the Cuban Missile Crises

When I was nine years old, I had one of the most powerful personal communications from Ashtar which occurred during the "Cuban Missile Crises." Throughout my early years I received so many Channelings from my "Friends Upstairs" that after a while they faded into the back of my mind, even though at the time I received them they had quite an impact upon me and my life. Often, they were specific communications giving me insight and an "inside scoop" of certain events, so that I would not be too concerned about the outcome.

The Cuban Missile Crises had quite an impact on my life. As I listened to President John F. Kennedy's famous Press Conference on October 22, 1962, I realized the serious and, potentially, fatal consequences for the United States of America, as well as for the entire planet. I knew that a full scale nuclear war (WWIII) would be the result if the Soviets did not agree to Kennedy's demands to remove their missiles from Cuba. I also knew that if that happened much of this planet would be destroyed and the rest of the planet would be horribly contaminated by radiation from the nuclear fallout.

Over the years, I had forgotten about most of this experience until I was recently watching a rerun of the "Quantum Leap" television show. The theme of this episode was about the main character (Dr. Becker) doing a "quantum leap" back in time into the body of a young teenager who lived in a typical American family in Florida in 1962 during the Cuban Missile Crises. In this show, he was trying to calm down his family because nuclear war seemed eminent. When I watched this rerun, it reminded me that this was a very scary and uncertain time for Americans, because they did not know whether or not there was going to be a nuclear war.

I have been told by my "Friends Upstairs" that, oftentimes, Higher Forces use the "special effects" of Earth's movies and shows to "interphase" certain types of "Higher Light Encodements" to help Light Workers lift their "Cosmic Amnesia." They also use these "special effects" to transmit certain messages and visions to remind us of things we have forgotten or to help spiritually Awaken us in regard to future things destined to occur on Earth. I have personally found that many times when I am watching particular themes, such as time-travel and related concepts, certain things get "triggered" and come flooding back into my conscious mind. And, it was, in fact, during this particular "Quantum Leap" episode, that the memories of my experience were "triggered" and came flooding back intensely into my conscious mind of what Ashtar had specifically communicated to me that day. This awakened memory included the concern for being aware of any possible future nuclear war, nuclear accidents, or "terrorist extremists" possessing nuclear weapons.

I remembered that when I was first given this information, it was a powerful relief for me at the time. This was because I was reminded of the Laws of the Federation which include what are called "Galactic Protocols" (Galactic Pax) that allow the Federation to step in and neutralize nuclear weapons so that the planet and all life upon it cannot be destroyed. While totally respecting free will, this exception may be made if people allow their free will to "get out of control."

This was Ashtar's main communication at that time:

Hello, this is Ashtar, wanting to calm any fears that you may feel, my son, to what you have just heard from your President (Kennedy) and to what the leader of Russia (Khrushchev) will do in response to this. I will assure you, that everything will turn out okay and nuclear war will **not** occur. This will, in fact, **not** be allowed by we of the Federation, the space people, for we have certain Authority to stop and neutralize such destructive events before they would even start to occur, so such concerns are **not** necessary.

We know, of course, that most of the Earth's population do not have access to us as you, and others like you, do who have strong connections with us off the planet. And, yes, there are other contactees who are also receiving similar positive communications. Unfortunately, all we can do is attempt to influence and Overshadow them with vibrations of hope and Inner peace to help calm their fears of a potentially destructive outcome. So, be at peace and know of our close monitoring from behind the scenes of these events and that we will **not** allow nuclear war to occur and that there **will** be a peaceful outcome for both the United States and Russia.

Later, I also remembered Ashtar informing me that one of the things that influenced President Kennedy to take the firm stand that he did against the Russians was because the Federation had communicated directly to him that he should be firm and that they (the Federation) would **not** allow nuclear war to occur. They also conveyed to him that the leader of Russia would back down and even if Russia did attempt to launch missiles, the Federation would neutralize them.

Ashtar informed me that the Federation had also communicated directly with Khrushchev, informing him that they would **not** allow him to start a nuclear war. Obviously, he took what they had communicated to him seriously, which is why on October 28, 1962, he agreed to remove the missiles from Cuba.

Throughout the past thirty years, due to my public appearances speaking about ETs, I have had numerous former military personnel who have told me about their first-hand knowledge and/or experience of UFOs landing or hovering near major military bases, including NORAD. Many of these individuals were retired from high level security jobs that had Top Secret classifications. They confirmed much of what I had been told by Ashtar and other Space Brothers about the ETs neutralizing the military's nuclear weapon systems on many occasions. They did this to demonstrate to the Earth officials that they could stop nuclear war, if they needed to. At the time of the Cuban Missile Crises, as well as in more recent times, the Federation has continued to make it clear to the world leaders of all the major countries on Earth who have had nuclear capability (including North Korea, India, Pakistan, etc.) that the Federation will Divinely Intervene and will neutralize any nuclear weapons, as many times as necessary to avert nuclear war. They have also made it clear that the Earth officials will not be allowed to militarize space as the power elite have planned for quite some time.

At that time, Ashtar told me that in the future there would be compact nuclear weapon systems that would be small enough to fit into a suitcase, though he also emphasized that these weapons too would be neutralized by the Federation. He stressed that these "nucs" would be used by our world leaders and the power-elite in an attempt to terrorize the population and that there were extremist individuals and groups who could activate these nuclear weapons. But, he also stressed that the most important aspect of this was not to be manipulated by the F.E.A.R., but rather to remember that we are always protected by the Higher Forces.

A Final Note about These Experiences

These personal experiences were of tremendous importance to me as I knew that in the future I would be sharing this first-hand knowledge with the world through public lectures, seminars, and media interviews. For even though I cannot physically prove these experiences occurred, I know that my memories are truly authentic and not some psychotically-emotionally induced mental state that I had conjured up as an escape from the everyday harsh realities here on Earth.

These "Higher Beings" have intervened on my behalf at various times and they have communicated with me throughout the years as they have done for Volunteers throughout earth's history. It is also important to know that, during the current critical time on the planet, they are intervening in the lives of all beings who truly want "Divine Intervention" in their lives. And yes, they are helping everyone *Prepare for the Landings!"*

CHAPTER 2

AURORA'S COSMIC EXPERIENCES

Touching On a Few of Aurora's Cosmic Experiences

I have had many Cosmic-spiritual experiences and I will share all of them with you as I can throughout The Divine Blueprint Series. Here are a few to inspire and uplift you and to let you know that we do, truly, have "Friends Upstairs" that care about us.

My Childhood

Coming into Earth embodiment is always a challenge, even for the most enlightened amongst us. I have yet to meet anyone who just sailed through it all. The inequities, along with vastly different consciousness levels, make this planet a very unique place for all of us to try and coexist together. However, most of us also have one commonality, the fact that we want to be loved and supported by each other.

The fact that I was born into a uniquely dysfunctional family sharpened my survival instincts and my spiritual connection to a Higher power at a very young age. Prayers were oftentimes my only hope and that hope for a better tomorrow was what kept me from feeling despair.

I was tested professionally and found to be a precocious child genius at age two. Though still a small child, this obviously manifested itself as my being conscious beyond my years and somewhat adult-like in my humor, communication skills, and interests. The arts, science, history, religion, psychology, philosophy, metaphysics, and politics were of great interest at an early age. Though I did not really have anyone to actually discuss these important topics with, I studied and contemplated them on my own.

Basically, my parents were considered to be middle class American's. My mother was an attractive woman, who was uncomfortable looking into life's big questions and not interested in self-analysis, unlike myself. Our common interest was our weekly shopping trips. My father was a handsome man, soft-spoken, and with a dry sense of humor, though emotionally detached, unavailable, and introverted. He worked for the Old Bell Telephone Company as a PBX repairman.

One day, I decided to snoop though my parents' strongbox to find out if I was adopted. I had a hard time believing they were actually my real parents. What I found was my father's Army induction papers that showed the results of his IQ test as 160. Though he never spoke of it, he was a genius. My father would often attempt to answer my numerous prying questions, but his information usually was limited to what he read in newspapers or heard on TV. However, there were numerous articles in the Detroit News about UFOs, and he did confide to me that he felt we are definitely not alone in the universe and that there is life on other planets.

Even though I was recognized as a gifted child, I was stuck in the public school system, where I was not challenged and was bored with the slow pace. On my first day of school at age five, I came home and announced to my mother that I was from a more advanced planet and that on my planet people learned much more quickly. I also told her that I felt that I had gotten off at the wrong stop and wondered why I was here on this backwards planet.

She laughed, taking it as a joke, but I was actually being serious. I realized it was useless to express any further what I was truly feeling on this subject. I told her that it was going to be difficult for me to have to go to school for the next thirteen years and that I felt sentenced to a type of jail. I also said that I was a foot taller than the rest of the kids and no one even got my jokes!

I just did not feel that I was going to fit in easily. I knew that I was doomed to intense boredom at school, so in order to kill time I daydreamed a lot. Forced to endure year after dull year, I became the class clown to amuse myself. I am sure that my humor and daydreaming saved me from going batty.

Both philosophically and spiritually, my parents and I were always miles apart. Every week from five years old on, my little girlfriends next door and I would take the Baptist bus to Sunday school where the people were very nice and I loved it. There I learned about love, morality, and many interesting Bible stories, mostly from the New Testament. I felt that I needed spirituality in my life; God was there for me to grasp on to and provided me with guidance and protection.

Although my parents were not aware of how spiritual I was, I always prayed to God for help. From a young age, I learned not to bother discussing anything spiritual with my parents, because I realized that I was just frustrating myself trying to communicate with them about matters of a Higher nature.

Most of the time things were extremely difficult at home, because my mother was emotionally out-of-control in many ways, including drinking alcohol which made things much worse. I was harshly punished constantly and physically beaten for the smallest infractions or for no reason what-so-ever. This being the chaotic routine that my mother created in our home, I left home and went out on my own at an early age, not wanting to look back.

My First Experience

When I was eight years old, a freak heat wave hit the Detroit area during the first week of May 1956, which sent the temperature soaring above 90 degrees. This was totally unprecedented as we never had sweltering heat at that time of the year. Even the large black June bugs had not yet made their appearance, and since this was so unexpected, my father had not put up our window and door screens yet. However, the extreme heat forced us to toss out caution and open the doors and windows, so we could possibly get some sleep.

My mother was gone for the evening. My infant sister, who had been born earlier that year, was in her crib asleep in the bedroom next to mine. My father was in the bathroom at the end of the hallway with the door closed. As he did every evening before retiring, he was completing his routine using his electric shaver with the water running in the sink to catch his whiskers.

While I was lying on my bed, I glanced at the new digital clock on the dresser and noticed that the glowing red numerals read 9:15 pm. At last it was starting to cool down somewhat. Suddenly, I heard footsteps and knew that someone was walking through our open front door. My mind was racing wondering who it could possibly be. My parents never had unexpected guests, so it probably was not a person that we knew. Besides, I thought, if it was people we knew, wouldn't they say something like "Hello" to let us know they were here? I wondered who it could be.

The footsteps sounded heavy to me, like a man's. Having heard of one or two burglaries in our Royal Oak suburban neighborhood over the past few years, I reasoned that it could be a burglar. If it is a burglar, I thought, he will open the drawers in the living room and look for something of value to steal.

I realized, after looking back at this event, that he must have read my mind because everything I was thinking that he would do, he did. I thought if he is a burglar he will open the drawers in the living room. Then, I heard him open a couple of drawers in the living room. Next I thought, he will come up empty-handed and go into my parents' room and open drawers, which I also heard him do. I decided that this guy had definitely picked the wrong house to rob, because I could not think of a thing that he would be much interested in taking.

I laid there quietly not wanting to create any unnecessary problems. I knew if he tried to harm me or my baby sister that I would scream, but otherwise I would let him take whatever he wanted. I felt that my Scottish dad, who was only

5'7" tall and weighed about 145 pounds, could very possibly get injured or perhaps even killed in a serious confrontation. It was better to just let the intruder take whatever he wanted, as long as he did not try to harm any of us.

As he entered my infant sister's bedroom, I could hear that he was not disturbing her. Our walls were thin and with my rather extraordinary hearing I could hear a sheet rustle in the next room.

Then, he started down the hallway and headed directly towards my room. This was suddenly getting even scarier. I wondered if I could possibly be dreaming or if this was really happening. I tried to think of what I could do to prove that I was not dreaming as I felt that I definitely needed scientific proof. All I could think of to do was to bite off the tips of my fingernails on my left hand. I figured that when this was over, if I had the nail tips inside my mouth, I would have some real tangible proof that I was indeed awake and not having a very vivid dream. So, that is exactly what I did.

By then, he was in the doorway and I felt it was much safer for me to pretend to be asleep. Having watched plenty of "Perry Mason" episodes, I knew that if a person could identify the criminal the witness might be killed. With the hallway light on, I could barely see the man silhouetted in the backdrop of the dim light as I peaked through my mostly closed eyes. To my astonishment, the man looked just like the actor Robert Young from one of my favorite 1950's TV shows "Father Knows Best."

This is weird; I thought why is this intruder carrying a leather briefcase? And why is he dressed up in what appears to be a felt hat and a heavy cashmere overcoat when it's 90 degrees out and we are all sweating bullets? What strange attire for a guy to be wearing who is robbing our home and, especially, in this awful heat!

As I look back on this experience, it appears that this visitor must surely have known that my favorite living male on the planet at that time was the "father" character actor that Robert Young played. This architect prototype, that the visitor portrayed, was non-threatening and was a comfortable image to me, and the way he was dressed was like what I believed a more cultured and educated gentleman might wear.

When he was silhouetted in the doorway, I really was not able to see his face very well. As he approached, I felt some fear and closed my eyes tightly as I was afraid to see his face and look into his eyes. He stood next to my bed, while I pretended to be asleep, still much too afraid to look at him close-up. I was afraid that he might be ugly and that I would never be able to get his face out of my mind afterwards. I was also fearful of his reaction, if I did anything to confront him. Looking back to that moment, I often wish that I had summoned the courage to look at him close-up, but at the time I had no clue that I was experiencing one of the most fantastic keynote events destined to shape my life.

After standing next to my bed for a few moments, I heard him walk over to the open window next to my bed and leave thru it. Our one-story family home had four steps up to the porch. So, from the window, there was only about a six or seven foot drop to the ground, easy enough for him to accomplish. I thought I should give him a chance to leave, not wanting any further interactions, so I waited a few moments before going to the window to see if he had left. I went to the window hoping he was gone and was relieved that he had left without an incident.

From the window, I was shocked to see two large neon-looking objects that were hovering slightly above the tall evergreen trees in Memorial Park and just behind our street. One object had a bright pinkish-red glow and the other had a bright light-blue hue. Both objects were round and seemed to be very large as I estimated that they were 30 to 40 feet across. I was very excited to see them and thought that they must be spaceships! I still get a thrill when I think about seeing them.

I stuck my head out the window and I could see up and down the row of my neighbors' backyards. I hoped that others were seeing what I was, but I was disappointed as I did not see a soul. I kept my eyes on the beautiful Lightships and began trying to telepathically communicate with them. I said, "Hey, I'm not afraid! Come on over and play! I really want to meet you!" Then, I waited for something to happen. Only a block and a half away, I could readily see busy Woodward Avenue that was eight lanes wide with many cars going by. I wondered, "Why doesn't anyone else see them but me? Why did you guys choose me?"

Nothing telepathically came to me. I still had the nail tips in my mouth and knew that I was indeed awake. As I was standing at the window looking at these fantastic spaceships, I thought, "I have had eight totally dull years, so why, all of a sudden, am I experiencing a burglar and spaceships all in the same night?" At that point, I had not yet made the association that the man was actually from the spaceship. I continued to stand there, afraid that if I went to get my father they would be gone by the time I returned.

Within a few moments, the pinkish-red or "rose colored" Lightship ascended approximately 100 feet upward while making a high-pitched noise. Then, the blue ship followed making a lower frequency sound, and then they disappeared! I was amazed that they instantaneously disappeared. I could not wait to tell my father, who was still in the bathroom shaving.

The Response I Got

I knocked on the bathroom door and he opened it. There I stood with my hair in pigtails, wearing only my Carters underpants, telling my dad about the whole incident. When I finished my story and asked him what he thought, he looked down at me said, "I think you might have been hallucinating." I responded, "Why? I have never hallucinated before have I? I know for sure it occurred because I still have the nail tips in my mouth that I bit off as the man walked down our hallway." I showed him the nail tips which did not impress him, but it was proof enough to me!

I told him that I wanted to report what happened and make some calls to the police, the newspapers, and the television stations and let them know what I saw. I then walked to the other end of the hallway where the telephone was. As he followed me, he suggested my plan to illuminate the world would probably not be a very good idea. I picked up the receiver part of the big black '50's phone, held it in my hand, and said, "But the world needs to know!"

He sternly ordered me to put the phone down, which I reluctantly did. I determinedly asked him, "Why can't I call them?" My dad replied, "Because they will think you are crazy! They will lock you up in a mental institution and I will not be able to do a thing about it. It will be out of my hands and you will be stuck in a nuthouse! So, give up on the idea, just forget it."

This did make some sense to me and he frightened me enough with his reasoning that I gave up on the idea of reporting the experience to the media and police. I replied, "Well, tomorrow I am going to school and I will tell my story at "Show and Tell" and no one can stop me from doing that!" My father chuckled and shook his head, "Then you will see for yourself that no one will believe you. Trust me, it is better that you keep this experience to yourself."

The next day at school, our rather new second-grade teacher asked, "Who would like to share something today?" Eagerly I raised my hand. Now is my chance, I thought. The teacher could see my enthusiasm and called on me first.

I told the whole story while the class sat listening, transfixed on every word. I thought that this was good as they were all paying close attention. When I finished, I asked, as we were trained to do, if there were any questions, and to my amazement, everyone just sat there staring at me. To me that was a very strange reaction. I assumed that I would have to answer many interesting questions, but everyone just sat there like bumps-on-a-log with blank looks on their faces. I repeated the question, "Does anyone have any questions?" Still nothing! I was very surprised that I had just shared this fantastic story and no one, including the teacher, asked anything.

There was never a response from anyone at all, ever. None of the kids spoke of what I had just shared with them, even at lunch time and recess. I was shocked! I just could not believe their reaction was complete un-interest, as though they were all in some strange trance unable to respond. Were their minds that closed? Did they think I had fabricated the whole story that I was clearly very excited about?

At the dinner table that evening, I told my dad what had happened at school. He responded, "See, I told you so! People will either think you are nuts or that you are not telling the truth. Save yourself a lot of pain and just keep quiet about it."

Since no one ever spoke of it, I decided not to bring it up again to my class. I did, however, try to tell a couple of friends, but their reaction was disappointing as well. I could tell that they just did not want to go there. It was a topic that they just could not handle. I did not share much about my experience with anyone again for many years, until I had my second experience at the age of sixteen.

My Second Experience: Time Space Warp

I never felt blessed as a kid. I had what most people would classify as a challenging childhood, but that's a different book. I was already out on my own at the tender age of fifteen. My nineteen year old boyfriend was from a very nice family that owned the Superior Door Company in Detroit, Michigan. My boyfriend, Michael Siefman, was very generous to me and frequently let me borrow his new car.

His car was a fabulous powder-blue Pontiac Lemans convertible. Even though I had just turned sixteen, he convinced the Driver Education trainer to fill out some paperwork that allowed me to get my license without having to take the driver's course. Consequently, I was driving without any real training and I was petrified about driving when there were a lot of large trucks surrounding me on the busy Detroit streets.

On a particularly busy spring weekday, I was driving my boyfriend's coveted convertible on my way to pick him up from the door company. I could not be late again or he said he would revoke my car borrowing privileges and I sure did not want that to happen.

On this remarkable day, I was in Southfield, Michigan, a suburb of Detroit. I was traveling south on Southfield Road approaching the Eleven Mile Road intersection. I was surrounded by heavy rush-hour traffic and I was desperately searching for a sign that would indicate where the newly-built extension to the

John Lodge Freeway entrance ramp was located. I was going around in circles, unable to spot it, and getting more and more frustrated by the minute. It was approximately 5:30 p.m. and it was difficult to see because the setting sun was in my eyes. At the same time, large trucks loomed all around me making it even more impossible to find this new freeway entrance.

I began getting more and more frustrated as I was determined to find it quickly so I would not be late again. I was out in front of the pack of vehicles on my third try, again heading southward, when I looked up and was surprised to see the light at the intersection had already turned red. I was shocked because it had just turned green and I normally had the ability to time lights very accurately. Now, what was I going to do in this bumper to bumper rush-hour traffic? I knew that it was impossible for me to stop in time and avoid hitting the other cars. (FYI - I found out many years later that the light at the intersection was ill-timed which lead to many deaths and that it was rated the number two intersection for deaths in Michigan.)

This was a horrible moment as I saw that cars were now coming into the intersection right in front of me and I knew that this could be very nasty. I saw a woman with a car full of kids approaching directly in front of me and I was afraid that I would impact their car and kill them all. I quickly said a prayer, knowing I could not possibly stop my car in time. I prayed: "Dear God, please don't let me hurt or kill anyone!" I then threw myself face down onto the floor of the passenger side while still feebly holding on to the steering wheel with my left hand and still holding my foot on the brake, not an easy feat.

Suddenly, while still lying there face down, I noticed there was no noise or movement of any kind. This was highly unusual, to say the least, and I really thought that I might indeed be dead. I was lying face down on the car floor when I took my left hand off the steering wheel and I pinched my right hand that was placed over my head to see if I could feel the pinch. Surprised that I could feel it, I thought, "Well, gee, being dead isn't so bad; I'll get used to it." But, I thought, "I certainly had a short life!"

I was frightened that I might be dead, in purgatory, or worse yet, hell. In my family, I figured no one was going to make it to heaven but my grandmother who was "the pillar of strength and dignity." Even though I was filled with fear, I wanted to know what had indeed just happened, so, after a few seconds, I finally gathered the courage to sit up and look around me.

I was shocked to find that my car had been moved without my knowledge of anything happening. Now, I was perfectly parked next to a gas station pump that was in the complete opposite corner (the southwest corner) of the intersection from where I had been approaching. Somehow, I had moved over all the lanes of traffic to this spot. I looked around and was shocked to see that no one, in all the numerous cars surrounding me, was moving. There was no sound or movement of any kind and everyone looked like they were frozen in suspended animation. I thought, "Oh my God, I am the only one moving!"

Talk about a "Twilight Zone Moment!" This was just too weird! I spoke out loud to myself and God and hoped to get an answer. I said, "Who did this? How did I get here?" Surprisingly, an answer immediately came as a clear voice in my head. The female voice spoke, "Chalk it up to Divine Intervention." I replied, "Why did you save my miserable life when everyday so many people die?"

The answer to that question did not come at that moment. I continued to look around and noticed that there still was no movement or noise at all. How strange, I thought! I saw an old guy that had been frozen in stride while he was walking back to the gas station. I called out to him hoping to bring things back to normal. I spoke loudly enough for him to hear me, "Hey Mister, fill it up!" To my relief, he reacted, turned around, and started walking towards me. The traffic started up again and no one looked at me strangely at all. No one, but me, seemed to realize what had just happened.

The old guy came up to my window and said, "Yeah, what will it be?" I looked at him and noticed that he did not seem to realize anything unusual had just occurred. I said to him, "Mister, did you see or hear me pull in?" He looked at me confused for a moment and I repeated the statement. "Did you see or hear me pull in?" He just looked at me blankly and I knew it was no use trying to get any information from him, so I said laughingly, "Just fill it up! When God parks you next to the pump, yeah, just fill it up!" He looked a little confused, but went about his business gassing my car. I paid the old gent and continued heading south on Southfield road. At last, I spotted the entrance ramp I had been so desperately seeking. I recognized that my ramp problem was that I had not gone far enough south. Well, now I knew!

For the rest of the trip to the door company, I contemplated the miracle that I had just experienced. By the time I got there, I was indeed late again. When I arrived a few minutes late, as I usually did, my boyfriend approached me with a look of both anger and amusement on his face. I scooted over into the passenger seat so he could drive. When he got in and looked at me I said, "Well, have I got a great excuse this time!" Somewhat amused, he said, "Oh really, I can't wait to hear it!" As we drove along, I told him the whole story and ended it with, "So, do you believe me?" I looked intensely for his reaction, not knowing what to expect. To my surprise he said, "Yes, I do!" I was shocked! I said, "Why do you believe me?" He laughingly replied, "Well, this is the first time you have ever put any gas in my car. A miracle would have had to occur!" He was right!

Years later, I came to the understanding that I had been teleported through a "time-space warp" by a group of benevolent extraterrestrials who were monitoring me and my situation. These advanced ETs had indeed saved my life and the lives of the others who would have certainly died, as well. This realization of advanced ETs was a fact that was obvious to me and could not be denied. But it was to be many years later before I found out more information concerning who they were and why they were so interested in my life.

Aurora's Camping Experience

When I was in my early twenties, I found myself teaching metaphysics and psychic development in the Detroit area, where I still lived at the time. It was the early 70's and my husband, Marvin Myers, and I had bought a nice home in the upscale neighborhood of West Beverly Hills, Michigan where we lived with our darling son, Bradley.

I loved metaphysics and enjoyed teaching the classes in my home to the people who showed up each week. It was a small group and close friendships developed amongst us. One of the gals in my class, Sharon, and I became good buddies and started hanging out together, going to parties, and doing other fun things.

Sharon was always bugging me to go camping with her. So, finally at the tail-end of that Michigan summer, I relented and agreed to go up north with her to the Traverse City area for the weekend. It was the first week in September when we finally headed out for our big adventure. Sharon assured me that she had packed everything we needed and all I had to bring was a blow-up mattress. I was not really interested in camping and was praying she might have a change of heart and we could get a hotel room on Lake Michigan. We filled up my beloved Audi 500LS, which is not a camping car at all, and headed out with plenty of supplies for our three-hundred mile trip.

On our way to the Lake Michigan area, we decided to stop at a little German town in the middle of the state to have dinner at a restaurant. The food was satisfying and we were feeling happy and content as we continued on our merry way. It was getting quite late by the time we approached the remote area that Sharon said was "it." "It" turned out to be beautiful grass and trees, as far as the eye could see, and in the middle of nowhere. It was truly lovely, but, unfortunately, as we drove up to the area it was sprinkling out and we did not want to get wet and cold.

The first strange thing happened when we got out of the car. We started walking around the large grassy area and were shocked that we were not getting wet at all. We could clearly hear and see that it was pouring rain all around us. As I walked around a large circle that was perfectly dry, it was shocking to see that there was not even a drop of rain within the circle. This was very bizarre and conjured up images of the Jews in the Bible who were protected by clouds from the sun and rain by day and kept warm and protected from the elements by balls of fire at night, as they made their journey for forty years through the desert.

As strange as all this was, the reality was that it was getting very late and we still had to get the tent set up. Sharon's expertise in this matter turned out to be sorely lacking, due to the fact that her boyfriend was the one who always assembled the tent. So, it was left up to me to figure out how to put up the tent and, even though, I had only seen tents while walking through a Sears store, I managed to figure it out by the Grace of God.

During all this time, it was still "dry as a bone" in our circle, which I esti-mated was approximately 150 feet across, yet, outside the circle it was "pouring buckets" all around us. I felt that this phenomenon was unique and wondered if "Someone Upstairs" was influencing this scenario, but I was too busy to think about it. It was late and I was getting tired and I still had to blow up my air bag, without a pump, I might add. As I blew up the air mattress that Sharon had told me to buy, I realized that it was only three-feet long, so when I crawled into my mummy sleeping bag, I ended up sleeping half-on and half-off the mattress.

Even though I was tired, I could not sleep. Sharon, on the other hand, had no trouble falling asleep. After she had been asleep for a couple of hours, I decided to get up as I was just miserable. We had a dim lantern in the tent, so I took it with me when I stepped outside. To my shock, I saw the most unusual sky of my life. From horizon to horizon, there were thousands of these little white lights, about the size of a dime, in perfect rows, close together.

I couldn't believe my eyes and had to wake Sharon so she could verify what I was seeing. It was about 4:00 in the morning and she reluctantly came outside mumbling that, "It better be good, whatever you have to show me." I did not tell her anything first as I did not want to influence her mind. Then, I asked her, "What do you see?" After she described the same thing that I was seeing, I then asked her, "What do you think they are?" She said, "Spaceships!" I said, "Well, it looks like an assembly line at GM." I was joking, but it was shocking to see so many spaceships surrounding the Earth.

Years later in April 1981, when I met Michael Ellegion at Arizona State University and told him the story, I asked him, "Could there really be so many spaceships surrounding the planet?" Unsurprised, he quickly replied, "Oh yes!

'They' are in 'Guardian Action' surrounding the planet in case there are any negative aliens trying to invade the Earth or in case of other serious planetary problems that require their intervention."

Sharon and I stood there watching the ships until dawn, when they faded from sight. She went back to sleep while I planned my escape. I waited a couple of hours and then announced that we were heading to the shores of Lake Michigan and to a hotel at my expense. She reluctantly agreed and tired as we were we began to pack and load the equipment.

All of a sudden, a tall and very handsome man appeared out of nowhere. The stranger was beautifully dressed in attractive designer-type sports clothes, like a GQ magazine model. He came up close to me and said, "Can I be of help?" Stunned, I managed to only say, "Sure!" He quickly packed and loaded everything into my Audi in a matter of minutes, then smiled and waived as he walked off into the woods.

I realized later that given the circumstances, this unusual man, who appeared in the middle of nowhere, was more than likely a "Space Brother." From the dry circle, to the spaceships, and, then, to the handsome designer-clad woodsman, it was a heck of a trip that I was not going to forget.

At the Sign of the Dove

I was married and living with Michael Ellegion on McCormick Ranch in Scottsdale, Arizona during the early eighties. One afternoon as I was backing out of the garage with the top down on my red Lebanon convertible, I felt compelled to look up into the eastern sky.

It was a clear day with hardly a cloud and my eye caught a white object that was moving about in an unusual way. I wondered at first if it was an airplane, but it was gliding around in a way that planes do not usually do. I was wondering what it could possibly be, when it started coming down lower. Then, it got so low that I was able to see what looked like a giant bird. It then hovered about three or four feet from me and I could see it was a beautiful shiny-white Dove. The Dove had about a five-foot wing span and did not have feathers, but appeared to be made of a substance like pure-white alabaster stone.

I was amazed! I just sat there in my car staring at this other-worldly bird for a few moments and, finally, I spoke to it, wondering if it would answer me. The Dove hovered for a few more moments, then started gliding up and away, all the while getting larger and larger until it was the size of a 747 before it left my viewing range. I knew it was a message from "Upstairs."

According to the Bible Dictionary, the Sign of the Dove was the prearranged means by which John the Baptist would recognize the Messiah at Jesus' baptism (John 1: 32-34). Also, before the creation of the world, it was instituted that the sign of the dove was to be a witness of the Holy Ghost and that the devil could not come in the sign of a dove.

The "Sign of a Dove" was given to John to signify the truth of the deed, as the dove is an emblem or token of truth and innocence" (Joseph Smith, HC 5: 261). Although we usually associate the "Sign of the Dove" with John the Baptist, from the latter reference, we know that it manifested to Abraham as well. It is written in legends and throughout history that it has been similarly made known to other prophets on occasion since the time of Adam.

I believe the "Sign of the Dove" appearing to me to mean that Christ is returning to Earth during my lifetime. Excited about the experience, I drove the car back into the garage and went inside to tell Michael what had just happened. He felt, as I did, that this unusual Dove coming to me was a "Sign" concerning Christ's return.

I decided to call two of our favorite Channels for the Masters; one was the famous Mt. Shasta channel and author Sister Thedra, and the other was a famous channel and author named Tuella. Both of these great channels wrote many books about the Masters and I respected them and their opinions. When I spoke to each of them, they both said the same exact thing: "This is 'The Sign' that I have been waiting for." They each felt that this was a "Sign" that Christ's return was imminent.

Some people think that the story of Lord Jesus Christ is unimportant or fictional; perhaps designed to control and manipulate the masses. One should keep in mind that the manipulation side of some religious organizations, along with the fear aspect that is used, is, obviously, not Christ-like and alienates many people. In this case, it is important that you "do not throw the baby out with the bath water," so to speak, as that would be a huge mistake. For, "Signs" have been given to many current-day prophets and historians, in addition to what was given to me, and these "Signs" reflect that the "Time is at Hand" for "The Return."

CHAPTER 3

CABAL'S ATTEMPT TO KILL MICHAEL

Influence of Edgar Cayce

If our first UFO encounters with the benevolent human-appearing ETs were eventful and memorable, as it always is for us and other contactees, the experiences that we were to have later on as we grew older were even more noteworthy, to put it mildly. Many events have happened leading up to my second experience, which I want to describe briefly, so the reader can more easily understand why this encounter occurred. But, first, let me explain a bit more about my background.

As mentioned previously, my Earth parents were followers of the famous psychic channel Edgar Cayce. In fact, my father was a professional hypnotist for a number of years. During his study of Edgar Cayce's life, he discovered that a hypnotist was the one who helped "activate" Cayce's abilities to go into a trance and to channel the vast amount of information that he did. My father's research found that Cayce went to see a psychiatrist because he was having a personal psychological problem. This psychiatrist was also a hypnotist who proceeded to put Cayce into a hypnotic trance to help his conscious mind "get out of the way," so that his subconscious and super-conscious minds could help him overcome his personal problem.

The rest was "history," as they say, for Cayce then became known as the "Sleeping Prophet." He learned through his early sessions to easily put himself into a trance to access important information for himself and, especially, for the thousands of people he "read" and channeled for. Many of Cayce's clients were people with specific medical or health problems and/or psychological challenges who had first gone to orthodox "medical and psychiatric experts" who were not able to help them with conventional medicine and therapy. But when Cayce channeled information for them, those individuals who followed his "advice" had great assistance in overcoming their problems. The information that he gave them specifically dwelt with karmic situations from their past Earth lives that were still influencing those people's present lives.

Oftentimes, when people encounter certain challenges in their lives, it is because they wrote that challenge into their own life-script prior to taking embodiment. Later on during embodiment, when the situation occurs that they "signed up for," they have the opportunity to deal with the situation, overcome it, and become spiritually stronger and more attuned to their life's Mission and purpose.

Getting back to my experience, prior to taking Earth embodiment I had written into my own life-script that by the time I turned 15 years of age my father had already taught me to do a similar type of trance readings like Edgar Cayce did. These readings, which were basically what I refer to as "karmic readings," helped people get off the "wheel of karma" during this lifetime. Sometimes, the channeled information was about diet and nutritional needs and, sometimes, it was mostly psychological and philosophical in nature. Much of the information that I channeled for these clients, like Cayce's readings, described their former Earth lives and the connection that these particular lives had with certain karma or dharma (positive karma) in this present life.

Although I was glad to help these individuals with these karmic-type readings, I did not feel the very strong spiritual-Cosmic connections with them that I do now. Since 1979, I have been doing a different type of sessions that I call channeled "Transformational" Cosmic Readings. I believe that the strong connection that I now experience with those I do sessions with is due to the fact that I am channeling information for fellow Volunteers in Earth embodiment that are more evolved souls who have come here from other intergalactic worlds. This change, in the type of readings that I was doing, came about as a result of my second encounter with the benevolent human-appearing ETs which occurred in '79.

Reasons for My Second ET Encounter

There are two major reasons why this second physical encounter occurred. First, this encounter (aboard the Merkabah Lightship) occurred for the purpose of "activating" me to do channeled "Transformational" readings for other Volunteers on planet Earth. I always knew deep down that my real Missions in this life would be to do channeled readings for these Volunteers, as well as preparing humanity for mass planetary Divine Intervention and Worldwide Evacuation. As mentioned in Chapter 1, these fellow Volunteers are also known as "Star People." In fact, many people may be reading this book because their own Inner Self has drawn them to it.

The other reason for my second physical ET encounter was to create a "force-field" of protection. This protection was necessary as I began to lecture to the public exposing various government cover-ups and the "Conspiracy of Silence" surrounding these cover-ups. Many of these cover-ups are directly attributed to those of the "secret or shadow government", the illuminati, the power-elite, and the industrial military complex, which I have in more recent years, simply referred to as the cabal. This group has suppressed the truth about the more advanced, beautiful, and benevolent human-appearing ETs. Yet, these same forces have "stuffed the 'grays' down everyone's throats" through their agents of disinformation in the UFO community and through UFO documentaries on television.

These same forces of the cabal will try almost anything and do whatever they have to (including either character or physical assassination) to silence anyone who attempts to openly speak the truth. The type of technique that the cabal has used to silence a particular person varies. Depending upon the circumstances and the person's job or career, the forces have used either bribes, threats, intimidation, and/or blackmail. Then, whenever these methods did not work, assassination of different types was used.

When most people have heard the terms "physical assassination" or "deadly force," the image of an expert sniper or professional "mafia hit man" has come to mind. There has also been another form of assassination of which people may not have been aware. In recent years, much evidence has surfaced regarding psychic assassination (connected to "remote viewing").

For many years through "black-budgeted projects," the cabal trained certain military "special forces" in remote viewing and took these techniques one step further. These remote viewing techniques were combined with advanced forms of radionic devices termed "psychotronics" which could literally kill, or at least incapacitate, individuals from a long distance. The effects of these devices may have been physical, mental, emotional, and/or psychic, depending upon the individual's circumstances. This information was shared with me through various sources including: conversations with ex-undercover and intelligence agents, channeling and telepathic communication with my space contacts, sources of recent alternative publications, and what has been confirmed to me personally while physically aboard the Lightships.

In fact, some of the agents that I met actually trained for and participated in "psychic assassination hit squads" that were set up in the sixties and early seventies. The purpose of these "hit squads" was to secretly get rid of the "Light Workers" (Volunteers in Earth embodiment) who were a threat to the cabal's hidden agenda of bringing in the New World Order. Fortunately, this secret plan of the power-elite was not very successful and it began to break down in the late seventies. This was due to the fact that many of the guys who trained to be part of these assassination teams actually turned out to be Light Workers themselves. These types of Light Workers (also referred to as "Cosmic Deep Undercover Agents of Light" or "Secret Agents of God) were, literally, on "Spiritual Espionage Missions of Light" from the Intergalactic Confederation and Spiritual Hierarchy. As a result, the more extreme destructive potential of these weapons was actually lessened by these Light Workers.

Along with this vast psychotronic "arsenal" that the cabal developed, they also developed many advanced techniques (such as the "clipper chip" and the global "echelon" satellite system) to monitor millions of telephone conversations made by the unsuspecting public. The CIA, NSA, and DIA are just a few of the agencies who were engaged in this type of eavesdropping, supposedly for "national security" purposes. This monitoring of phone conversations has been going on covertly for many decades even before President George W. Bush officially authorized it. But, unlike in the past when the phone companies were not aware of how their own equipment was being used for covert phone monitoring, now they are conscious participants in this illegal un-constitutional activity.

Several years ago Nexus publication had a very insightful article about the ability of the cabal to eavesdrop on any phone conversation practically anywhere in the world that they wanted to. The article in this "cutting-edge" publication confirmed what I have been stating for many years about governmental cover-ups and the "Conspiracy of Silence." This article also confirmed that the cabal, through major phone companies (unbeknownst to them), has used "automatic voice-recognition or phonetic-activated technology." This technology used advanced equipment and computer systems that automatically started recording phone conversations whenever specific words, terms, or phrases were used. This was done, obviously, for the purpose of monitoring peoples' conversations without their knowledge. Furthermore, this article also confirmed another thing that I was told (both telepathically and in person) by my "Friends Upstairs" while onboard the Lightship. They conveyed that eventually the public would be informed about the phone monitoring through publications and lectures by those who were courageous enough to help expose this suppressed information.

Personally, I have never been one to go looking for trouble or to try to tempt fate, but neither am I one to run from trouble or be intimidated by other forces who might wish to silence me for ultimately speaking publicly about this "Conspiracy of Silence." In fact, many times, during the years prior to the UFO contact in 1979, when I mentioned over the phone that one day I would publicly expose the details of this vast cover-up at many events and by being interviewed for many radio and T.V. shows and newspapers all over the world, I realized that my conversations were undoubtedly recorded and monitored by psychics and others working for the cabal. I was aware that I could ultimately pose a threat to their position of power, if I was allowed to live and do all the things that I have been able to accomplish with the media and with this book.

I realize, now looking back, just how deadly earnest the cabal was about eliminating me, because of my efforts to expose them. In the last 20 years or so, I have met well over 200 retired and ex-intelligence agents who have ethically and morally rebelled against the original intent of their own organizations that had the goal of bringing in the New World Order. These agents have shared a great deal of information and documentation with us, and we, in turn, have shared this same information, naming names, places, and events on more than 1,500 radio and T.V. stations and in numerous newspapers. We also presented this information on our own L.A., California radio and T.V. shows in the early '90's (Vortex Network News).

This is just part of the reason for my second encounter and the need for these more advanced, human-appearing ETs to intervene by physically beaming me aboard the Lightship and saving my life from the organized psychic assassination hit squad of the cabal, whose negative force was projected at me in the early morning hours of March 25, 1979. And, now I understand that I wrote this experience into my life script (just as it was in '59 when my first physical encounter took place) as a part of my destiny in order to confirm to me the existence of ETs by their physical presence.

Information from Commander Korton

I was told by my "Friends Upstairs" that the reason I became a "psychotronic target" was primarily based on the fact that the cabal was monitoring countless phone calls of mine in which I had mentioned (very sincerely and passionately) that I would ultimately be able to expose the entire UFO cover-up and how the benevolent human-appearing ETs could intervene. The fact is that much of the information in regard to the benevolent human-appearing ETs has been suppressed and anyone attempting to expose this to the public would be a major threat to the cabal. And, even though I might not be able to show proof, the fact remained that I could create doubt in the minds of millions of people because I was aware of much evidence that was contradictory to what the official government reported to the main-stream corporate-controlled media. Therefore, the cabal considered me a threat.

They could tell that I meant what I said and they knew that I was in a position to bring this information to the public's attention. They were aware that I would be meeting many people from high security levels with great knowledge of "sensitive" material and that I would have the potential to expose this to millions of people. These people, in turn, would become "activated" and start asking questions and so on. It was because of this possibility that I became a target.

Prior to this assassination attempt on me, I had been living in a small town in southern Oregon. I had spent several months in Cave Junction, Oregon, just "attuning to nature" and enjoying a carefree and unstressed life. I now am aware that my time there was psychologically preparing me for the intense stress of what I was about to experience.

In early March '79, I received a very strong telepathic message from my "Friends Upstairs" that it was now time to begin a new (and more powerful phase) of my Mission of being a Volunteer on Earth. One of the many beings who I had been communicating with throughout the years (and knew previous to this life) was a human-appearing ET known as Commander Korton. Commander Korton is the Communications Officer of the Ashtar Command and one of his roles is to "activate" channels.

For many weeks prior to my journey back from the southern Oregon area, I had been receiving messages from Commander Korton about the need to start wearing (and to utilize more seriously) natural quartz crystals and other natural gemstones. These crystals and gemstones can be combined to form a spiritual-psychic strengthener. I was also instructed to be stricter about what I was ingesting and to do certain powerful color meditations and Light Decrees. All this was important because I was going to need to be a lot stronger both spiritually and physically than I had even been up until then. I was told to prepare myself, not only for what would be occurring in the coming weeks, but also for a greater phase of my Mission that involved physical UFO contact that was going to occur very soon. Looking back, I remember that I had a "bewildering" feeling and questioned whether I needed to do all the things that Korton (and others with him) were strongly urging me to do. I wondered if I "was above it all" and could survive what was to come without the advice and direct Intervention from my "Friends Upstairs."

A few weeks before I moved back from Oregon to Los Angeles, I received a very strong telepathic message from my "Friends Upstairs" to telephone a friend of mine immediately and "that it was urgent for me to do so right then and not wait another moment." So, I called my friend Ron Rowens and told him that I was planning to move back, but was not sure exactly when that would occur. I just knew that I had to get back soon. Of course, this also alerted the cabal of my plans (I found out later that they were monitoring my calls.) I did not know, at the time, when I was to have my second ET experience or any circumstances that would lead up to it, but I had been telepathically informed (through other channels, as well as myself) that it was going to happen soon.

Ron Rowens

One of my closest friends (and one of the clearest channels that I have ever known) was an African-American named Ron Rowens whom I had gotten to know about a year before. I witnessed Ron's spiritual abilities several times and could attest to how remarkably clear and powerfully he received information, both through direct-voice and as a telepathic channel.

About a year prior to this time in March '78, Ron and I were with a group of more than 30 individuals near 29 Palms, California that attempted to have physical contact with these benevolent human-appearing ETs. Our group was guided to take a "car caravan" out to a particular hotel where we would all be staying for a few days. We had originally met about a half-hour earlier at the famous "contactee hang-out spot" known as the Giant Rock Airport. This is the place where George Van Tassel used to hold the famous "Flying Saucer Conventions" during the decades of the '50's and '60's.

When we left that location, I decided to ride in the van that Ron was driving. Within a few minutes after we pulled away, I was suddenly urged (telepathically) to look up into the sky. After a few moments, I saw at a distance some kind of aircraft that was flying above and slightly behind us. This was the only aircraft in the entire sky that I could see, but I also sensed that there were Lightships from the Confederation up in the sky nearby. The Lightships were not in physical form at that time but were on a Higher dimensional or "ethereal" level. Next, I received the strong telepathic message that this visible plane was from the CIA and that it would be following us until we got close to our next destination which was 29 Palms.

Ron did not know what I had just seen or about the personal telepathic message I had just received, but, a second later, while driving down the road he received a direct-voice channel from one of the "Space Brothers". "Yes, as our brother Michael just telepathically received from us, it is true and we now confirm this verbally thru our brother Ron, as you Michael just sighted, there is a plane overhead and behind you which is from the CIA and will be following you to your next location!"

There was no way Ron could have known (at least not on a conscious level) what I knew and, yet, he had spontaneously channeled a very strong confirmation of this from our "Friends Upstairs." Ron was a bit shocked about what he had just verbalized. However, he was not shocked that he had channeled this while he was driving for he had done this many times before. It was just that he was not expecting this particular message and was surprised to be informed in this way of what was "going on behind the scenes."

For another half-hour or so as we continued on our journey, I kept scanning the sky for any airplanes. During that time, I only saw that one airplane that had continued to follow us. It was in basically the same location above us as it had been in since first sighting it. At one point I briefly looked down, and then, a few seconds later I was telepathically urged to look back up at the sky. When I did, I was shocked to see that the plane had disappeared. It was as if it had suddenly vanished from view. I now saw a plane or aircraft of some kind that was way over in an entirely different area of the sky where there definitely had been none before.

I had a strange feeling about this. At first, I did not understand what had happened and my conscious, rational mind tried to explain it. But I knew deep-down that there was no logical explanation for this. Then, I received a very strong telepathic message: "We just teleported the plane across the sky!" And, a moment later, Ron verbally direct-voice channeled: "Yes, you just observed and have received telepathic confirmation of this from us, Michael, and it is true that we just teleported the CIA plane across the sky to this new location!"

So, this confirmed the telepathic message that I had received. And, as incredible as it may seem, the CIA plane that had been following us was suddenly teleported across the sky into a different location. This particular scenario was only one of many instances that demonstrated Ron's ability as a very clear channel and it was this kind of interactive-synchronicity that confirmed so much of what was truly "going on behind the scenes."

And, as far as our efforts that day to personally contact the benevolent human-appearing ETs, our attempt failed because of the cabal (CIA, NSA, and possibly Russian KGB agents) who was nearby to make sure that this attempt did not occur. We found out that they were prepared to use deadly force had these benevolent human-appearing ETs attempted to land and to make physical contact with those of us who had specifically gathered there to do so.

There have been a number of "attempts" made (with many witnesses present) to have open physical contact with the "Space Brothers." I learned, then, in the late seventies, that this was not destined to be for a while. That is, until, the upcoming eminent "Worldwide Evacuation" occurs.

Floyd and Rita Selman

About six months prior to my second ET encounter, I had another relevant, and very important, experience. I had the pleasure and privilege of meeting Floyd and Rita Selman. The Selmans were very clear channels for the Spiritual Hierarchy and the "Space Brotherhood." They also knew George Adamski and were a part of the original "sincere and authentic" pioneers of the early contactee movement of the '50's and '60's.

They were a very warm and charming couple and you could sense their true sincerity, as it had also been with the other well known contactees of the '50's. This is unlike the bias and hidden agendas of most of the prominent UFO researchers of recent times.

Within days after having first met them, Rita received a very strong telepathic message. She was told by our "Friends Upstairs" that within approximately six months I was definitely going to have physical contact with the "Space Brothers." And, it was, in fact, at the end of that six months after Rita telepathically received the message and conveyed it to me that my second ET event actually happened.

Two Days Prior to My Second UFO Contact

From the start of the 23rd day of March, 1979, and up to the actual physical UFO encounter itself, some of the events are a little "blurred" in my conscious memory. Part of this lack of clarity, I attribute to the fact that my "Friends Upstairs" knew that within 48 hours the cabal was going to use psychic "deadly force" on me, so, they caused me to experience a type of "physical-emotional-psychic detachment" for the two days leading up to the actual contact in the early morning hours of the 25th. My space contacts were aware of what was about to occur and of the terrifying nature of being "psychically zapped" and "spiritually violated" by whatever type of "black budget" psychotronic device the cabal planned to use on me.

This detachment was like an extreme case of being "spaced out." I honestly cannot remember much about where I went or what I did during those two days before the actual encounter. In a way, it was as if I experienced some sort of strange "time-space" warp in my consciousness that blanked out large portions of what was transpiring on this third-dimensional level of being. This "detachment" was very similar to that which I experienced prior to my first UFO encounter in '59, except perhaps this was even more intense, especially on the day before. My understanding of this now is that my "Friends Upstairs" were partially, psychically shielding me, as well as preparing me for the ultimate full attack.

I have been told that during this time the team of "psychic assassins" were actually vibrationally "tuning-in" to where I was. They were using the "normal" espionage physical-auditory-visual and verbal monitoring of my approximate whereabouts through monitoring the many phone calls that I made from different friend's houses in different locations. During these two days, I was guided to go and reconnect with several friends whom I had not seen since having been gone for several months to Oregon. Unfortunately, I don't remember much about whom I saw or where I went exactly, but I do remember making several phone calls. Unbeknownst to me at the time, part of this monitoring was being conducted in a hidden, unmarked government van that was moved and parked within a few blocks from wherever I was during those two days. Later on while aboard the Lightship, I was shown a few brief and periodic movements of this vehicle that may have helped the team of psychic assassins to more easily tune-in to me and my whereabouts.

As I came to find out, "Big Brother" has been constantly monitoring and recording phone conversations and they have even trained many agents in the past to read people's minds. These agents have been referred to, literally, as the "thought police." The cabal has been especially watching and listening to those who have posed a major threat to their agenda. It actually has given me comfort in knowing that I have been fulfilling my Mission very effectively, if they have been so "threatened" by the work that I have been doing including the publishing of this book. And, while "they" may have been monitoring me, guess **Who** has been monitoring them at the same time, our "Friends Upstairs," of course! In fact, I have specifically mentioned this over the phone many times to let them know that I know that they are listening. Or, as I like to humorously state, "Yes, Big Space Brother is monitoring them!" And, as I have also stated many times, "as long as they can never take away my sense of humor, they can never destroy me."

Although I do not remember most of my movements during those two days, I very clearly remember a phone conversation that I had with Ron. I believe that I remember this important verbal interchange because of the particular significance of what occurred while I was speaking to him. Even though I don't remember anything else from our conversation, what I do remember is that Ron direct-voice channeled a message to me from Commander Korton.

"This is Commander Korton of the Ashtar Command of the Intergalactic Confederation. My brother Michael, I am channeling and coming through our fellow Light brother and Volunteer Ron to confirm to you that you are to have physical contact with us within the coming hours. You, and Ron, are to go out to the Upland area (near L.A.). Prepare yourself, our brother, for this!"

As stated, I am uncertain whether this phone call happened on the 23rd or the 24th. Regardless of the day, Ron and I went to the Upland, California area on the following afternoon. I remember getting into Ron's van and traveling to a specific location in Upland where Ron said he had received one or more telepathic messages that told him where to go. The location was supposed to be where this physical encounter was to take place.

However, it seems that our "Friends Upstairs" were just giving the government a "ride for their money." They must have only been pretending to have physical contact at that time for when we got out of the van and stood around for awhile nothing, of course, occurred. One thing that I do remember about the situation was feeling this intense negative feeling, as if someone was very powerfully and negatively monitoring and attempting to "probe" our minds and consciousness. I also had a feeling of some "imminent" negative event that was about to happen. At the same time, what I was mostly experiencing was strange "disassociation" or "detachment" feelings.

After we had waited for awhile, Ron mentioned that it was getting late and that he had to work in the morning. So, he took me back to where he had earlier picked me up and we ended our little sojourn.

At Sylvia Wilson's House

Soon after Ron and I returned from Upland, I got the feeling that I should call a woman whom I had met prior to going to Oregon. Her name was Sylvia Wilson. Sylvia was a woman in her late twenties or early thirties who had had an interest in UFOs and metaphysics for many years. She lived in the town of Aguora, California which was not too far from the L.A. area.

When I called her on the phone, she invited me to stay at her place for a couple days as she said she had a lot of information that she wanted to relate to me. This information was about some of the UFO and metaphysical experiences that she had had since we had last seen each other. She related that she wanted to get some metaphysical insight about her experiences as she knew that I was a very clear channel.

Interestingly, the strange disassociation-detachment I had been experiencing went away for a few hours. But, even when this happened, I still felt an intense "psychic probing" that seemed to come and go. I realized later on that what I was feeling was the cabal making final preparations for their psychotonic assault on me.

Sylvia picked me up and drove me to her home in Aguora. After we walked inside, I began feeling the incredible "spaceiness" again. It would come and go over the next several hours as I began to feel what was coming my way from the cabal.

Sylvia and I talked for hours about our individual UFO and metaphysical experiences. Finally, in the early morning hours, she excused herself and went to her bedroom to get some sleep. I, on the other hand, planned to crash on the living room floor or sofa as I had brought my sleeping bag with me. For a few minutes, I just sat there thinking about all that we had discussed.

I must have fallen asleep for a short while when, suddenly, I woke up needing to go to the bathroom. As I was stumbling back out of the bathroom, things got very dramatic. I was unaware that I was about to be physically beamed onto the Merkabah Lightship that was hovering above Sylvia's home. Fortunately, the beings in the Lightship were closely monitoring what the cabal had been doing to me.

Once again I was in that strange disassociated-detached state and it was more intense than ever. At that point, I experienced two totally conflicting states of being. One was a very negative and overpowering force of biological destruction to my physical body as if someone (both spiritually and biologically) had violated my very essence with death and destruction. It was as if a negative dark hand reached right into my physical body and literally ripped the life-force out of me, causing all (or most) of the chakras or main energy vortex centers of my body to be "ripped to shreds." The other state of being that I was simultaneously experiencing was like a very calm and soothing force that allowed me to become "detached" for those last moments of my physical life.

Then, these benevolent beings intervened and physically teleported me aboard their ship and, in doing so, they saved my life. Or, perhaps, it would be more accurate to say that they brought me back to life from having physically died on Earth for a brief moment before they physically beamed me onboard. There is a scene from "The Day The Earth Stood Still" (the original '50's flying saucer motion picture classic, not to be confused with the recent *negative* and *disgusting* remake of the movie) where the benevolent human-appearing space-being Klantu (played by the actor Michael Ranie) is killed by the Earth's military and he is taken immediately back aboard his ship (by the giant robot) where he is brought back to life by a rejuvenator device. That particular scene reminded me of what I experienced in real life.

I do want to emphasize that it was most definitely a physical encounter that I had, just as it was in '59. I had been taken up into a Higher realm (6th dimensional) rather than what happens in the case of abductions (which occur on the third or fourth dimensional levels) where the renegade grey aliens kidnap Earth humans for their negative genetic experiments. It was also not just a "very vivid dream" as other ufologists might want to believe. I can clearly tell the difference between this encounter and vivid dreams that I have had. It was also not an "out-of-body-experience" (OBE) as I have experienced when I have "ethereally" traveled aboard the ships.

My next conscious memory was waking up aboard the Merkabah Lightship. At first, my memory of all that occurred was somewhat incomplete, because of the intensity of what I had just experienced - literally dying and being brought back to life aboard the craft. I often use an analogy to explain how I (physically) felt upon coming back to consciousness aboard the craft in a state that was very near physical death. Imagine a sponge being wrung dry of water; that was like my energy having been taken from my physical body due to the psychotronic attack.

At that time, I didn't remember much that occurred aboard the Lightship and I had to wait awhile before I remembered most of my experience In fact, when I was physically beamed back to Earth, I was induced into a relaxed and semi-sleep state. The purpose for this was to help me adapt vibrationally and to allow my physical body to continue with the biological strengthening process that was started aboard the Lightship. This involved strengthening my DNA/RNA to help shield and protect me from any future attempts on my life and, also, to help prepare me for the work I was to do. Over the next few days when I returned to full consciousness, I obtained more complete memories of this encounter, but, to begin with, I had very little memory of what occurred while I was aboard the Lightship.

When they physically beamed me back into Sylvia's home, I was basically returned to the same location on my sleeping bag as I was when they teleported me aboard the ship. As I tried to sit up and, then, stand up, I experienced a strange dizziness and light-headedness. Along with that, I was feeling very weird sensations as if I was literally feeling the blood running through the veins in my body. As I was getting onto my feet, I moved a little too fast and almost fainted. Medical experts would state that this physical sensation was just the blood rushing to my head, but this was definitely something more than that. I remembered a warning that I was given by my "Friends Upstairs" about physically moving too quickly after they worked on stabilizing me. I was told that for approximately a month, I would be experiencing these "irritating" physical sensations. They said it was because it would take that amount of time for my blood to "physically stabilize" from the unique harmonic DNA/RNA "Consciousness Technology" procedure that they had put me through. Furthermore, they related that my entire system, both physically and spiritually, would be greatly strengthened when the process was finally complete.

DNA/RNA Consciousness Technology

This DNA/RNA strengthening procedure was done for two reasons. One reason was to help protect me from any future attempts of "psychic deadly force" by the cabal. Even though all Volunteers who come to Earth on "Cosmic Spiritual Espionage Missions of Light" already have "Higher Protection" from the Spiritual Hierarchy, this stabilization process would now make it even easier for them to protect and "Overshadow" me.

The harmonic DNA/RNA "Consciousness Technology" procedure that I went through altered my blood. This procedure used the harmonic "Consciousness Holographic Computer" aboard the Merkabah that is directly "plugged" into the Godhead, which I would describe as a computer with a consciousness system from a Higher source.

I also was equipped (internally) with my own high level security system. This system, which is much more advanced than what the cabal could possibly conceive, detects anyone attempting to use any kind of psychotronic weapon on me and automatically changes my own harmonic-biological vibrations to a different frequency. And, even if the attackers are able to readjust their system to my new vibration, by the time they do that, my system would automatically and instantly readjust to a different harmonic vibration. This would continue on for as many times as necessary in order to protect me so I can continue with my Mission on planet Earth. It works on any level of reality, whether it is psychic, spiritual, biological, or physical in nature. And, it doesn't matter if the attack is coming from an alien or Earthly source. The result is that the weapons used by the negative forces will not work on me because they are tuned into a different frequency (so to speak).

I was also made aware that this "Cosmic" protection is only at it's most powerful and totally failsafe level, if I adhere to certain requirements. This "energy recipe" requires that I maintain a specific diet and a natural holistic lifestyle and, also, that I live my life with conscious intent and follow certain spiritual lifestyle practices. In other words, I have to assume total and disciplined responsibility in regard to all I think, say, and do. And, if I follow this "energy recipe," I would literally be immune to attacks for the rest of this lifetime.

Probably, most Earth people will feel that these dietary requirements are "too strict." But, as we all have free will and choices, if I want to have the maximum level of Higher protection and empowering that I need for my Mission, then, I know that I must adhere to the requirements. After all, "God helps those who help themselves!" (I heard this phrase several times while I was on the Lightship.)

The second major reason for this procedure was to help me assist other Earth Volunteers to "Cosmically activate" their own DNA/RNA consciousness levels. This would be accomplished through my channeling work. Part of my Mission is to help individuals (for whom I am destined to do channelings) gain a conscious understanding of their own Earthly Missions. Also, they may receive information from the channeling about their soul's galactic or planetary origins and about future opportunities that may be coming up so that they can take advantage of these possibilities and help manifest them more abundantly.

Whenever I do a reading for someone, there are positive "galactic subliminals" that are harmonically and cellularly interphased on the cassette tape of the channeled reading during the session. When the Volunteers listen to these powerful harmonic recordings, the "subliminal-subconscious programming" helps them consciously awaken. There is also the potential for a Higher biological and psychic protection that is available to them when they play back the recordings. This protection is available only if they choose to accept responsibility for following a disciplined dietary and natural-holistic lifestyle (just like I have been required to do).

So, does this mean that they would be "depriving" themselves of all the things (in regard to their diets) that they supposedly enjoyed before? The truth is that what they are truly depriving themselves of presently is a higher quality of health, well being, and better energy levels. From a dietary point of view, the "crap" that most people in our modern society eat is nothing but "empty" calories and a lot of chemicals and additives. The effect of this keeps them totally "numbed and dumbed out," as far as their consciousness is concerned. Eating like this means that they also will develop weak immune systems and pollute their bodies with toxins. Then, they wonder why they get sick, why their bodies begin to break down, and why they start to age. And, they are probably spending a lot of time and money on doctors and pharmaceutical drugs, as well.

What they are truly depriving themselves of is a more productive, empowered, healthy, and vibrant physical life and, due to their low energy, they will never be able to achieve their dreams and aspirations. Also, they will not be able to have the ultimate experience of the "Spiritual Ascension" as their vibrations are much too low since they are "literally" out of tune spiritually.

My Veiled Memory

After I was beamed back to Sylvia's house, I was initially bothered that I could not remember more of the UFO encounter though I was told very strongly through my own telepathic communications that before the day was over much more would be unveiled.

Later, when Sylvia came into the room, I told her (very excitedly) all that I could remember of what I had just experienced during the last few hours. In regard to my lack of memory, she said that she had a very strong feeling that I would be able to remember more of the total experience very soon. She mentioned that there was a "cutting-edge" metaphysical meeting that evening in the L.A. area that she felt very strongly that I should go to. I sensed that she was receiving a type of telepathic message from our "Friends Upstairs."

Throughout the day, I continued to have the disassociated-detached feelings and most of the day was a "blur." At one point, I remember calling Ron to tell him about my experience. And, I am sure the cabal (who I am sure were monitoring the phone call) were shocked to discover that I was still very much alive.

Early that evening after Sylvia returned from work, we headed to the meeting. Sylvia mentioned that she felt I should meet a friend of hers (also named Michael) who might be at the meeting. Later on, I discovered that this meeting was arranged by my "Friends Upstairs" to help educate me about the need to wear (and utilize) natural quartz crystals (combined with other gemstones) for Higher protection and empowerment. The benevolent human-appearing ETs and the Spiritual Hierarchy use these natural crystals and gemstones to transfer important information to us here on Earth. The crystals act as a powerful "tuning-fork" to help, protect, guide, and empower the Volunteers that are here on Earth assignments (On Earth Assignment was a popular 1980's book by the famous, very-clear channel Tuella.). More information on crystals will be discussed in another chapter.

I remember very little about the meeting that we attended, but about halfway through it we took a short break. At that time, Sylvia's friend, Michael, came over and introduced himself. He stated that on the previous day he was guided to drive from L.A. to a small town named Fallbrook (about 50 miles south) and to go to a specific metaphysical store. In the store, he was supposed to purchase a couple of natural quartz crystals that he would be very strongly drawn to. (Crystals have different harmonic-vibrations and some are definitely more powerful than others.) When he arrived at the store, Michael said that he was drawn to two crystals that felt like they were extremely powerful and had certain rare and unique qualities for quartz crystals.

As he was explaining this to me, he reached into his pockets and pulled out the two crystals. They were both a little over two inches in length and about an inch in width. He handed them to me, putting one in each of my hands. Then, he directed me to put the one in my right hand up against the center part of my body. This is where the seven main chakras or energy vortex centers are located.

He told me to hold the other crystal away from my body and somewhat above me. (People receive energy through their left hands and then send this energy through their right hands into themselves [or others] that they are in the process of healing and activating.)

This was my first usage of natural quartz crystals, so I did not know what to expect. As I closed my eyes and "tuned-in" to see what I might feel, I experienced an awesome and powerful transfer of Higher knowledge from my "Friends Upstairs." It was what I call a "spontaneous-synergistic activation of empowerment" or to put it another way, a powerful "Cosmic Epiphany of Self-Realization" had just taken place! In simpler terms, in that instant most of what I had experienced (and hadn't remembered) while aboard the Merkabah Lightship flooded into my conscious mind.

Medical Treatment on the Merkabah

The following account is what I recalled as my memory returned. The first thing I was aware of (beyond my physical condition that I described earlier) when I gained consciousness aboard the ship was that I was lying on the most comfortable padded couch I have ever been on (at least on planet Earth). It was literally like lying on a cloud. I had the telepathic sensation that what I was lying on was more than an inanimate material substance. It was like touching a living entity.

I felt a strange sensation, as one does when they are about to astrally leave their physical body and have an out-of-body experience. Then, I floated out and above my physical body that was below me on the couch.

Four very handsome human-appearing beings dressed in shiny blue metallic jumpsuits, were standing around my body. I felt beautiful energy, serenity, and unconditional love that they were sending me.

I noticed that the chamber walls and the floor of the room had the same glowing white and pulsating appearance as I had experienced before. Then, I watched the wall open up and a small container with a clear glass covering appeared. Next, the beings guided a couple of long, slender clear cords from the wall and stuck one of them into my arm and the other one into my leg. I watched (from my detached astral state) as they began to remove the blood from my body. It flowed through the transparent cord into the glowing, light-filled container. I saw intense light rays of different colors being projected through my blood and it was being altered in some way. It appeared to be "slashing around" similar to what it looks like when oil and water are being mixed together.

The beings were very aware of my astral body floating near them. I tele-pathically asked what they were doing with my blood. Even as I asked the question, I sensed that something very positive and wonderful had transpired. It was conveyed to me that certain harmonic energies, rays, and other elements were being projected through my blood which would strengthen me on many levels.

One of them was holding a device in his hand that appeared very similar to the one that was used on me 20 years before on my first visit. This device was projecting rainbow-colored rays into my body from the end of a long slender flexible cable. As he continued this "treatment," I began to feel my life-force rapidly increase as once more my weak chakras began to strengthen. Within about 15 to 20 minutes, I had regained all of my energy and vitality and my chakras were strong, aligned, and balanced. In fact, I had even more energy than I normally do and I felt like I could have "jumped over a building."

I noticed a horizontal shelf that was extended out from the wall that ap-peared to be levitating. There were a number of translucent appearing objects on the shelf that were approximately one-half to one inch in diameter. I noticed that there were seven of them and that each was glowing slightly with one of the different colors of the rainbow. I recognized them as some type of crystalline or crystal lens, but they were so transparent that they appeared to be etheric rather than physical in nature. As I learned later on, they were, in fact, of a Higher vibration or frequency level.

Next, one of the beings telepathically directed one of the crystal-appearing objects to levitate up off of the surface and over towards my body. The objects, as they were being levitated, moved over about an inch above my body for a moment and then descended towards each of my seven main chakra points as they began to glow and light up. When they came into contact with the rainbow rays being emitted by the other device, the seven etheric crystals merged into my physical body. I felt a slight tingling and warm sensation as they did this. I instinctively knew that this was a type of Higher etheric bionics" that was helping strengthen and balance the seven main chakras in my physical body.

Then, the beings standing around me pushed the device and the cable it was attached to back into the wall. When it went back into the white glowing wall, it was as if it just merged, molecularly, into the wall. It became a part of the wall itself with no apparent crack or aperture. After they completed the treatment, my astral body immediately floated back down and joined my physical body.

I am estimating "time" on this Higher 6th dimensional realm aboard the Merkabah, but I probably was in that astral state right above my physical body for about 15 to 20 minutes and it was unique to have an O.B.E. while having been taken physically aboard the ship.

During the time that I had been lying on that very comfortable couch, the four beings had been telepathically speaking to one another. I kept (telepathically) hearing them comment on my refusal to follow their "suggestions," that, in a sense, had gotten me into this predicament. They mentioned how important it was that their Emissaries in Earth embodiment (like me) needed to follow more closely what they suggested to do. They were not speaking in a critical or judgmental way, but rather it was like an unconditionally-loving reminder of what each of us needs to do in order to make our Missions "failsafe" and to be more successful in the process. They conveyed a very important understanding that we (Earth beings and our Space Brothers) are "all in this together." At the same time, I sensed that they were speaking with a "dry sense of humor," despite the very seriousness of what I had just gone through. In fact, many contactees have noted from first-hand experiences that the more advanced a being is, the more well-rounded their sense of humor is. I mention this because I sensed them very gently and chidingly reminding me of my responsibility whenever they made the comment, "God helps those who help themselves."

The Holographic Crystal Computer

Once they had finished their work on my physical body, one of the four beings told me (telepathically) that I could now get up and go to another part of the ship. I got up, feeling amazingly good after my "life saving experience," and followed him. We immediately entered a hallway with walls that were emanating a glow of warmth and unconditional love. I sensed that this corridor led to the center of the ship and the central control room. We traveled approximately thirty feet when a door suddenly appeared before us. I knew that this was the entrance to the main communication-control room of the ship.

I entered a huge chamber which was about 60 to 70 feet across and at least 20 feet or more in height. One of the first things that got my attention was a crystal-clear tube that surrounded an intensely-brilliant and pulsating shaft of light extending from the floor to the ceiling. I knew that this was the "holographic crystal computer" (consciousness technology) that is the direct link to the Godhead of the Universe (the I Am That I Am or Heavenly Father-Mother God Force). The shaft of brilliant, pure light and energy was like an aspect of this great God Force that was focused through this crystal computer. This computer is aboard most of the more advanced Intergalactic Command starships of the Federation of Light known as the Merkabah.

There were about 20 to 25 crewmembers (about as many males as females) working on the computers and monitoring screens that were placed within the chamber. Although they did not look in my direction, I sensed their telepathic greetings of hello and welcoming me aboard their craft. They were all dressed in either blue, silver, or white jumpsuits, except for one being who was dressed in red with gold epaulet. The one in red was standing against a wall with his back turned slightly toward me and was speaking to the Commander of this craft. I knew that this was Commander Korton.

As I approached him from across the chamber, Korton turned toward me and began to approach me. He walked up with a grin on his face and he grabbed my arm and gave me a familiar arm shake (a gesture of Universal friendship). His eyes were intensely focused upon me with great concern in regard to what I had just gone through. He welcomed me aboard, and then made the comment "God helps those who help themselves." I was somewhat embarrassed for I knew exactly what he was referring to. He was "rubbing it in," as they say here on Earth, regarding the predicament I had gotten myself into. And, I had to admit that I had made the mistake of ignoring his telepathic suggestions about doing what would make me less vulnerable to the psychotronic attacks. My ego had assumed that since I was a "Cosmic Spiritual Rainbow Warrior of Light" (before this lifetime) and because I was specifically linked to the Cosmic ancestry of Archangel Michael, then, I must be superior and, therefore, I rationalized that I did not need to wear the natural quartz crystal and gem stones which I was telepathically told I should. This would have strengthened my auric field, including the seven energy vortexes (chakras) in my body. So, obviously, it was my own responsibility, on a conscious level, that got me into this dangerous predicament.

Korton then reached over to one of the nearby computer systems and retrieved a small disk-shaped object (called a "universal credit chip") about the size of a quarter that was a silver-gold color. He held it up briefly in front of me and then slipped it into a slot that I sensed was connected to the shaft of light before us. What occurred next could only be described as the ultimate holographic video and sound system that one can imagine. What happened was that the pulsating shaft of bright white light changed dramatically to very clear colorful images within the tube. Instantly, colorful images merged with the entire room becoming an advanced "virtual reality" 3-dimensional, holographic picture with depth, sound, and smell. It was as if I was there in person looking in on what was going on around me. (In the New Generation of Star Trek TV series, the crew uses a similar type of technology [aboard the Enterprise] called the "Holodeck.")

The first holographic images that appeared were scenes from my recent human embodiments (before this one) prior to returning to the Higher worlds. I then saw myself in my own galactic "immortal physical Light body" which is a "physical" body with a Higher vibrational density than my Earth physical body. This galactic Light body is the same type of "etheric-physical" body that is used by Korton and the advanced human-appearing ETs of the Intergalactic Confederation.

Through this scene I relived the experience of lying upon a flat white crystalline slab with a clear crystal cover over it as my original extraterrestrial body was put into a type of "energy deep-freeze storage." My body remained in this state until I was ready to use my body again at which time my soul and spirit were literally beamed from the starship (while it hovered over the Earth on the Higher 6th dimensional level) into my Earth mother's womb about 20 minutes before I was born into my present life.

The next holographic scene that was recreated was my visit to the Merkabah in '59 (my present lifetime) at six years of age. What followed were several more scenes of other events that I had experienced up until the UFO encounter that I was presently experiencing. I now know, literally, what was referred to in the Bible when it describes the "Book of Life" as containing "everything one has experienced, thought, or done."

Because this "consciousness computer" taps directly into what one on Earth would describe as God or "Divine Intelligence," these computers have been programmed to be in alignment with the Divine Will and the Divine Plan of the Universe and to always, automatically, be attuned to each Volunteer's Divine Will. This depends, of course, upon the Volunteer's own personal lessons that he/she is supposed to experience, his/her Mission, and any Earthly karma that he/she has created in this life or any past lives on Earth. Sometimes, too, the computer has the capacity or "Higher authority" to automatically intervene in situations that would stop one from completing his/her Mission.

In respect of our privacy, the ship's consciousness computer is "impersonally" monitoring Volunteers in Earth embodiment all the time so that if anyone is in any kind of danger, the computer instantly can tell what needs to be done to protect the individual.

This is the opposite extreme from what the "grays" have done of abducting people against their free will. Actually, these Higher, angelic forces of the Federation of Light do not "invade our privacy" nor are they looking in on us all the time.

That which is described as intent or motive of the individual is the deciding factor that specifically affects the operation of these advanced "consciousness computer systems." For example, one does not jump out of a building, as if to test this protection, and say to the Higher Forces "Save me!" For there would be no protection afforded one in that kind of situation. It is only when one has done the best he/she honestly could do in a given situation and something occurs that threatens him/her (physically or psychically) with the danger of being severely hurt or killed, then this Higher protection automatically comes into effect. This protection will also be intensified whenever one uses Light decrees and prayers, such as "Not my will, but Thy Will be done." Additionally, an even Higher level of protection is provided for those who have taken full responsibility and are dedicated and devoted to improving themselves physically and spiritually for the sake of uplifting humanity.

After I was shown these vivid holographic scenes from the past to help re-affirm this Higher protection, Korton quoted a statement in the Bible. He said, "I will send my angels charge over thee." Then, with a twinkle in his eye (like "I told you so"), he made the statement, "Now wear crystal! And, tell the other Light Workers, Volunteers, and Emissaries in Earth embodiment how they are protected by those of us who surround the planet in 'Guardian Action'." (This was a very interesting term that he specifically emphasized as a few years later Tuella [famous channel and contactee] named her Earth-based organization "Guardian Action Publications.")

Information Conveyed by Korton

Korton explained how the combination of natural quartz crystals and different natural gemstones strengthens one's auric field and chakras. He conveyed information about doing very powerful color meditations and certain Light decrees to strengthen the auric field, the spiritual-etheric immune system, and the physical immune system. He also discussed a number of important things about diet and nutrition which included eating only natural, organic foods and staying away from refined and processed foods with chemical additives (more in a later book of this series). As he explained, it is everything that one does (macro-view) physically, mentally, emotionally, psychologically, and psychically-spiritually, ("energy recipe") that either raises one's energies and life-force, or lowers and weakens it. It's basic Earth common sense or as Korton would state, "It is also 'galactic common sense' to strive for this higher quality of life and consciousness."

I was then reminded by Korton of many things that I had been told through previous telepathic and channeled communication from him, Ashtar, various Ascended Masters and Cosmic Beings of Light, and other benevolent ETs. Much that Korton "reconfirmed" at that time, **is, in fact, much of the information contained within this book.**

He specifically mentioned the secret plans of the illuminati, otherwise known as the cabal. Additionally, he shared details about the particular negative renegade group of ETs known as the "grays" and also the reptilian aliens (referred in the Bible as the "Nephilian"), as well as those referred to as the "Men in Black" (MIB). He said that some of the "Men in Black" are actually shape-shifting reptilian aliens, while others are part of the NSA's 'black budget project" section. These gray aliens have made agreements with the cabal to secretly share their technology in exchange for resources which includes abducting whomever they want to for the purpose of conducting genetic experiments.

Korton confirmed (what I already knew) that part of my Mission on Earth was to act as a "troubleshooter" or "whistleblower" to assist the Intergalactic Forces of Light by uncovering, documenting, and ultimately stopping the vast planetary "International Conspiracy of Silence" concerning the benevolent human-appearing ETs. This would also include uncovering and documenting anything planned by the cabal that attempts to enslave humanity through a one world government, otherwise known as the "New World Order."

I was told that some of this documentation and information was of a top secret security level and that it would be released through declassified means. Sometime after this experience, I heard for the first time about the Freedom of Information Act (FOIA) and how a number of attorneys and retired government and military individuals were instrumental in helping get thousands of pages of highly-classified documents released. Allowing this kind of information (about benevolent human-appearing ETs coming to Earth) to be readily available to the public, was, of course, a threat to the cabal. An example of this type of information is the Air Force Cadet Manual which was actually taught for over 20 years to the cadets during their fourth year at the Air Force Academy in Colorado Springs, Colorado (Introductory Space Science 370).

He mentioned that I would be meeting many former military intelligence agents and ex-undercover operatives who would be sincerely sharing this information, along with documentation, and in turn, I would share it with the public through major media interviews over radio, TV, and in the newspapers. Korton said that I would be instrumental in helping enlighten the public of these facts and that eventually a "popcorn-effect" would occur. The "popcorn effect" meant that many retired government and military personnel, who had been at top secret and "above" security levels, would start "coming out of the closet" to officially and publicly divulge such information (Yes, courageous individuals, like William Cooper, who wrote the book Behold a Pale Horse.)

This "popcorn effect" would occur partly because of an increase of new "Cosmic Light energies" hitting the planet which would help to vibrationally lift people's consciousness (**This is now happening!**). Another reason that the "popcorn effect" is occurring is due to the large number of "Walk-in" souls that are coming into human embodiment. A third reason for this to occur is that the Higher Forces are sending down "tensor-activation beams" from the Lightships to open up our synoptic centers, which are the psychic-spiritual centers of the brain. All of these things are occurring to spiritually awaken Earth's humanity to the Higher realities.

While I was in the communications-control room, I noticed a number of interesting things that were happening. Many of the different computer screens were showing Earth scenes that were happening right at that moment. One screen showed the downtown L. A. area. I telepathically sensed that the ship was studying and recording levels of physical pollution, as well as vibrational (spiritual-psychic) pollution and the effects upon the consciousness of those who were living there. Other scenes were of various cities around the world, forest and wilderness areas, and even different military bases. (I was aware that the Intergalactic Confederation was keeping a close eye on the development of nuclear weapons, as well as all types of psychotronics, mind control, weather modification, and other "black budget" projects.

One of the more interesting scenes that I viewed was of a 60 to 70 year old woman writing down a telepathic message (also known as "inspired" or "automatic writing") that she was receiving at that time from the Beings onboard the ship that I was on. I realized that similar scenes happen millions of times all over the world every day and night as different Volunteers in Earth embodiment receive telepathic messages from different beings (on different ships of the different fleets of the different Commands of the entire Universal Federation) that surround the Earth (in parking orbit) in Guardian Action.

As I was watching this woman receive the message, Korton telepathically confirmed what I was thinking. "Yes, as you are observing from our physical presence on a Higher dimension aboard this ship, this female Volunteer presently upon Earth is receiving another message from us. Despite the skepticism and bias of all those, as you term it, 'UFO investigators' who have trouble accepting our particular existence, we do, never-the-less, constantly transmute different types of messages, some definitely spiritual and esoteric in nature, as we previously did for many of the courageous contactees of the '50's and '60's." At this point, he specifically made reference to certain famous contactees to confirm their authenticity.

Then, he made a personal remark to me: "I would specifically make a comment to you, our brother Michael, that as you suspected, you definitely have been telepathically guided by us in discovering printed documents and books (out of print or hard to find) about the earlier contactees. You have also been guided to meet some of these early pioneers, as well as many sincere people who personally knew many of these individuals." He spoke at length about the UFO community and the "Flying Saucer Movement" which will be addressed in the next book of this series.

Korton very passionately stated: "We of the Federation have a message for you. It is a most important point for you to make to those with whom you will share this present experience. Many Earth UFO investigators have criticized the early authentic contactees of the '50s and '60s for what appeared to be 'contradictions' when sharing their personal real-life experiences with others. The important thing is that just because one contactee seems to have had an experience that appears to contradict the experience of another contactee does not mean that both of their experiences are not valid. Rather, the so-called "discrepancies" are due to the lack of understanding on the part of the UFO investigators. This is partly because they do not see the bigger picture and also because of a continual hidden agenda of ridiculing and maligning the courageous pioneers who have had contact with us. They need to also recognize that we are all unique individuals and we sometimes see things quite differently."

After lengthy communication from Korton, I was guided to sit down in a padded chair in front of one of the computer screens. Korton reminded me that these Higher consciousness systems were mentally-telepathically controlled and operated. I knew that I had operated them previously, when I, too, was a starship Commander on these Higher dimensions of the Universe. I began, almost automatically, to mentally activate this very advanced system. For a brief instant, I caught sight of a 3rd-dimensional image beginning to form on the screen. Then I suddenly lost consciousness for awhile during which I knew that I had experienced a relay of knowledge of some kind that was programmed into my mind and consciousness at a very deep level. I knew that I would not be able to consciously access this information (even under a deep hypnotic trance) until the time was right, when I needed access to it.

After I returned to a full conscious state, Korton explained to me what I was experiencing and the reasons for it. He said that they vibrationally-harmonically altered my blood. This was necessary to cleanse it and to activate the "electrolytes" within the blood which would raise my vibrational level. Additionally, the activation of the "electrolytes" would help open up my synoptic centers (the spiritual-psychic centers of the brain) so I, in turn, would be better able to assist other Volunteers in becoming activated.

He then gave me a significant message, "From now on, you will specifically be doing channelings for other Volunteers who are the Eagle Commanders and Commanderesses in Earth embodiment." This expression "Eagle Commanders and Commanderesses" was one of the statements that Tuella (and others) channeled from these same Space Brothers and Sisters. It refers to spiritual responsibilities that many of the present day Earth Volunteers have had on a Higher Cosmic level before they took Earth embodiment. These Volunteers may have come in either at birth (incarnates) or as "Walk-ins" (soul mergence or soul transfers in later years), as is well described and documented in Ruth Montgomery's two books, Strangers Among Us and Aliens Among Us. In fact, there may be many individuals who are reading this that are Volunteers.

He communicated to me that after I returned to Earth I would soon discover a list of traits that would help identify those of us who are extra-terrestrial souls in Earth embodiment. These highly-evolved Volunteers are on Missions from more advanced worlds to help the Earth in its spiritual Ascension process and to liberate the planet from the control of the imbalanced forces. And, in fact, I did discover a list of characteristics about two months later that will be thoroughly described in Chapter 5.

The information that Korton shared with me is quite significant for those who feel a strong rapport with the information in this book and/or who know inwardly or suspect that they are Volunteers (in Earth embodiment) from another world. It is also significant, because a few years later I met and became close friends with the channeler Tuella, who published several excellent books about her own experiences with Lord Ashtar and others of the Ashtar Command. Prior to her ascension back to the Higher realms in 1993, Tuella formed the Guardian Action International which was based on the experiences and information that these benevolent forces of the Light had shared with her and others. One of her greatest books was a very accurate and detailed account of the upcoming Divine Intervention called Project: World Evacuation by the Ashtar Command.

He emphasized the seriousness of my work as a channel and said that fellow Volunteers would be guided to me for channeling sessions. He explained that the total number of Volunteers or "Star People" in Earth embodiment was approximately 11% to 12% of the total Earth's population in early '79 (It is now over 17%.) and that I would only have time to meet a small percentage of them. He said that these individuals were usually from the original "Core Group" of 144,000 Volunteers who first took Earth embodiment many millions of years ago to start the long process of ultimately liberating this planet from the hands of the dark forces. (Since this experience, I estimate that I have done several thousand of these "Cosmic channelings" for fellow Volunteers.)

In the back of my mind throughout the time that I was aboard the Merkabah, I realized that I did not "hate" those who had tried to psychotronically assassinate me. I also knew that I would not be afraid or intimidated in any way by these negative forces for I had first-hand knowledge/experience that I had a very powerful "Cosmic Back-Up Team." Furthermore, I knew that I was now prepared to move forward with my Mission and that one of my jobs was to "officially" inform the "powers that be" that the human-appearing ETs and the spiritual, angelic forces of the Universe will always protect their own Emissaries (who are technically representing the Higher Councils). Moreover, they will be taking more direct action to make sure that their "Cosmic Sons and Daughters" are totally protected, guided, and Overshadowed to help fulfill their Missions. This fulfills the promise that was agreed on prior to incarnation that as long as one is true to the Higher spiritual code of ethics, ideals, and principles, then these Higher beings will always Intervene when called upon.

After Korton finished giving me this information, he explained that they were about to physically beam me back down to Earth and that I had to be careful over the next month or so. He warned me not to make quick movements or I might experience "side effects" such as mild fainting spells or dizziness. He also explained that I would feel much stronger and more balanced and centered within my being. A short time later, I was physically beamed back down to Earth where they had first beamed me up.

Back On Planet Earth

I remembered all of the foregoing experience after I returned and was holding the natural quartz crystals that Michael (Sylvia's friend) had handed me. When I "tuned-in" to the crystals, I experienced the powerful transfer of Higher knowledge from my "Friends Upstairs." This triggered my recall of all that happened during my time on the Lightship.

The "Cosmic amnesia" veils that had been placed over me (when I left the ship) were totally released. I also received a strong telepathic message from Commander Korton that the main reason they placed the veils over me was to provide me with this experience of utilizing natural crystals. Their hope was that I would be inspired and start using them as a resource with my work in activating and empowering fellow Volunteers.

So, from this experience, I learned first-hand about the effects of using crystals for activation, amplification, and empowerment. And, I knew that it was time for me to start utilizing this technology, synergistically, with the other things that Korton had shared with me aboard the ship. I knew this experience would help me and the others that I would be working with on our "Cosmic Spiritual Espionage Missions of Light." I also knew, especially with the publication of this book, that I could help enlighten others (on a far greater mass level) about the cover-up and the plans by the Higher Forces to effectively counteract this with a

"Divine Intervention" and "World Evacuation." And, I knew that the main focus of my Mission was now to help others ***"Prepare for the Landings."***

CHAPTER 4

DR. RAY BROWN & THE ATLANTEAN CRYSTAL

This rare and fascinating story is, in our opinion, one of the most unusual and significant events to occur in our modern times. I assure you that the story you are about to read is factual to the absolute best of my ability to recall and relate it to you. The following is an account of what both Michael and I recall concerning Dr Ray Brown and the fantastic Atlantean Crystal. This includes our own experiences, as well as, what Ray personally related to us.

Edgar Cayce's Prophecy

One of the most captivating and, also, perhaps least-known prophecies of the famous "Sleeping Prophet" and seer Edgar Cayce, relates that sometime "In the years of 1968 or 1969, an underwater Atlantean pyramid will be uncovered on the ocean floor." Cayce went on to say that, "A person will penetrate the pyramid and retrieve a crystal and will bring this remarkable Atlantean power-crystal back to the surface. Many remarkable things will occur to the people who experience its powerful transformational presence."

It was, in fact, in the year 1968, when Dr. Ray Brown, a Naturopath Medical Doctor and professional diver, fulfilled this famous prophecy. Dr. Brown made this discovery while on a scuba diving expedition with the famous Jacques Cousteau team. As one will learn, the circumstances surrounding this spiritually-destined and historical event are extraordinary. As with so many of Edgar Cayce's famous prophecies, this one too was destined to be fulfilled.

This unusual event has been the theme of several television documentaries in years past. During the '70's, the "In Search Of" television show did an extensive investigation into Dr. Ray Brown's experience and documented his retrieval of the Atlantean crystal. In recent years, this show has been replayed a number of times because of its fascinating nature.

Their Diving Expedition

The adventure story begins as Dr. Ray Brown and several members of the Jacques Cousteau team were on their way back to Miami, Florida after an extended treasure-hunting expedition to South America. While returning from their initial expedition, the diving team was approaching the Bimini Islands in the Bahamas.

Note: This is the notorious Bermuda Triangle area where vast numbers of ships and planes have, literally, disappeared throughout the years. They simply vanish, never to be seen again, that is, at least for now. But, who knows, perhaps in the future all these missing airplanes, ships, and even the people may reappear from another dimension as the earth manifests the upcoming prophesied Golden Age.

Just as the divers were approaching this area, a threatening storm suddenly came out of nowhere. Dr. Brown, and the crew, observed one of those dreaded water-spout storms developing close by. These types of storms are sometimes referred to as "water tornadoes," because these potentially destructive and violent storms take on the form of a tornado. Unlike the tornadoes which occur on land and uproot everything in their path, these types of water spouts can violently (like a Hoover vacuum) suck up and disrupt areas of the ocean floor. These storms are relatively common in the Bermuda Triangle and they usually last only a few minutes before dissipating.

According to Dr. Ray Brown in this instance, the storm seemed more powerful than normal. The crew was particularly frightened, because they knew how these storms can destroy a boat. Dr. Brown, and the crew, watched as the storm began to cross the ocean and head directly towards them, as if something was specifically guiding it straight to where they were.

In regard to this event, Michael channeled an interesting insight from Lord Ashtar of the Spiritual Hierarchy. Ashtar stated to Michael that it was he who activated and guided this storm, because of the important destiny that was to be fulfilled. This storm occurred and was so intense in order that it would uncover what was to be shortly discovered on the ocean floor off the coast of Bimini. The Spiritual Hierarchy wanted to make sure that Dr. Ray Brown would fulfill his Mission that, in fact, had been prophesied decades before by Edgar Cayce.

All those aboard Jacques Cousteau's boat were quite concerned because of the intensity of the storm and its observable trajectory towards them. They knew that they were in the path of destruction and their survival instinct kicked in. Since they were near the coast of the island of South Bimini, they decided to anchor their boat there until things calmed down, rather than risk heading through the storm to Miami. In the intense storm, the crew managed to anchor and firmly tie the boat to the dock, and, then, they ran for cover to a nearby hotel bar to wait things out. As the storm raged on, the crew decided to spend the night at the hotel, hoping that the weather would be more suitable for travel on the following day.

According to Ray, this storm was the most powerful he had ever experienced. The storm continued to rage throughout the long night with its center near the island. The crew felt very fortunate and were grateful to be safe and dry at the little island hotel. They wondered if their boat would survive, considering the length and intensity of the storm. Normally, this type of storm would produce extensive damage to boats. However, when the storm had passed, it seemed obvious that the same Higher Forces who had activated the storm, also had protected their boat from being damaged.

After the storm subsided, the crew was interested in diving as, oftentimes treasure and other ancient objects are uncovered on the ocean floor as a result of these types of storms. However, the crew's air tanks were quite low, because they had already completed the required diving activities for that expedition and they were returning home. Despite the ordeal, a new excitement began to manifest within them, after all, they were treasure hunters. They decided that at least they could go down for a few minutes to see if anything interesting had been uncovered. Ray stated that the crew was feeling strongly, for some unknown reason that something unusual had surfaced.

By the time they got things back to normal on the boat, the sand that had been wildly stirred up on the ocean floor had begun to settle down, but it was still very hazy water which made it difficult to see more than a few feet away. The crew gathered the oxygen tanks that they had left and found that there was only enough oxygen for Ray, and five other divers, to go down for about thirty to forty minutes. They were determined to check out the area for a possible future expedition.

Finding the Pyramid

As the divers began to descend, Ray ended up being the last diver to go down. After he dived, he was surprised that he could not find the other divers. However, the water was very cloudy and visibility was extremely poor. Then, he spotted what, at first, appeared to him to be a vision, as it was so surreal. What he saw in the near distance, was what appeared to be a pyramid structure. He thought his eyes were playing tricks on him; that perhaps what he was seeing was a mirage of sorts. At first, it looked like a hologram that appeared eerily out of place, rather than a real object.

When he swam closer, Ray realized that it was, indeed, real. Before him, protruding out of the ocean floor, was a huge, glowing white-stone pyramid with what appeared to be a beautiful blue lapis lazuli capstone. Although the pyramid seemed to be approximately 80 feet tall, he had the distinct impression that the actual size was considerably larger with much more of the pyramid hidden below in the depths of the ocean floor. The beautiful white walls were glowing intensely with a slight pulsation. He touched the surface and discovered that it was solid and, yet, he could actually feel the slight pulsation, as if it was filled with an intense energetic light force. The way that Ray described the pyramid's surface was similar to that which Michael described from his two experiences onboard the Merkabah: "The walls inside both Lightships had a similar type of sensations, as if the very walls themselves were alive and pulsating with life-force."

Note: Michael relays that he has been told by the Spiritual Hierarchy that the Great Pyramid of Egypt was once coated with a similar type substance. This substance made it capable of receiving the intense energies of the life-force of the universe and it was definitely a type of Higher consciousness technology.

After swimming around the four sides of the pyramid structure a couple of times, Ray suddenly found a portal that was large enough for a man to go through. It was as if it opened on its own accord or, perhaps, the Spiritual Hierarchy had, in fact, activated this portal so Ray would be able to go inside.

Later on, in the numerous lectures that Ray gave about this awesome experience, he stated that he initially hesitated to go through the portal because, "There was concern, that even though I had just seen this portal appear in the wall, as if beaconing me to come in, the thought had also entered my mind--what if once I got inside, it might then close and I could be trapped inside, with no way out." He was also concerned that he had a limited amount of air left in his tank, which made it an even more difficult decision.

In spite of this, his curiosity of what he might discover began to overcome his hesitation. He decided that this was one of those once in a lifetime opportunities, and that he must take the risk. After all, he had been a treasure hunter and a diver for many years, and he was used to going down onto the ocean floors. He had previously entered sunken Spanish galleons and other ships in search of treasure, and his experiences had always presented some danger, so, in a way, this was just one more such experience. He did know, however, that this was a much more uncertain and dangerous situation. Ray stated, that when he finally made the decision to go for it, that: "It was not an experience I could run from or ignore, due to the intense curiosity of what I might discover, being so overwhelming."

According to what Michael received in communication with the Spiritual Hierarchy, they said that this was an experience in his life that Ray was destined to have. They also stated that they had spiritually "Overshadowed" Ray to influence him to go inside the pyramid. For those unfamiliar with the term

"Overshadowed," it refers to a person who is being strongly-influenced spiritually and inwardly guided.

So, Ray made the decision to enter the pyramid and trusted that the portal would stay open long enough for him to explore as much as possible with the little air he had left. Once inside, he stated that there were no words that would adequately describe what he saw spread out before him. The architecture of the large chamber that he entered appeared to be a blend of Grecian and Egyptian with elegant pillars and ornate frescos built into its walls. This is significant because, according to many sources of channeled material and legends, both Greece and Egypt were actually colonies of Atlantis.

He also noticed a number of strange hieroglyphic symbols on the walls, and that the inner walls were glowing with life-force, just like the outside of the pyramid, making it easy for him to see. Ray noted that, "Though the inside of the pyramid was filled with water, everything was still in a perfect state of preservation." This Atlantean pyramid had been submerged and covered in water by the cataclysm, over 12,000 years before, yet, as Ray surmised, it appeared to be as perfect as the day it had originally been constructed.

Because of the direction that the circulation of the water seemed to be flowing once he entered the pyramid, Ray felt that he was being gently pulled up and forward. Next, he realized that he was in the upper chamber of the pyramid. Inside the upper chamber, there was a large, elongated white table that was glowing and was, apparently, made of the same substance as the walls. There were seven large, high-backed chairs along one side with the center chair being larger than the rest. This seemed to Ray to have been part of a council chamber during Atlantean times.

From the middle of the pyramid's point, there was a large golden rod. This round rod was several inches in diameter and was hanging downward. On the very end of the rod was a brilliant red ruby stone that was very large and round-shaped. On the table, directly underneath it, was a golden pedestal of hands that were holding a clear quartz crystal ball, approximately the size of a baseball.

At the time, Ray was determined if he had enough air left, to take something with him to prove that he had discovered the pyramid. He knew he must allow for enough air to get through the portal opening and back up to the surface. Keeping this in mind, he first attempted to pry loose the golden rod and found that it would not budge. Then, he took out his knife and attempted to cut off a piece of it, only to discover that, though it looked like gold, it was definitely much harder and he could not even make a scratch on it.

Next, he attempted to pry the large ruby-colored stone loose, but to no avail. He then tried to pry the golden hands loose from the table, but that was futile as well. Then, he felt himself drawn to the largest of the seven high-backed chairs, and, even though he was wearing his air tank, he was able to partially sit in the chair. When he sat down, he noted that: "It felt so familiar, as if I had sat in that chair many times before."

According to the Spiritual Hierarchy, it was familiar to him because, in an earlier Atlantean life, he was a member of the Council that met in this chamber, and he did, in fact, sit at this council table with other High Priest-scientists. These High Priests initiated energy-activation ceremonies and directed Higher energies from the tip of the pyramid through the golden rod into the red ruby-colored stone and, then, into the clear crystal ball. This activation ceremony, which directed the Cosmic energies of the universe, helped energize the Earth with these Higher frequencies. Michael also picked up through his channeling that Ray, as one of these original Guardians of Atlantis, had returned to retrieve the crystal that was used in these healing-power ceremonies. Though he did not consciously remember at the time, Ray spiritually awakened a short time later as his veils of Cosmic amnesia lifted.

Retrieving the Crystal

For a moment, Ray sat in the chair trying to catch his breath from the attempts he had been making to remove an object to take with him. All of a sudden, he experienced a booming voice in his head. The firm-sounding voice said: "Reach into the hands, take the crystal, and go--and never return!"

Ray was taken back, never having experienced anything like it before, but he knew that this was not his imagination. He was even more surprised when he reached inside the hands he had been tugging on and the crystal came out easily. As he rotated the crystal in his hand, he saw a holographic image of three pyramids which only appeared at a certain angle. Then, the voice spoke intensely again: "You have gotten what you came for, now leave, and never return!"

Stunned by what he had just experienced, he decided not to test fate and to respect the voice. And, besides, he had no time to linger and explore anyway, because he was almost out of air. Perhaps, this too was part of the script that was written by the "Higher Beings Upstairs." He left the upper chamber of the pyramid, passed through the lower one, and exited through the open portal, quickly heading up to the surface.

Initially, upon returning to the boat, Ray shared his experience with the crew about finding the pyramid, but he kept secret about the crystal ball that he had recovered until sometime later. He told them about going into the pyramid and, also, about the stern warning given to him not to go back. When he did reveal the crystal to the crew, perhaps because of jealousy, he was bombarded with all kinds of accusations from his fellow divers. The divers were skeptical and some even accused him of having brought it with him on their expedition.

However, in spite of the difficulties he experienced initially, things were about to change. He was once again in the presence of this powerful healing crystal that was destined to impact millions of Light Workers all over the planet.

Meeting Dr. Ray Brown

I, Aurora, began to spiritually awaken at an early age and was officially "saved" at eight years old while attending a Baptist church camp. My uncle, who was a Baptist Minister, had invited me to a summer camp in Traverse City, Michigan. Later on, I graduated beyond what they were teaching and began developing my spiritual attunement and psychic abilities. This included learning to follow God's Divine Guidance and reading a lot about metaphysical realities. I developed into a Muse and health intuitive, guiding others in overcoming their challenges and achieving their goals. In 1981, Michael and I began traveling throughout the U.S. and Great Brittan where we spoke to thousands of people on many subjects. I talked about electrical-magnetic-fields (EMF), quartz crystal modalities, healing with light and sound, and other advanced technologies used in balancing and healing.

I also spoke many times before the National Health Federation. I was spiritually guided to use the title "Amusing Muse." I learned that I have the ability to assist people in overcoming numerous life-challenging situations and I really enjoy helping people transform their lives. This, in turn, helps them to release old karmic blocks which allows them to fulfill their true life Missions. (See Highly Recommended Websites at the back of the book for resources to physically rejuvenate and eliminate toxic conditions.)

Back in 1975, I was living in the suburban Detroit area with my (then) husband, Marvin Myers. I was guided to go to Phoenix, Arizona for a little getaway. As is usually the case for me, I have to go on faith a lot, and I did not consciously know at the time that an important spiritual experience was going to occur in my life while I was there.

When we arrived from our journey, Marvin and I stayed at the San Carlos Hotel that was located in the middle of downtown Phoenix. This was an old renovated hotel with lots of interesting history surrounding it. The San Carlos was next door to the Hilton Hotel, so, on our first day there, we decided to go to the Hilton for a nice breakfast. However, we never got to eat, because upon entering I noticed a sign that read "International Psychic and Yoga Conference."

To my utter delight, it was starting that day at the hotel. I could not have been more excited, as I had studied psychic development for years and had a great interest in the subject. Marvin, on the other hand was less interested, being much more mainstream traditional than I and he was basically just along for the ride.

We walked over to the registration table and found out that there were many speakers from all over the world who were scheduled for presentations over the next two days. One of the speakers listed was Dr. Ray Brown whose presentation was to be about the Atlantean Crystal. What was so interesting is that Dr. Brown was giving his very first public presentation since finding the Atlantean Crystal and his presentation was scheduled to begin within a few minutes after we had arrived. Talk about timing, folks, I mean really!

We attended Dr. Brown's presentation, along with about two hundred other people. At that time, we were also introduced to the awesome Atlantean Crystal and its truly remarkable powers. Almost everyone in the huge ballroom sensed the power of the Atlantean healing crystal. The crystal had been placed in a glass display case in the front of the lecture room and everyone who looked into it from one specific angle could clearly see the holographic image of three pyramids.

Initially, Dr. Brown's story seemed almost too incredible to be believed, even though I, like most people there, thought we could feel a force-field of energy emanating from the crystal. I had some questions and wanted to know more, but I definitely planned to be cautious and not gullible in my approach to investigating this further. There was definitely some evidence that what Dr. Brown had shared was true.

After he ended his presentation, he invited everyone to come up and take a closer look at the crystal, to tune into it, and see what they were feeling. He then made an announcement that later that afternoon there was going to be another presentation and that he had invited a very famous psychic medium from Great Britain to join him. Unfortunately, I do not recall her name and she has most likely passed on from this life by now as she was quite elderly in 1975. Dr. Brown had scheduled for her to do a session that afternoon to see what she could tune into with the crystal. He invited everyone who was at his seminar to attend the session that afternoon.

The Pulsating Crystal

I made sure, by arriving early, that Marvin and I would have front row seats for whatever was going to occur. Over one hundred people were present, when the elderly medium entered the conference room. After she sat down at the front of the room, Dr. Brown handed her the crystal and she proceeded to go into an altered state of consciousness, almost like going into a trance.

Over the years in many seminars and lectures, Michael and I have shared the experience of what happened next and it was definitely one of the most incredible things that this group of people probably ever experienced in their entire lives. Right there in that fully-lit hotel conference room, one of the most awesome things happened.

As the medium went into this altered state, she spoke to everyone in the room saying: "Gather around me for "the Most-Highs" (Masters of the Spiritual Hierarchy) want to put on a demonstration for you, so that you will know that what I am about to say is the Truth."

I jumped up with Marvin behind me and hurried to the medium's side, wanting us to be as close as possible. I was standing right next to her right side and had a very clear view of what happened next. A few moments passed, then, to everyone's astonishment the crystal ball, which was resting in her open palms, came alive. It changed into every color of the rainbow, while its shape altered into a pulsating jelly appearance. All the colors lit up, like brilliant neon iridescence, while it continued to pulsate.

Right after the crystal started to go through this awesome transformation, I asked Marvin if he saw it. I specifically asked him this question as a reality check, because Marvin was a very grounded and balanced-type person. I figured that if he was also seeing it, then, it must be happening. Marvin, who was as stunned as the rest of us, responded: "Yes, I see it."

After a few minutes, the crystal ball returned to normal. At this point, the medium again began to speak: "The Most Highs have put on this demonstration for you today, so that you will know that this crystal is truly from Atlantis. It is truly from the Temple of the Great White Brotherhood of Light and has been brought to your surface world. We want you to know that it is no accident that you are here today. We want you to tell the others what you have seen today, so they will know that 'Now is the Time' that the 'Army of Light' is being formed and when you are 'Bright enough and Light enough' that will be our 'Signal' to remove you from this planet!"

Along with the stunning other-worldly display, this heart-opening (and mind- opening) message had all of us amazed. It is interesting that throughout the years when Michael and I have shared this fabulous experience, we have met at least a half-dozen other people who were also present that day when the incredible metamorphous of the crystal took place. (I want to invite those people to contact us for a communication reunion.)

In 1981, which was two years after my ten-year marriage with Marvin ended, I met and married Michael Ellegion. As the years progressed, Michael and I became close friends with Dr. Ray Brown. Michael and I were privileged to have him stay at our home in Malibu, California, and sponsored him, throughout the years, for events in Sedona, Phoenix, and Scottsdale, Arizona. Also, while Ray was staying at our Malibu home, he allowed us, for over a month, to energize one of our large crystal clusters off the Atlantean crystal.

Years later, the Spiritual Hierarchy channeled more information about why they had activated the crystal that day. They said that there was a reason that they activated the crystal to transform into every color of the rainbow. This was done because it symbolized the Light Worker's seven main "chakras" (energy centers) of our physical body, as well as the chakras that are located above our Crown Chakra (the more Etheric Chakras for Cosmic Activation, Protection, and Empowerment). When these chakras are opened, activated, and balanced, then we each emit the Rainbow Rays of Light and these merge together into the pure White Light, which when mellowed with wisdom, becomes a bright golden hue.

It was interesting that the medium used the expression "being Bright enough and Light enough." Michael was told by the Spiritual Hierarchy that this was a specific reference to our auric fields becoming balanced and much stronger. Following this impressive display of power and the inspirational message by these obviously Highly developed Beings, I felt guided to design a very special balancing Rainbow Crystal pendant. As a result, I have designed and produced these pendants since 1981. The pendants are specially charged by the Spiritual Hierarchy to powerfully amplify and balance one's auric field. We were told by these Beings of wisdom that these custom-designed pendants, should only be made available to fellow Light Workers who we were destined to connect with through our work. There is more information about these pendants in the next chapter.

The Spiritual Hierarchy confirmed that their inspirational message and the comment "that will be Our signal to remove you from this planet!" was an obvious reference to the upcoming "Rapture" (Divine Intervention and Worldwide Evacuation) that is Destined to occur soon for the people of planet Earth. This "Atlantean Crystal Activation" event, and, the message from them, was one of the most dramatic and inspirational experiences in my life, a life that, I might add, has been filled with Cosmic experiences.

Dr. Ray Brown was knighted by the "illuminati" in Great Brittan and showed Michael and I photographs of the event with royalty and famous stars in attendance. Ray was a little naive about the people he was dealing with at first, but after they knighted him, he soon found out their true natures. They demanded that he hand over the Crystal to them. When he refused to do so, they stole the Crystal and threatened him.

However, the story does not end there, because the Crystal remarkably teleported back to him every time "they" managed to steal it. Dr. Brown passed on in the mid-1990s and the Crystal is now sequestered in Sedona, Arizona. I would like to share more information about its location, but, unfortunately, I am not able to at this time. It is my deepest hope that the reader will remember the "Message" from the Spiritual Hierarchy and take it to heart.

CHAPTER 5

CRYSTAL POWER

Aurora's Move to Phoenix

In 1980, I (Aurora) was told by those "Upstairs" that my mission in Detroit was over and that it was time for me to move to Phoenix, Arizona, where I would meet my other half and where my true "life mission" would began." I wisely followed this Higher Guidance and moved to the Phoenix area in late 1980 where I met Michael on April 28th of the following year while he was lecturing at Arizona State University. As strange as it sounds, when I told Michael about my experience with the Atlantean Crystal, he informed me that a spiritual group, that he and some friends had formed, was sponsoring Dr. Ray Brown in a couple of weeks. This was the first of several events that Michael and I did with Dr. Ray Brown in the ensuing years.

Excited about the opportunity to reconnect with Dr. Ray Brown, I could not help but think about my life changing experience with the Atlantean Crystal and, how at last, I was about to be in its presence again. It was during this second encounter with Dr. Ray Brown's Crystal that I received a strong impression from the Spiritual Hierarchy that they wanted me to design a uniquely beautiful CHAKRA-balancing, power-crystal pendant. The "Masters" said that this unique crystal pendant design had not been on the Earth since the early Atlantean and Lemurian times. They told me that they would charge the crystals with their Higher Cosmic energies and that the design of the crystal would help balance, amplify, and increase the frequencies of Light Workers.

Marcel Vogel and the Power of the Crystal

As a matter of fact, Michael and I were shown in a very pragmatic and scientific way just how powerful this particular design of Rainbow crystal pendants actually was when we connected with the late Marcel Vogel. He was a very famous IBM research scientist who spent many years designing numerous components for IBM Research Laboratories. Marcel, who started out initially as a very "left-brain" type person, had a very analytical and scientific genius brain in which everything needed to be scientifically proven and documented in minute detail in order to validate any theory.

In his work, he conducted intense and thorough scientific research that proved the power of natural crystals and gemstones and the effect they have on individuals that wear them. He stated, "If it were not for quartz crystal and other natural gemstones, we would literally not be able to have electronics such as TV's, stereos, and computers, and even watches would be unable to work or function."

What Marcel was referring to was the scientifically proven fact that quartz crystals and gemstones are energy anchors and amplifiers. Crystals are keepers of knowledge and wisdom, and Quartz, specifically, is used in computers to program information (data). In fact, a couple of decades ago, IBM was able to program over one billion (1,000,000,000) pieces of data into a quartz crystal the size of a sugar cube, and then extract it at any time they wanted. And, since then, this capacity has greatly increased.

Quartz grounds electric-magnetic energy and that is why it is used in watches. Quartz crystals are made of this same electromagnetic energy called Piezo Energy which can amplify and ground more energy in one's electronic body. A couple of decades ago, this was scientifically proven by a German doctor who was later nominated for the Nobel Prize for his findings.

Marcel also spoke about the properties that make a quartz crystal more powerful. "For example," Marcel stated, "the most powerful and balanced a quartz crystal point can be is when it is totally optically clear and when it is perfectly cut and polished on all six sides. This would definitely be the most powerful way for one to wear them as a crystal point," as he was able to determine through his research with Kirlian photography and applied-kinesiology. However, even if individuals wear a very rough piece of foggy-looking quartz crystal along the main energy of their bodies, within about 20 minutes, their auric fields will be increased approximately 30 percent. This is where the seven main chakras are located.

Marcel continued, "And if one were to place different types of colored gemstones, with each of these corresponding to the main chakras of the body, around this very optically clear and perfectly balanced quartz point, sort of like a modern form of Aaron's Breast Plate--well, the auric energy activation and increase of one's natural energy field around them, if one was to measure it-- would be way off the chart!"

This reference, regarding the intense increase in one's auric field due to this type of design, became very obvious to us and to thousands of others who have experienced wearing these powerful Rainbow pendants through the years since we first started making them available to Light Workers in 1981.

As time went by, Marcel, like the great genius Nicola Tesla, become increasingly "right brained," as he was introduced to such things as "Kirlian photography" (which produces photos of one's auric field) and applied-kinesiology (muscle-testing). After meeting many powerful shamans and natural healers, he began to spiritually awaken and opened up to metaphysical and Higher realities such as UFOs, extraterrestrial contact, and channeling.

Marcel Vogel, as mentioned in the second book of The Divine Blueprint Series - "The Cover-Up on Human-Appearing ETs," actually examined the crystal-metal samples that were given to the famous contactee Billy Meiers from his human-appearing ET contacts, as documented in the book "Contact from the Pleiades." One of the chief investigators for this series of ET contacts was Lt. Colonel Wendelle Stevens. After he received these crystal-metal samples from Meiers, he gave them to Marcel, who rigorously analyzed them at the IBM Research Laboratories. Marcel determined that these particular metal samples could not have been manufactured on earth because of the advanced sophistication level that existed within the samples. This experience was only one of many that opened Marcel up to other realities and subjects that many other Earth scientists choose not to examine.

Rainbow Crystal Pendants

We were privileged to have Ray stay at our home more than once and, while he was there, he allowed us to energize one of our large quartz crystal clusters off of his own Atlantean crystal. When other crystals are charged off of Dr. Ray Brown's crystal, these new crystals individually pick up the exact energy that the main crystal contains. New crystals, including the Rainbow pendants, that are charged for 30 days (a whole lunar cycle) continue to hold this energy charge forever and they also experience this same "Ceremonial-Initiation-Energy-Charging" so that the overall effect of balancing, aligning and energizing for each person is definitely enhanced because of this.

Throughout the years, there have been a few companies who attempted to duplicate this original design that I was given from the Spiritual Hierarchy, but they have been unsuccessful in creating the same powerful effect. Not only were these imitations not as esthetically beautiful, but they also lacked this special factor.

I was also specifically told to have the individual gemstones placed onto the different sides of the optically clear and perfectly cut quartz points without using prongs (which is a much cheaper way of fitting individual stones), because the Spiritual Masters wanted the energies to "flow" smoothly around and over the point. Therefore, our jeweler uses a method that is more time-consuming, but produces a higher level product. We were also instructed not to use facetted gemstones, which is actually a more modern way of finishing gemstones, which allows a jeweler to hide inclusions and imperfections within the particular stone. Instead we were told to use a rounded and smooth cabochon, which has to be AAA quality which is the more ancient and traditional way to attach gemstones to pendants.

Because of how powerful these Rainbow pendants are, Michael and I were instructed by the Spiritual Hierarchy to act as Guardians to these very unique and precious pendants. In doing so, we are not allowed to sell these through "normal" distribution methods, such as in jewelry stores. They stressed that we are only allowed to make these available to the Light Workers that we meet on our individual missions while preparing humanity for the eventual Divine Intervention and that there would be no exceptions. They said that "Each person's crystal is uniquely and vibrationally attuned to the person who orders it." In a sense, the Light Workers have to "pass through the Cosmic Security Code" which, normally, includes that the Light Workers must first experience a Transformational channeling session from the Masters that helps vibrationally attune them to the Higher Cosmic Energies. This also provides them with a greater understanding of their individual Missions on planet Earth. The Light Workers then have a greater understanding of the significance of these powerful special pendants and it is assimilated much more into their total awareness levels. Wearing the pendants also reactivates their DNA/RNA which results in other abilities and powers manifesting.

The Masters have explained to us that whenever a Light Worker is guided to order one of these pendants, they Overshadow the master artesian jeweler from the start to the finish while creating this Rainbow pendant. This Overshadowing of the jeweler by the Spiritual Hierarchy assures that the individual receives the specific gemstones, that come from totally different parts of the world, that are harmonically and vibrationally attuned for that specific Light Worker. Furthermore, the different cabochon gemstones in the pendant represent the basic color energy of each of the main chakras of the body and, thus, they specifically match the Light Worker's major chakras of his or her body.

As mentioned in the last chapter, the Spiritual Hierarchy activated Dr. Ray Brown's crystal to transform into every color of the rainbow to symbolize the main "chakras" of our physical bodies. The following is a list of the seven main chakras, the color ray that they each vibrate to, and the particular gemstone that we use for our Rainbow crystal pendants.

1. The Creative Chakra: Vibrates to the color Red and is located in the genitals. When fully open, it represents "Divine Creativity." The gemstone that vibrates well to this chakra is Garnet.

2. The Vitality Chakra: Vibrates to the color Orange and is located in the abdomen, or intestinal area. When fully open, it represents "Divine Service." The gemstone which vibrates well to this chakra is Carnelian.

3. The Security and Clarity Chakra: Vibrates to the color Yellow and is located in the solar plexus or stomach area. When fully open, it represents Security, Clear Mental Processes, and Clear Communication. The gemstone which vibrates well to this chakra is Golden Citrine.

4. The Heart Chakra: Vibrates to the color Green and is located in the heart area. When fully open, it represents the uniting of the Spiritual and Material Worlds, manifested together: "As Above, So Below." It also represents kindness, generosity, abundance, and prosperity. The gemstone which vibrates well to this chakra is Jade Chrysophrase.

5. The Will Chakra: Vibrates to the color Blue and is located in the throat area. When fully open, it represents an individual's free will aligned to the "Divine Will." It is also called the Ray of Power (deep blue) and Peace (light blue). The gemstone which vibrates well to this chakra is Lapis.

6. The Third Eye Chakra: Vibrates to the color Purple or Violet and is located in the center of the forehead. When fully opened, it represents Visionary Insight, Emotional Balance, and the Ability to Transmute Energies to the highest level possible. The gemstone which vibrates well to this chakra is Amethyst.

7. The Crown Chakra: Vibrates to the color White (because it is a combination of all the colors of the complete rainbow merged together, which makes up the total White Ray, and this chakra is usually the last chakra of the seven main chakras to be opened in Higher spiritual initiations and activations). It is located in the center of the top of the head. When fully opened, its attributes are Purity and Protection. The gemstone which vibrates well to this chakra is Quartz Crystal.

8. Chakras above the crown chakra are "Etheric Chakras". They vibrate to Gold, Silver, Copper, Turquoise and Pink. For this we were guided to add an AAA quality full spectrum Fire Opal that assists in creating Higher "Intergalactic Activation's and Initiations."

Whenever a Light Worker starts to wear one of these Rainbow crystal pendants, that person experiences a very important Cosmic Spiritual Initiation. This also helps raise the frequency of the planet as it begins to experience its own mass Spiritual Ascension process. In a sense, we on the planet all actually benefit from the process of the individual Light Workers as they boost they own vibrational levels.

Another interesting thing that often occurs to those who are financially struggling and who decide to order one of these pendants is that after they have made a small deposit to order a pendent, they experience a sudden increase of prosperity and the ability to manifest whatever they truly desire in life. What we are aware of is that there is a powerful phenomena occurring on the etheric level. Once the person takes action to purchase the pendant, then the "etheric wheels" start to turn and the etheric counterpart of this powerful pendant begins to merge with that person on his/her etheric level of existence, and begins the process of amplifying a greater level of abundance in his/her life.

Programming One's Crystal

When an individual decides to program a crystal (mentally and spiritually), it is a simple matter of visualization and invocation. Since every thought and word spoken is considered a "prayer or mantra," one simply invokes, whatever one desires to manifest by thinking a strong positive thought. In fact, when one speaks this desire and intent out loud, it will greatly increase the power and authority surrounding this thought, as it makes the ethers reverberate which affects one's surroundings. Then, couple this with visualization of the desired result by visually planting these desires in your crystal.

A good affirmation is: "Every time I wear my crystal, my auric field is increased and balanced! My entire life is in total Oneness with the God-Force and Universal Christed-Energies in all I think, say, and do! I AM now manifesting all my dreams and desires, easily, effortlessly, joyfully, and powerfully, and this Energy now goes out into all my relationships and all my affairs healing with Divine Love and Light! This Energy now surrounds Mother Earth and instantly manifests throughout the Universal Realms! And so it is! Amen!"

Chicago Convention Experience

A short time after connecting with Marcel Vogel in the early '80's, we went to Chicago to participate at a New Age type show. At this particular event, which was a "Dowser Convention," there were lots of different energy machines and devices being displayed and promoted, including various tools and technologies that were being shared and demonstrated by individuals and organizations from all over the world.

Unbeknownst to those entering the building, one of the convention exhibiters had set up a type of Kirlian device to measure the auric fields of the attendees arriving through the front doors. A Kirlian snapshot was taken just outside the entrance doors to the building and, within seconds, the auric fields of everyone entering the building was displayed for others to see. The exhibitor was inside the entrance and was explaining to the convention guests how the Kirlian device displayed auric fields. When we walked through the entrance, we heard gasps of surprise and excitement from the people that were standing by the Kirlian device. It showed that our (Michael and Aurora) combined auric fields was actually larger than the size of the entire building! Needless to say, it "blew" their minds, because they had never seen such a reading before from anyone else.

This reading, as registered upon their instruments, did not really surprise us for we had each personally experienced a major energy shift after we had started to wear the powerful Rainbow crystal pendants.

Muscle Testing

Michael and I have both been trained (by one of the top experts of kinesiology in the world - the same one who taught Marcel Vogel) in the technique of muscle-testing. We have demonstrated this technique of "applied-kinesiology" thousands of times, before large audiences and in front of TV cameras, at numerous public workshops and lectures during the past two or three decades. On these occasions, we have always tried to find the most muscular or strongest-looking person that was in the audience to volunteer for the experiment. During these demonstrations, individuals are presented with the opportunity of personally experiencing the "power of crystals" first-hand. The truth is that Applied Kinesiology goes way beyond one's "conscious beliefs, opinions and concepts." One's own mind can fool oneself, yet one's own body never lies. That is, the subconscious mind, through muscle response, causes reactions of the body, which may be seen as either a "strong" or "weak" reaction through the muscles. Regardless of what one may consciously believe, muscle-testing, when applied and used correctly, allows one to determine responses quite accurately rather than what their conscious opinions or beliefs may lead individuals to believe.

When we are conducting these kinesiology demonstrations on people, we have them hold one arm out in front of them and they are told to hold it as straight and as firm as possible. We then ask them different types of questions, while simultaneously attempting to pull downward on their arms. Depending on the type of questions asked of them, there is a difference in how the body responds. It is first determined what a "yes' or a "no" answer is for that particular person. After a few times testing the arm, this is obvious based on whether the arm is able to stay up or is pulled down, and the difficulty involved, i.e. how difficult or easily did the arm move based on the ability of the person to resist.

What is fascinating in regard to muscle-testing, is that it has been shown that different individuals will react differently to tests done while holding certain foods or substances, indicating that some individuals may be "allergic" to these items. Also, there are some things that everyone is shown to react to (be allergic to) including white refined sugar, artificial chemical sweeteners, coffee, pork, fluoride, GMOs (genetically modified foods), and many other substances and foods as well. Individuals holding these substances always get a "negative" or "no" response, i.e. a weakening response to the body's normal level of strength, health and well being.

One of the basic muscle-testing demonstrations that we love to do is have individuals place one of these substances in their hand and then place their hand on their solar plexus area, which is in line with the main energy meridian of the body. We then pull down on their arm and every single time (it does not matter how strong they happen to be!) their arm will show a "negative" or "no" response by being easily moved downward. This is because these type of substances cause a weakening effect (basically, an allergic reaction) on the body. Somehow the body knows through the subconscious (which is connected with the Super-Conscious Mind of God or Divine Intelligence and our I AM Presence) what is good or bad for it.

This demonstration is then followed immediately with another demonstration in which we place a piece of natural quartz crystal in their hands--along with the substance that they were already holding--and the person doing the testing again pulls down on the individual's arm, but, now, the individuals are able to resist their arms being pulled down. This demonstration always seems to "blown everyone's mind" when they first experience it. As a result of the experience, the individuals tend to alter their view of reality and change their "old" perceptions in regard to the power of crystals.

We wish to make it clear to those who are hearing about muscle testing for the first time, everyone should not assume that they can eat anything that they want to without it affecting their bodies as long as they are wearing a natural quartz crystal or other gemstones to overcome the weakening effects of negative substances. Instead, it behooves us to at least consider the concept that "God helps those who help themselves." It is more a matter of recognizing that we are made up of "everything we think, say, and do." Consider that our bodies are "the Temple of the Holy Spirit" and, they should be treated as such, and since we have been given free will to make choices about what we consume, we should think of food as either "lower-grade octane fuel" or "higher premium-grade octane fuel" for our bodies.

Dr. Brown and the Cabal

Getting back to some of the incredible experiences surrounding Dr. Ray Brown and his Atlantean Crystal, throughout the years Ray shared his story of how he found this incredible crystal in the underwater Atlantean Temple of Light with hundreds of others whom he met at conferences in the late '70's and early '80's. In our case, we got a chance to sponsor him at several main events before he passed away in the late '90's. As a result of making the crystal available to people, many Light Workers have greatly benefitted from having contact with the crystal, which, for some, has brought about powerful healings and life transformations.

After Ray found the crystal and started speaking to others about it, he told us that on at least eight different occasions the cabal attempted to steal the crystal to use it for evil purposes. He explained that each time they were successful in capturing the crystal it always reappeared back with him afterwards. Unfortunately for Ray, he experienced personal difficulties with the imbalanced forces constantly attempting to steal the crystal from him or to attack and weaken him in other subtle ways. They believed that if they could weaken him enough then they would be able to steal the crystal and it would not be able to keep reappearing back to him.

Having been around Ray for considerable periods of time, it is our opinion that a lot of the difficulties that Ray experienced were directly related to his bad dietary habits which led to his body becoming increasingly toxic. As the old saying goes, "It's hard to teach old dogs new tricks." He was definitely set in his ways and he even admitted, on more than one occasion, that the Spiritual Hierarchy had tried to get him to radically change his diet. The purpose for doing this was so he would not be as vulnerable to the actions by the dark forces to weaken him. However, by his own free will, he chose a dietary lifestyle that shortened his life.

In fact, one time in the early '90's while Ray was staying with us in Malibu, California, we spent time helping him improve his health habits by making him fresh organic raw juices and cooking high quality natural organic food for him. After a few weeks eating this higher vibrational food and nutrition, he began to feel better and we could see a major rejuvenation starting to occur. Unfortunately, after he left and went back to his own home in Mesa, Arizona, his health rapidly declined because he went back to eating the same old toxic things that he had eaten previously.

Ray also shared with us that he had secretly worked for the CIA and the intelligence community for a number of years. This created a personal conflict for him, because he was often ordered to do things that he was, morally and ethically, opposed to. He shared some true "hair-raising" stories of being involved in CIA covert "political" missions while on many of his expeditions for treasure. He stated that he realized that some of the things he was ordered to do were ultimately "Karmic producing" and attempted to get out of his intelligence work. We realized that Ray, like many other covert intelligence operatives that we have met through the years who really wanted to end their careers in the "intelligence community," had some negative Atlantean karma that he was attempting to totally overcome, and that this Spiritual mission (being the Guardian to the Atlantean crystal and sharing it's positive healing and transformational qualities with others) was able to help him overcome and ultimately transmute his own past negative karma from the Atlantean times.

Actually, on one of these covert missions, he was taken prisoner, tortured, and held by the government of Niagara until the CIA special ops showed up and rescued him. He would not give much detail except that he and others experienced the "cattle prods on certain very sensitive areas of his body." Of course, torture can also psychologically scare a person for life, but Ray was a very tough and self-reliant type of person who refused to give up in any way.

On another occasion, Ray showed us photographs taken at his knighting by the illuminati for the "Bach flower holistic remedies" that he had created to help others holistically. He knew that the illuminati was only playing on his ego by honoring him for his contribution in the holistic health field and, then, would want something in return. Of course, when they asked him for his crystal they assumed that he would actually give it to them, but he flatly refused as he was the Guardian to it and he was not about to let it be used for evil purposes.

So, they created false charges against him and had him arrested for the very thing for which they had earlier knighted him. He was placed in the "tank," which is a very dangerous maximum-security prison cell, where the worst murderers, rapists, and other evil types are placed, and they assumed that he would be dead within a very short time, because of where they placed him. Also, their plan was to steal his crystal while he was there. But, instead of being killed, the Spiritual Hierarchy had other plans for him and they allowed him to survive this horrendous ordeal. During his time in the prison, by a series of "strange events" and while defending himself, he ended up killing the worst criminal in the cell. This meant that he was symbolically "in charge of" the entire cell and, therefore, the other prisoners left him alone. Eventually, the officials released him, when it became obvious that the other prisoners were leaving him alone and he was going to survive.

The Earthquake in Malibu

Another experience that we had with Ray was when we were living in Malibu, California in the early '90's. Several years had gone by without seeing Ray, when suddenly I was guided to call and reconnect with him.

Because of what occurred, it is important for the reader to have an understanding of where we lived. The large Malibu apartment where we lived had an incredible architectural design. It had been built by our landlord who happened to be one of the chief architects at UCLA. In fact, he won the prestigious "sunset award" for the design of this apartment. It was definitely one of the most beautiful and breathtaking places we had ever lived. "The Launching Pad" was what we lovingly called our place.

This apartment, which was connected with three other apartments, was built into the side of a small mountain overlooking Pacific Coast Highway and the Pacific Ocean. It had a 50 foot balcony from which the BBC actually filmed a couple of New Age TV specials.

In order to reach our apartment, which was the top one, people either had to walk up 65 steps to get to the front entrance or they could get into what is called a "vernacular." This is a type of elevator that goes diagonally up and down the side of the mountain, allowing one to get out at each apartment.

On the same street as our apartment complex was the entrance to the old J. Paul Getty Museum. Shortly after we had moved in, we heard from some of our neighbors that J. Paul Getty originally built this museum specifically at this location because he knew that there was a very powerful energy vortex centered under the small mountain there.

Right after we first saw our new apartment, Michael tuned into the fact that over 25,000 years before there was a beautiful Rainbow crystal temple of Lemuria that was built in approximately the same location where our apartment now stood. One of the reasons that the temple was built there was because spiritual structures are usually constructed in areas where very powerful energies exist, as in vortex locations and upon certain energy meridians and ley lines that cross Mother Earth's surface.

The fact that there was a very powerful energy vortex underneath our apartment was a significant factor in regard to all the events that occurred leading up to and during the earthquake. It was no coincidence that we were directed to reconnect with Dr. Brown just prior to the very intense earthquake that occurred in Southern California on January 17th, 1994.

After I called him, Michael made a six hour drive to Mesa, Arizona to pick him up and, then brought him and the crystal back with him. They arrived in Malibu just hours before the earthquake hit the area that evening. That evening after dinner, we decided that Ray would sleep in our bed, since he was quite a large man and was too big for the narrow couch.

Scattered throughout our home, we had many large pieces of both quartz crystal and amethyst clusters, each about a foot or more in diameter. One of these was a large cluster which had many jagged quartz points jutting out of it. We had placed this particular crystal on top of the headboard of our bed.

We had wondered before whether an earthquake might cause this large cluster to come crashing off of the headboard and became a dangerous projectile that could impale us, but, like most people, we always assumed that that "couldn't happen to us." And, we thought, even if that happened, we would be "Divinely Protected."

No sooner had we gone to sleep on that historic night, when we were suddenly awakened by what sounded and felt like a "locomotive train" was barreling right through our home. It was an earthquake that seemed to go on and on with an "up and down" motion to it. After the quake subsided, we checked on Ray to see if he was all right. The story he told us was quite amazing.

He said that he was experiencing a very vivid dream moments before the quake occurred. In this dream on a more etheric level of existence, he saw his physical body lying in bed sleeping. There were human-appearing ETs, throughout our home, as well as, all around him that were standing beside some type of "special energy devices" (Higher Consciousness Elohim Technology). The ETs told him in this dream that they were there "because the cabal was about to activate a very horrible quake that would cause a lot of death and destruction if they did not intervene as they were doing at that moment." They also explained (which confirmed what Michael had tuned into) that this quake was being artificially created by the cabal as a part of their hidden agenda of attempting to create massive martial law with the objective of gaining more control over the citizens. They confirmed the need for Ray to be where he was presently with his special crystal and said that they were utilizing it's unique and special energy (with it positioned there in the energy vortex) to neutralize a much worse quake than what was actually happening. Obviously, they were utilizing the power of Ray's crystal to amplify their own "etheric energy consciousness machines and devices."

Ray stated that one Being mentioned that within a few moments (of third-dimensional time) the cabal was going to activate the quake, and that Ray should immediately sit up in bed as soon as his physical body woke up. He was told that he needed to do this so that when the quartz cluster was knocked off the headboard by the sudden movement of the quake that he would not be impaled by it.

So, as Ray woke up, he immediately sat up, and, sure enough, the quartz cluster came crashing off the headboard and landed where Ray's head had been on the pillow just a few seconds before. Not only had the Being warned Ray about their Divine Intervention on behalf of humanity, but they also saved Ray's life or at least prevented him from receiving a horrible head injury.

According to the corporate-controlled mainstream media, the quake measured approximately 6.7 on the Richter scale, which was supposed to be an average of the overall areas that the quake affected. That is why we were surprised when we obtained a copy of the actual level of the earthquake from Cal Tech. This sheet of paper recorded the actual level on the Richter scale of the earthquake in all the different areas of California. We noticed that some areas of California had readings over 9 and even 10 in a few places and, when we averaged these figures, it appeared that the officials had manipulated the data to make it appear below the real level of what the reading should have been.

We also found out that California has a "loop hole" in the tax laws that states that if a quake is seven or more in magnitude on the Richter scale and there is a certain amount of damage caused to homes and other structures, then the citizens do not have to pay certain taxes for a while. It appears that the government did not want to lose all that revenue, so this may be one of many reasons that they manipulated the data. Perhaps, it also was an attempt to downplay the full spectrum of destructive potential that this quake should have created had there not been "Divine Intervention."

Both Michael and I felt that this quake was not a "naturally occurring" earthquake created by Mother Nature. We spoke to many others who had experienced earthquakes and most everyone commented about the particular movement of the earth during this quake and how it seemed different and much greater than previous quakes. Instead, we learned later on that it was actually a "failed attempt" by government black-op forces to cause a much worse earthquake than what occurred. The black-ops sometimes use HAARP technologies which are capable of creating an artificially-induced earthquake.

Although we cannot prove this hypothesis, we believe that the circumstances surrounding this event warrant this conclusion. At least three people we spoke to after the quake, told us that "a split second before" the shaking started, they observed what appeared to be a very short and intense "red flash" sweep across the sky. This had the "earmarks" of a laser-activated system in which a bomb, placed at a significant location along or near to the San Andreas Fault, would cause a quake. Furthermore, the attunement that Michael received was that this was actually an attempt by the cabal to generate a much larger and more destructive earthquake which would lead to martial law being enacted and create a more destructive outcome.

The sudden guidance that we received to bring Dr. Ray Brown and his powerful Atlantean healing power crystal to that exact location helped the Higher Elohim Forces of Light transmute the level of intensity of the earthquake by the black-ops. The Forces of Light knew about the cabal's evil plans and Overshadowed us in bringing Ray and the crystal to the specific energy vortex location that would be the most effective area to lessen the effects of the quake. An analogy of this situation is that the powerful crystal acted as a "safety valve on a pressure cooker" or, in other words, a "pressure point of planetary acupuncture" for this major vortex point along the energy meridian that crosses that area.

The destructive outcome of this quake would most likely have been far worse had the crystal not been at the vortex area, if not for this case of "Divine Intervention." It is also obvious that the cabal was unable to perceive that the Higher Forces were aware of their actions and that they would take counteractive measures.

Just as we have, many individuals on the planet are now waking up to the hidden plans and agendas of the cabal and they are also becoming aware of the help from off the planet that comes from these compassionate and loving beings who value freedom and sovereignty. More and more earthlings have begun, like the "hundredth monkey" effect, to call on these Cosmic Forces of Light to help rescue Earth from the hands of the forces of the cabal and to "help us help ourselves" take back this planet for the Light and to liberate it once and for all. As a result, these Higher Forces are beginning to step in more and more in some very powerful and unique ways to neutralize numerous attempts of mayhem and destruction. Afterwards, we knew that what occurred was all in Divine Order of the Divine Blueprint of life.

The Sedona Event

It became very obvious that the cabal was more determined than ever to steal Dr. Ray Brown's crystal, because of how powerful it was. It was also obvious that the Spiritual Hierarchy was not about to allow this special crystal to fall into their hands, despite the cabal's attempts to steal it.

A few months after this incident with the quake, we were guided to sponsor Ray for another event. This time the event was in Sedona, Arizona, which is famous for its powerful vortexes. (Michael was the first person to openly and publicly talk about the many vortexes in the Sedona area.)

We set about preparing for the event in Sedona, printing up flyers advertising the event, and placing ads in New Age publications. During this time, Ray experienced another very determined attempt to steal his crystal. Part of the cabal's plan was to target Ray with their Psychotronic-radionic technology, which was used to psychically weaken him so that he would not be aware of their actions. Regardless, Ray was aware that someone was sending him very negative energy, and he responded by sending back his own intense energies from the source. For a while, this seemed to help, but as they continued this ongoing deluge of psychically zapping him, he began having difficulty counteracting this very powerful psychic attack and he started to weaken from the intensity. As a result, the Higher Forces began putting up shields to help protect Ray and counteract much of the attempt by the cabal to weaken him.

A few weeks before our event while Ray was traveling in Canada, he called us, extremely upset for once again his Crystal had suddenly disappeared. In earlier times when the cabal stole his crystal, it would soon reappear back with him. This time, however, it had not reappeared and he was very concerned. He wondered if the cabal had actually been able to accomplish their evil deed of taking control of it.

Right after speaking with Ray, Michael received a very powerful "Transmission" (channeling) from Ashtar, who explained that the cabal had not been able to get it even though this time they had attempted a combination of more "exotic or unconventional ways" of stealing it. Now, not only were they using a very powerful psychotronic weapon upon Ray to weaken or kill him, but they were also utilizing the services of their black-op remote-viewing teams, who were attempting to take control over the Crystal and to actually teleport it into their possession at one of their numerous underground cabal facilities.

Because the Higher Forces were aware of what the cabal was attempting and before they were able to accomplish their nasty little deed, the Ashtar Command beamed Ray's crystal up aboard one of their Mother Ships. Then, during Michael's channeling, Ashtar stated that "by or before the date of your upcoming event in Sedona, we will return it to Ray so that you will be able to display it at the event, and so the cabal will finally realize that all attempts that they make to acquire the crystal will fail." The Spiritual Hierarchy is not about to allow this powerful and special crystal to ever fall into the hands of those forces who would only use it for evil purposes.

As the days and weeks went by and the Sedona event approached, Ray began getting nervous and concerned because the crystal had not been returned to him. All the other times that the crystal had been taken, it had also been returned to him within a few hours.

Ray woke up early on the morning of the Sedona event, having acquired very little sleep due to his concern about the missing crystal. When he walked out of the bedroom, there was his crystal in the middle of the living room floor. Well, sure enough, (at the last possible moment!) it had, indeed, reappeared; just as our "Friends Upstairs" had promised us that it would. It was such a relief to recognize their protection and Higher Guidance and to know that they continue to provide and care for us all on our Missions to uplift the planet.

CHAPTER 6

VOLUNTEERS IN EARTH EMBODIMENT

Star People Characteristics

As I shared in Chapter 1 from the time I was born on this planet, I have had a conscious memory that my soul did not originate from here, but rather I came from a more advanced world. I also remember "the debriefing" that I, like all Volunteers, went through prior to my soul being beamed into my Earth mother's womb before my birth. Part of what I remember is that I would be lead to a list of traits that makes it possible to physically identify the Volunteers from Higher-dimensional Intergalactic worlds regardless of their race, culture, or the level of Earth society into which they are born.

In 1979, my "Friends Upstairs" guided me to read a copy of the February issue of the New Age publication East West Journal. (Note: This was approximately two months after my experience aboard the Merkabah where I was told that I would come across a list of characteristics that would help identify the Volunteers in Earth embodiment.) This was the first time I saw the complete list of "Star People" characteristics that Brad and Francie Steiger had compiled through their research with NASA engineers and scientists. The article by Brad Steiger was titled *Flying Saucers from the Middle Earth*. In addition to the "Star People" traits, the article contained an illustrated listing of several of the most "commonly seen" types of extraterrestrials that have interacted with Earth humans. In their book, The Star People, the Steigers list these characteristics.

As referred to in a section of this book, "The Beta Humanoid or Space Brother is described as tall, blond, light-complexioned and has also been referred to by some UFO researchers as Nordic appearing (though they have also been seen [and do exist] with the different skin-tones of every race upon this planet and they are totally human-appearing and beautiful in form) and often a native of Venus. They appear as benevolent entities, who seek to direct our misguided species along a more spiritual path. The Beta-F Humanoid is the female version of the Space Brother. She is often seen transported on a beam of Light, such as visions of the Blessed Mother at Fatima and Garabandal, and is seen as independent of any UFO-like vehicle."

"The Alpha Form humanoid is smallish in size with wide-pointed ears and large eyes (also known as the 'grays'). The Beta-2 Humanoids approximate the human form and predominantly have pointed chins, thick lips, dark complexions, and unusually long fingers."

These Star People characteristics, which were thoroughly explained and documented quite well in Brad and Francie Steiger's book, The Star People, were also listed in an article called: *Are You Really From Krypton?* As I first examined the complete list, it really did not surprise me to discover that I had most of these characteristics. Upon seeing this list, I knew that this was the list that I was going to find that Korton had told me about during my '79 encounter on board the Merkabah.

As quoted directly from the article: "About seven years ago, as I (Brad Steiger) was traveling about the country gathering research data and lecturing, I began to make the acquaintance of men and women who claimed either to have strange memories of having come to this planet from 'somewhere else' or to have experienced an interaction with paranormal entities since their earliest childhood. The Star People, as I came to call them, were both normal and attractive in appearance and seemed to be rather successfully integrated in contemporary society."

Brad Steiger's profile of the Star People contains the following elements. Few Star People on Earth have all of the characteristics, but all have at least several to a third of the elements. Star People Characteristics include:

- Compelling eyes and personal charisma
- Unusual blood type (such as A-, B- or AB-) (Aurora and I both have AB-, the rarest blood type upon this planet. Approximately one out of every 10,000 people has this very rare type. It is also the type of blood found on the Shroud of Turin. This brings up an interesting point in regard to those who have tried to explain that the Shroud was a fake created by Leonardo Da Vinci [or someone else]. If this garment [that supposedly covered the body of Jesus/Yesua right after His Crucifixion] is a fake, then why was the blood type (AB-) that was found on it not even in existence prior to that time?)
- Lower than normal body temperature
- Was an unexpected (or "unplanned") child
- Extra vertebrae, transitional vertebrae, fused vertebrae and lower back problems
- Extra or "misplaced" ribs
- Thrive on little sleep and do their best work at night
- Hypersensitivity (or feel more sensitive) to electricity, electromagnetic force-fields (may also be termed "environmentally sensitive")

- Unusually sharp (or above "normal") hearing and eyes very sensitive (or above "normal" sensitivity) to light (or sunlight)
- Seem to have been "reborn" in cycles--for example, 1934-38, 1944-48, 1954-58, and so on (Actually, the majority of Volunteers who have come to Earth have been born within a year or two of particularly "intense" times. In fact, the largest number of Volunteers to ever take Earth embodiment occurred right after the bombs were dropped on Hiroshima and Nagasaki in WWII. This happened because of the concern on Higher worlds [observed from Lightships] that the next generation could possibly destroy this planet, so it was decided that the Volunteers were to come "in mass" into Earth embodiment, thus, the "baby boom generation appeared," to make sure, once and for all, that never again would this planet be allowed to be destroyed.)
- Feel that their (Earth biological) mother and father are not their real parents
- Feel a great urgency (or strange "restlessness" of feeling like they have been in a type of "holding pattern" for too long), a short time to complete an important goal or "special mission" of some kind
- Lower than normal blood pressure
- Chronic (or "semi-chronic") sinusitis (also known as "irritation in the nose or nasal passages")
- Feel or sense that their true ancestors came from another (much more beautiful, peaceful and sane) world, another (Higher) dimension, another level of consciousness, and they yearn (or long) for their true place of origin, or their real home "beyond the stars"
- Had unseen companions as a child
- Natural (or "above normal" or "unusual") abilities in specialized areas, such as art, music, mathematics, healing, acting, natural sciences, etc.
- Experience a buzzing or a clicking sound or a high-pitched mechanical whine in the ears prior to, or during, some psychic event or warning of danger
- Had a dramatic or unusual experience around the age of five (or six years of age or at least sometime before the person's early teens) which often took the form of a white light and/or a visitation by human-appearing beings who gave information and comfort
- Have since maintained a continuing contact with beings which they consider to be angels, masters, elves, spiritual teachers or openly declared UFO intelligences (that is, who are benevolent in nature, other than the

"grays", and have not been abducted--only contacted to help guide, inspire, uplift, empower, etc.)

- Had a serious accident, illness, or traumatic experience around the age of eleven or twelve (or early teens) which encouraged them to turn inward
- Their artwork, dreams, or fantasies often involve an alien, multi-moon (and/or multi-dimensional, inter-) planetary environment
- Children and animals are attracted to them
- May have "mystic crosses," "mystic eyes," or "mystic stars" on their palms
- Have unusual abilities, considered paranormal by their peers and family, (for example, such as being very psychic, doing channelings, and/or involved in psychic/spiritual healings and psychic-surgery, telekinesis, etc.)
- Experience a strong attraction to quartz crystal and natural gemstones
- Have flying dreams or out-of-body experiences
- The ability to take on the role of an empath (extreme compassion and feelings for what the other person or animal is going thru)
- Have a strong affinity to past eras of Atlantis, Lemuria, ancient Egypt, King Arthur & Camelot and other ancient, biblical or "mythical" times of history, when contact with multidimensional beings was conducted on a more open basis by the entities themselves
- Have recently received the message or inner feeling that "Now is the time!" (James Beal, a former NASA engineer, and Dr. Norman Cooperman, a psychotherapist from Miami, are currently researching this subject.)

This is the end of the NASA Star People list from Brad Steiger's work, but I would also add four more characteristics:

- Have experienced at least one or more "close calls" or "life threatening situations" through the years, in which one should have been either killed or at least severely injured, but instead was protected from it or should have died from either a severe sickness or disease but fully and quickly recovered, and have felt that they were "being watched over and somehow Divinely Protected" time and time again
- Have often experienced through the years, while glancing at a digital clock or watch, that the time, coincidently, just happened to be at "**11:11**," when they did so
- Feel that they are one of the "144,000" (In the fourth book of the Divine Blueprint Series - "Who's Who in the Cosmic Directory," there is a chapter on *The Arrival of the 144,000*.)

• Feel like they are <u>A Stranger In A Strange Land</u>. This was the title of a very famous science-fiction classic by Robert Heinlein which accurately describes what Volunteers intensely feel while here in 3-D Earth embodiment. Of course, reality is so much stranger than fiction, but truth has often been presented in so-called fictional form.

Walk-ins

It is my theory that these particular characteristics manifest as a result of Higher, more advanced souls of extraterrestrial origin taking Earth embodiment. These individuals may either incarnate near the moment of birth or they may come in as "Walk-ins" (soul transfer or soul mergence in later years). These Volunteers (Star People) have a more intense level of energy and consciousness than the average "mundane" soul on Earth usually exhibits. Their DNA/RNA genetic code is affected by the amount of energy that they are able to retain on the physical Earth level. As stated above, most Star People have at least a third, or more, of these characteristics, depending on their awareness, interests, diet, and nutritional habits. That is, their consciousness is affected by what they put into their bodies and how this causes them to be "numbed out," as far as their attunement goes.

As a matter of fact, it is my theory that there are very real and important reasons (for metaphysical, consciousness, and biological/genetic purposes) that the Jews and Moslems were given specific dietary laws through their religious teachings by the spiritual beings and masters who guided them. For these same reasons, the rest of humanity should also follow these dietary laws for the wonderful and positive benefits to be derived.

In the decade of the '80's, two of the more interesting and enlightening books to be published on "Walk-ins" were written by the well known metaphysician, Ruth Montgomery. <u>Strangers Among Us</u> and <u>Aliens Among Us</u> thoroughly explain and document her research in uncovering the fact that there are now millions of Volunteer extraterrestrial souls who have taken human embodiment. Many of these souls were born as part of the post WWII "baby boom."

Because the need on the planet is so great at this time, there has been a need for many more Volunteers. Since it takes too much time for souls to go through the normal biological birth process and then grow up and mature, there is another way that many have chosen to speed up the process. Because of the shortness of time (with the End of the Old Age cycle quickly occurring and a New, much more enlightening, Age beginning), many millions of Higher souls have made a mutual "win-win" agreement with souls (presently in Earth embodiment) who are willing to leave their physical Earth bodies in place for the incoming "Walk-ins." The souls who are leaving are usually ones who are "graduating off the wheel of karma" for the first time. Since they have been, more or less, stuck on this particular planet for lifetime after lifetime, they are now free to go on to the "other side" (the Higher realms) without negative karma holding them back anymore. The "Walk-in" souls come from more advanced worlds of the Confederation and they are more evolved and have greater wisdom and inner knowledge. As part of the arrangement, the in-coming souls (because of their greater abilities) will be able to quickly transmute the old negative karma of the souls that they replaced, which would have taken many years, or even possibly more lifetimes for the less-evolved Earth souls to complete. The extraterrestrial "Walk-ins" through this "Cosmic Lease Program," are then able to get on with their individual and collective Missions for the Upliftment, Transformation, and Liberation of this planet. In the case of soul mergence "Walk-ins" who harmoniously share the same individual's body, this strengthens their potential Mission and assists them in fulfilling their Destiny.

I have met literally thousands of "Walk-ins" through the years and most of them have many of these Star People characteristics. Yet, from what I have been able to determine, prior to the "Walk-in" actually "walking-in," the other less-advanced soul that had inhabited the body, did not have any of these characteristics. However, in the case of soul mergence, the individuals already have some of these Star People characteristics, but they manifest many more characteristics after the soul mergence takes place.

It seems to suggest that it is the energy-consciousness level of the soul that inhabits the physical Earth body that allows for many of these characteristics to "suddenly" appear after the Walk-in came in. Obviously, the DNA/RNA genetics have been altered to support the new level of awareness and knowledge that is now contained within the mind and brain of the individual. This realization was partly based on the fact that many of the "Walk-ins" that I have met throughout the years have came into Earth embodiment with partial or total conscious memory of being on the Lightship prior to coming in. In fact, some of them specifically remember searching around the planet to find the right type of Earth body that would allow adaptation to contain this Higher level of extraterrestrial consciousness and genetics. It had to be a positive change and mutation for these particular DNA/RNA genetic changes to take place.

Many of these "Walk-ins" also remember being members of Higher Galactic Councils (as part of the Federation of Light) and of planning to come into Earth embodiment. They specifically remember that the Higher density physical extraterrestrial body that they inhabited in those Higher dimensions was definitely human-appearing and usually more beautiful and perfect, as compared to their present Earth bodies that they walked-into.

One of the more interesting, and perhaps more extreme, cases of a Walk-in was a woman whom I met at one of the numerous public lectures and seminars that I gave in California in the early '80s. When I first met her, she showed up dressed in very colorful and flamboyant-type clothing with a very "mod" looking hairdo. She had a very out-going and assertive type personality with a great sense of humor.

I got to know her a little bit and she shared her Walk-in experience with me. She showed me photographs of what the original soul (who used to inhabit her physical body) used to look and dress like and it was most startling to observe the extremes from before to the present. Previously, she had dressed and acted very conservative and plain. Her original self had, obviously, lived a much simpler lifestyle with absolutely none of the same interests or inclinations that she was now exhibiting. Her personality, her clothes, and her lifestyle had all dramatically changed since she had "walked into" the Earth body. She told me that she remembered the very first moment after she first came into her new Earth body. (This is something that other "Walk-ins," over the years have also expressed to me.) She said that her body was lying in the hospital bed following a serious surgery that had just transpired, when she suddenly sat up, totally awake and alert, and turned to her "new" Earth family members (including her "new" husband and his Earth relatives) and very clearly informed them that she was no longer the same soul that had inhabited the physical body a few moments before. She told them to get used to the idea that this was true and she warned them about the changes, so as not to shock them too much when they observed her new personality. Eventually, after many years, this woman began to dress a little more conservatively and learned how to integrate more into Earth society, but she always thought that this planet was extremely backward in its customs and lifestyles. This is what usually happens with "Walk-ins" who's "before" and "after" personalities are so extremely different.

It appears, that in the majority of cases of "Walk-ins" coming in, that it is not as outwardly obvious at first to those around them that this has happened. There are, of course, always subtle changes in the person's personality prior to and after the "Walk-in" experience. Normally, only one person per Earth family becomes a "Walk-in," but I do remember a couple of families that I have met in which the entire family all became "Walk-ins" at the same time. In these cases, it appears that the particular Missions they were on required that it happen this way and this, no doubt, made it easier for the entire family to help each other adapt to "normal" Earth family life.

Divine Protection for the Volunteers

As with those of us who come in right before the time of birth, "Walk-ins" have the same Higher Divine protection that the rest of the Volunteers here in Earth embodiment have. The Divine protection and "Cosmic back-up" is always operating in our lives, whether one is aware of it consciously or not. And, both, incarnates and "Walk-ins," have total free will to either fulfill their individual and collective Missions, or they can become "casualties" along the way. This can happen by becoming "numbed out" or distracted from their Missions or they may "get lost in the masquerade" of all the diversions and temptations of the "Maya" (karmic level of being).

I have met (literally) thousands of Volunteers over the years and have found that most of them have encountered numerous life-threatening experiences in which they should have either been killed or at least severely injured, but, instead, there was some kind of Divine Intervention that took place. It was as if "God's Guiding Hand of Divine Providence" exerted influence in their lives and miraculously protected them from any major harm occurring to them. Many people can relate to having had at least one so-called "traumatic" event occurring at sometime in their lives which helped to spiritually awaken them to their "greater purpose" for being.

The physical UFO and extraterrestrial contact experiences that I have had, as previously described, were the fulfilling of a promise (that I also consciously remember) that I was given by the Galactic Council prior to my physical birth on Earth. All Volunteers experience similar situations where they make agreements and are given promises on the Higher worlds prior to embodiment. Those promises include protection from danger, so that we (the Volunteers) are able to fulfill our Missions. The Intergalactic Confederation agrees to Divinely Intervene and save us from any threats to our survival, whether those threats are accidental or intentional. (More information will follow in an upcoming book of the <u>Divine Blueprint Series </u>on the cabal's attempts to assassinate me.)

This aspect of personal "Divine Intervention" and "Divine Protection" is important to know for those individuals who feel deep inside or suspect that they are one of these Volunteer souls on a Mission to Earth. If you feel that this applies to you, then rest assured that you automatically have this protection, as your "Cosmic Back-Up Team" has agreed upon prior to taking physical embodiment. How much protection or "Sponsorship" we all have is dependant on each of our individual Volunteer Missions while we are here on Earth. Those of us who are here in this capacity are actually acting as "Ambassadors," "Emissaries," or "Representatives" from the different Councils of the different worlds of the Federation of Light. Specifically, this means those of the Cosmic species of human-appearing ETs throughout the Intergalactic and interdimensional realms, as compared to those of the "grays" or reptilian species.

Of course, countless Volunteers have taken this a step further than just the "basic" form of over-all Divine Protection. Many of us have wanted to get a "Cosmic Extended Warranty" to cover a lot more, so to speak!!! That fail-safe warranty includes all areas of one's life (every cell and molecule) and everything we think, say, and do on every level of being "24/7," from the moment we arrive on the planet until the Worldwide Evacuation and Divine Intervention occurs, when that phase of our Mission is accomplished.

On Earth Assignments for the Volunteers

Presently, it is extremely important that all the Volunteers Awaken, so they can fulfill their Missions. To this end, I have invoked and decreed through the power of the Great I Am That I Am (the Christ Flame, the Holy Spirit) that the Divine Will for all others (whether aware or unaware) now Awaken to their individual and collective Missions to help transform and free this planet from the control and manipulation of the dark forces and energies (whether astral, economic, or political). These dark forces have been operating on Earth for many ages.

At this time, the Earth is truly in "Cosmic Escrow." By that I mean that the control of the Earth is about to totally change ownership and no matter what the imbalanced energies attempt to do to stop this, it will happen, for this is God's Divine Will that this be so. It is only a matter of how long it will take before the total cleansing is complete. Light Workers (Star People) actions can be "part of the solution, rather than part of the problem" which will greatly speed up this process. After all, the Volunteers have individually and collectively chosen to come here "On Earth Assignments," after which they will return to their Cosmic homes amongst the stars, galaxies, and dimensions from which they originally came prior to this lifetime.

On Earth Assignment was a wonderful book written by Tuella. Tuella was one of the most dedicated Light Workers that I have had the privilege of knowing. She was an extremely clear telepathic channel for Ashtar and was a very intelligent person who had an Inner knowing coupled with a discerning and open-mind and heart. There are a number of very significant books about our Space Friends that she wrote and published.

As quoted from Tuella's book, <u>On Earth Assignment</u>, The Summons of Star Born Representatives: "An oversimplified term for these individuals refers to them as "Walk-ins." Ashtar has stated, "This program in assisting earth is not new, however past implementations have been scattered, even rare events. But in this generation and an important point in time in the transition of earth into its new frequency, multitudes of special helpers are needed. Walk-in souls are now appearing almost daily. Their acclimation to this dimension is sometimes as drastic as the new born. They need to be discerned and assisted. A severe or devastating illness or a tremendous healing experience may be in the record."

Other information in regard to "Walk-ins" was described in an article in the <u>Universal Network</u> (a quarterly journal formerly published by Tuella) as dictated by Nathan, a representative of the Great White Brotherhood. He spoke of this phenomenon, "When the exchange is made, often the body recovers completely but contains a new personality. The new awareness is aware of the memory patterns, which permits the recollection of all former life and environment. Therefore life can, for the most part, be resumed as permitted by the physical recovery. The new awareness is now possessed of a past, and conditions for an earthly environment, and the urgency of the purpose, or mission to be performed. The Higher awareness decides what amount of veiling of the 'true self' is required. Also at what rate the memory of the mission and the nature of the true self can be released. Earthman would be surprised to know how many of us are among your society. Eventually you will accept it as common place in your existence. Each representative thus privileged, must obey the same general laws in the process. The dominion of the Higher awareness realizes the conscious physical organism and function in the earth environment. Veils are lifted as the new awareness senses the Higher calling and pursues the purpose of the mission."

Ashtar makes clear that these representatives, "have a human consciousness through which they must pull their slow awareness and be helped as the infant is helped by its elders. A limited period of confusion is to be expected, but will pass swiftly with the timed release of programming within. They will find a light to guide their understanding and the early mists will clear away."

Unlike the numerous "Walk-ins" who have entered Earth embodiment by "soul transfer" or "soul exchange," most of the other Volunteers who came into Earth embodiment through the normal biological birth process must go through a "Spiritual Awakening" process. This requires that their "Cosmic amnesia veils" lift, so that they can remember their Missions. There are literally millions of these "late bloomers" also on Earth who may be confused by thinking of themselves as "Walk-ins" only because of hearing about or having read Ruth Montgomery's books on the subject. The point I am making here is that it does not matter which way a Volunteer arrives on the planet, whether as a Walk-in or as an incarnate, the important point is the work they have to do here.

These Light Workers are dedicated, courageous, and noble beings who have come on strategic Missions to uplift this planet (which is, literally, the most difficult and dangerous planet in the entire Universe) and to help Mother Earth experience the Ascension as it moves quickly into the Golden Age.

As I like to say, these Volunteers are here as "Secret Agents of God" on "Cosmic Spiritual Espionage Missions of Light" and we have "Cosmic Sponsorship" to make sure that we will be successful. This will happen, of course, as long as we remember that "God helps those who help themselves" and as long as our intent and motives are pure. For one day soon, when we have completed our Missions and are physically lifted back up to be with our "Cosmic Friends and Relatives," we will be standing before the Councils and **reviewing this life** holographically. At that time, everything we said, thought, and did while we were on this planet will be shown back to us. So, when we look back, will we be proud of what we did and did we use the time productively to bring more Light, love, truth and freedom to the planet? Were we able to assist in eliminating suffering by helping expose the dark forces of the cabal?

As the Higher Forces, and even I, have stated many times, it is not that we cannot forgive these negative forces; rather it is just that until these forces are effectively exposed and eliminated that the horrors will continue. Since the Volunteers come with the Mighty Authority and Blessings of the Higher Councils and the entire Intergalactic Confederation, we have the right and the responsibility of a Cosmic Mandate to do this very thing. We are to go "where angels fear to tread," to courageously expose, and then heal these horrible planetary wounds! For unlike many past lives in which we died as "martyrs," this time we can speak with Spiritual Authority that was granted to us prior to taking Earth embodiment. As Volunteers, our Light, our connection with our Cosmic Back-up Team, and our Destiny (of achieving our collective Spiritual Ascension) assure us as is Divinely decreed that we are protected and that we have the authority to challenge, expose, and ultimately transmute all forms of injustice, corruption, disinformation, and suffering, no matter where it comes from.

It is never our human mistakes or "frailties" that are judged by our "Higher Friends," rather it is our intent and motives that are of concern. It is not even in believing in them that makes a fellow Volunteer "chosen," but instead it is what is in one's heart, mind, and soul that matters. In the final analysis, this is what really counts for the ultimate Upliftment of humanity.

Tuella's Awakening

Tuella's book speaks of her Awakening:

The heavy stacks of mail at Guardian Action headquarters are filled with letters from dear souls who are attempting valiantly to find their way through those "early mists." It isn't easy! Often the revelation can be staggering to the uninformed, and it is our hope that this book will be of help.

My own unveiling was triggered by joining the Book of the Month Club. Strange? Not really. Included in the six free volumes being offered were two leading books describing the life and works of Edgar Cayce as well as two of Ruth Montgomery's popular books. After completing the Cayce books in one day, that night I became aware of a form lying on a suspended platform, draped and totally covered in a metallic like golden cloth. The floating form was suspended at level with my form, along the left side of my bed. Amazingly, I had no fear or anxiety, quickly associating this sleeping form with the description of the "sleeping prophet." I simply took this as a sign to my consciousness as confirmation of a true account of this person. As I sat up on the edge of the bed following the occurrence, in deep thought concerning this and many related subjects, I received a message loud and clear. The words were, "You are a volunteer on earth assignment." At that time in my life I did not have the foggiest idea what the words were talking about or what such a personal category might be. The "early mists" had begun to lift. Ruth's books, in turn, led me to A.R.E. in Virginia Beach where I then found the books of Gina Carminera. They truly triggered my understanding of reincarnation so beautifully. A 500 watt bulb lit up within my understanding and all the darkness was removed forever. It has been said that an understanding of re-embodiment is like the front steps of the Temple of Truth, and that following such as awakening, everything else falls easily into place.

Message to Ruth Montgomery

Ruth Montgomery received a message from her spirit guides regarding Tuella: "In the meantime I had been in touch with Ruth Montgomery by letter and by phone. In one of her letters she wrote: 'I asked the guides about you and they wrote: Tuella is a being from outer space. There is indeed an Ashtar Command guarding Earth to rescue those worthy ones who will contribute to rejuvenation of Earth after the Shift when they will return. Including outer space volunteers here to help others accommodate to changing times, to prevent war, to prepare for inevitability of the Shift. Take seriously what Tuella reports."

"Because of this, she (Tuella) graciously mentioned our work in her newest book, Aliens Among Us. This gesture produced a swelling in our mailing list of incredible response. The interaction between the Special Earth Volunteers has a wonderful way of coming to pass and helping one another. The obedient Volunteer, walking steadfastly in the Light of his own Mission can almost just stand back and behold the handiwork of God in his or her life. The Divine Program is the greatest commitment we can make during our embodiment."

Monka Speaks

In another very insightful quote from Tuella's book, she specifically addresses the Awakening, the lifting of the Volunteers' Cosmic amnesia veils, and the activation of their Missions:

> Monka to speak: The earth volunteer carries a very powerful tie to the upper levels of other dimensional layers of power that cannot be compared with other planetary dwellers. The volunteer has ties of incredible strength to the Hierarchy and whatever particular group or family (or command) from which he has come forth. There will be a powerful compulsion toward the truths that are implanted within the soul, and the first contact with them will result in instant recall and activated soul memory. Belief as such, does not take place for that is unnecessary. There will be a pure remembering that gives forth a definite knowing, so that no argument or proof is necessary to the volunteer - he knows! Thus it is, that in these days which are so limited and time is so short, and the process now being used for Earth Volunteers has changed during the last decade. No longer can we dare to spend the time in the slow unfolding such as you experienced. Now drastic action must be taken. The Volunteer is geared up to handle experiences which overtake him or her with the strength of a tornado. There is no longer time for the gentleness of revelation; the veils are being torn asunder at great haste but with loving care. The Volunteer of today is a new breed of Adventurer who must accept his or her des-

tiny and see life in an Armageddon world as a (consciousness) battle to be joined.

Therefore, the guideband of that soul will be fully stepped up to the twelve representatives almost immediately. Each and every one of which is an important cell of the group dynamic from which the Volunteer has come and upon which the objective will be focused.

It is the intention of the Hierarchy that the release of this manuscript (as it especially will be now with the release of this book) will assist untold hundreds **(millions!!)** of unawakened earth Volunteers to awaken to their soul purpose. THE INVISIBLE STEEL THREAD WHICH ANCHORS THEM TO THE PERSONAL POWER POINTS WITH THEIR GROUP IN OTHER DIMENSIONS WILL HUM WITH THE CALL TO THEIR SOUL. THEY ARE POSITIONED WITH A PURPOSE, **PREPARED FOR** A PROGRAM ONLY THEY CAN FULFILL, IN WHATEVER WALK OF PLANETARY LIFE THEY HAVE COMMITTED THEMSELVES.

Information from George Hunt Williamson

In the '80's and '90's, the terms "Star People" and "Walk-ins" were used to refer to extraterrestrial Volunteer souls in Earth embodiment on Missions from other worlds. But back in the '50's and '60's, the unbiased researchers, contactees, and channels (the real pioneers of UFOology) used the term "Wanderers" to refer to these beings on Missions for the Federation.

An excellent book that was published by George Hunt Williamson that specifically spoke of the "Wanderers" was In Secret Places of the Lion, which explained how certain advanced Higher souls keep incarnating at key times throughout Earth's history to help uplift the planet. The term, the "Wanderers", was not only received through telepathic communication with the "Space Brothers" during the period of the '50's and '60's, but it also was received by the use of short-wave radio, telegraphy, and International Morse Code. This information has been highly-documented in more than one book published during that time (but now highly suppressed). In fact, numerous civilian and private ham radio operators participated in and showed documented proof that such contact was possible between space intelligences and those on Earth.

What is amazing to me is the fact that such well-documented experiments of both radio, as well as telepathic communications, were attempted and proven successful (hundreds of times) by numerous sincere and unbiased researchers in the '50's. During these experiments, three forms of communications were used: actual extraterrestrial verbal voice communications thru ham radios, International Morse Code or telegraphy, and mental telepathy. These were used separately, and in various combinations, to prove that they could easily communicate through these various means with the benevolent human-appearing ETs of the Confederation. These experiments were also conducted to demonstrate to those sincere and unbiased researchers participating in these series of experiments that pure telepathic (i.e., mental, mind-to-mind communication) was just as feasible as is utilized on all the other worlds. The remarkable thing is not that such a series of experiments were attempted and proven successful numerous times by many different individuals, but how thoroughly this information has been suppressed by the modern day so-called "professional UFO investigators." These agents of disinformation or spin-doctors have been very prevalent within the UFO community during the decades of the '70's, '80's, and '90's. But, in the last few years, newer, less-biased, and sincere UFO researchers have begun to emerge who have provided more positive and spiritually uplifting information in regard to contacts with the benevolent human-appearing ETs.

In the second book of the Divine Blueprint Series, The Cover-Up on Human-Appearing ETs, I will be documenting the different forms of communication (One of the main sources of this information is from an out-of-print '50's book called The Saucers Speak.) that the Space Brothers have used during the '50's and early '60's, to converse with this planet, as well as more recent "communication transmissions" in which they have attempted to openly warn the people of this planet in regard to what the real world leaders of the Earth (the cabal) have planned for us. The truth is that the Federation has Intervened many times "behind the scenes" on our behalf and I will show how the communications were covered-up and suppressed. This suppression has been orchestrated not only by the government, but also by many prominent, so-called "professional," UFO investigators in what I term "the cover-up within the cover-up."

There are numerous other sources that address the Awakening of the incarnate Volunteers, as well as, the subject of "Walk-ins." The information that has been presented herein has merely been to expose one to the significance of the Volunteers that have come to Earth to assist in the uplifting of humanity during this crucial time.

CHAPTER 7

BARACK OBAMA

Fulfilling One's Mission & Destiny

This particular chapter was not originally planned for the book, but just as we were completing the final editing, I (Michael) was strongly urged by the Higher Forces of Light to include this information in regard to the recent events in the political, economic, and international scene. These insights are primarily about the 2008 Presidential Election, the financial bailout, and the true facts about the "so-called" Russian aggression against the country of Georgia, which the corporate-controlled mainstream media has totally suppressed. Much of this information is posted on my website "ChannelFortheMasters.com." This particular posting consists of a Channeling from the Higher Forces and my own opinion, as well.

The 2008 Presidential Race

This is another "Intergalactic Commentary" from the Higher Forces of Light, who are benevolent, human-appearing Elohim ETs that surround the planet in their Merkabah Lightships. These channeled commentaries give an Intergalactic and, often, "behind the scenes" perspective for the purposes of enlightening humanity about their Missions, helping us survive the challenges we are facing, and preparing the way for open Divine Intervention on our behalf.

I must admit that I was not specifically expecting a Channeling Transmission about recent events leading up to the 2008 Presidential Election or about the candidates running for the office. Over the years, I developed a "stereotyped" impression of Earth politicians and a "bias" towards the whole election process, knowing that the "power-elite" have manipulated these votes to their advantage. Both major political parties have been very effectively controlled by this hidden manipulation and others who have attempted to change this system have been forced into dropping out of the race when the negative forces have made it clear what will happen to them if they become the President, i.e. the assassination of JFK as President and Robert Kennedy running for President.

I have been "progressively Libertarian" in my political orientation. This was determined by my memories of living on more advanced worlds prior to coming to this planet. So, as a result of my awareness, I was never drawn to Earth politics.

On these more advanced worlds, the Higher Councils of Light have set policies termed "Intergalactic Rule of Law." The leaders of these worlds are in touch with the "peoples' needs and wants" and are not part of hidden agendas from anyone attempting to manipulate the masses. Unfortunately, on earth the "power-elite" have been secretly plotting for complete world control and have created numerous "false-flag" events which have resulted in the loss of more and more of our Constitutional Rights and Freedoms.

In December of 2007, I received a channeling from Ashtar about the manipulation of our votes. The Higher Forces stated that they wanted to help Overshadow the voting process to stop the manipulation of votes. They said that this manipulation has actually been going on in all the major Presidential elections since President Kennedy was assassinated. The sophistication of how this has been accomplished has changed throughout the years. There is video footage from over forty years ago that shows tabs being punched out by hand in voter cards in Dade County, Florida by the League of Women Voters (as documented in James Collier's book, "Vote Scam"). And, more recently, the technique being used is to manipulate the vote count through the use of computers in conjunction with the actual voting machines.

The Higher Forces said that they would help us get more accurate vote counts, as long as we, the citizens, do all we can in fulfilling our own responsibilities and "constitutional duties" to elect the persons who we feel are the best choice for this country. During this channeling, Ashtar made a "philosophical comment" regarding the candidates who were running for office as to who **their** best choice of a candidate would be: "who would **we** vote for, who would be **our** main choice for a Presidential candidate of the U.S (that is, if we were allowed to participate in this upcoming Earth electoral process)? We will only state, that as a major "Cosmic Hint," the only really good choices are less than the number of fingers on one of your hands. We, of the Federation, termed Space Brotherhood/Sisterhood, tend to be what you of Earth would say are extremely, **'Intergalactically-Libertarian'.**"

After I received this channeling, I wondered if this comment was a reference to Ron Paul or Dennis Kucinich. As a matter of fact, those like Ron Paul and Dennis Kucinich are often drawn to other Volunteers (Star People) because of this inner recognition and because they hold similar principles. Ashtar continued: "It is also no accident that Dennis Kucinich sighted one of our ships, which we purposely brought down to be seen. This sighting event, like most sightings of our craft, is not usually a mere accident. The crafts you of Earth refer to as UFOs are really IFO's (Identified Flying Objects) and these appearances are actually "Spiritual Visual Reference Points" and "Inner Cosmic" reminders, of our connections with those of you on Earth. We are your Extended Cosmic Family who are preparing for more open, mass appearances very soon over Earth.

After both Dennis Kucinich and Ron Paul dropped out of the race, it was obvious that the same old manipulation of the number of initial votes had occurred. The cabal manipulated the number of votes they each received as the first few primaries occurred. After a few of these primaries, it became clear to them that it was useless to continue their run for President.

I had to admit I was confused and depressed by this predictable outcome of these two men who had more virtuous qualities and who would have had the strength and courage to stand up to the power elite. On one level, I was not at all surprised, since both Ron Paul and Dennis Kucinich had made their positions and objectives extremely clear that they were going to challenge the power and influence of the power elite. On the other hand, having received this particular channeling from Ashtar and the Higher Forces, which had "implied" that they would help stop this manipulation of our votes by the cabal, I could not understand why they had allowed this outcome for both Ron Paul and Dennis Kucinich. I had assumed that these two men were the only good choices that were available because of their sincerity, their open and honest stands, and their true intent.

A short time later on, I ultimately lost respect for Ron Paul, when he was interviewed by the neo-con host Glenn Beck of Fox Network. During the interview, Mr. Beck was making fun of the "9-11 Truth Accountability Movement" and ridiculed those of us who knew that the government covered up the facts and totally distorted the truth about what actually happened. Ron Paul pretended that he had never heard about these "theories;" he agreed with the official version and explained any of the "discrepancies" as being caused by "irresponsibility's" on the part of the officials. I was flabbergasted by his response, for up until that moment, I had assumed that he was a truly honest and straight forward individual. It was at that moment, that I lost respect for him, and realized that he had been given a chance to "rise to the occasion," but had chosen otherwise. At the very least, he could have made a statement like, "Well, now that you've brought it up, any intelligent person who is not biased or with a hidden agenda and who truly examines the evidence, would have to conclude that there are an awful lot of contradictions and irregularities in the official version of 9-11, and, therefore further investigation is warranted." After that incident, I believed that he was definitely not the right person to represent this country as our President.

This was a very depressing moment, just as it was when Dennis Kucinich dropped out of the race. At that time, I initially lost interest in this election.

Furthermore, both my sources on Earth and the Higher Elohim Beings of Light have exposed the truth about the Clintons and the Bushes. The truth is that despite the outer public appearance of not liking each other, the Bushes (or as they are referred to as "the Bush Crime Family") and the Clintons have actually been secretly working together. They are part of the cabal and they are some of the most corrupt and evil people on the planet. President Bush Sr. used to take President Clinton to Mena, Alaska, to get deliveries of cocaine, which were hidden in the nose-cones of the CIA planes. More recently, Bush Sr., Bush Jr., and both Bill & Hillary Clinton have attempted to block the financial steps that would activate the new economic system known as NESARA (National Economic Security And Reformation Act) which would officially "do away with" the old Federal Reserve global banking system. NESARA would financially free all of humanity from any more unnecessary suffering.

Even though many who have been Hillary supporters will deny this information, I make no apology about what I have uncovered, because it is important to understand much of the "hidden dynamics" that have been going on during these last several months and the "bitter" tug-of-war between Barack Obama and Hillary Clinton. She actually believed that she would win the Democratic nomination, because her "controllers" were going to manipulate the votes for the primary and she was assured of winning the nomination. Yes, "these puppet-masters" have always chosen ahead of time who would be running for each party's nomination (as well as, who would ultimately win the Presidency), while the gullible public has believed in their naiveté that their votes actually made a difference. But this time, there was a "major problem" that the illuminati had not considered, and that is that the Higher Forces would **"manipulate their manipulation"** or to express it another way "two can play this game!"

I also recently envisioned a type of "Corruption Scale" that measures how corrupt Earth politicians are. The scale is numbered from one (1) (least corrupt) to eleven (11) (most corrupt). It is literally impossible for an Earth politician to be at the one mark, because seemingly all politicians have at least a few "skeletons in their closets". When I intuitively tuned into this scale, what I found was that most politicians fell between six to eight points on this "corruption scale." This scale is similar to the "Richter Scale" that measures the "intensity" of earthquakes and as the numbers increase, the intensity of the quake multiples. So too, with this scale, each number that is higher than the last one, actually multiplies the intensity of corruption and evil acts.

It was made clear to me that Hillary was the cabal's first choice of who they wanted to "win" the Presidential race and McCain (or "McSame," as I refer to him!) was their second choice. According to the "Corruption Scale," both Hillary and McCain are somewhere around the 10 to 11 point levels. And, by the way, both Dennis Kucinich and Ron Paul were at an extremely low level of 1 to 2 on this scale.

Barack Obama

Unknown to me, as well as to others, there were some very positive things happening "behind the scenes." I suddenly realized, very unexpectedly, that something awesome and extraordinary was happening. While I was watching Barack Obama give his "acceptance speech" for the Democratic Primary, I tuned into the "Corruption Scale" and found that he was around two to three on this scale, which is still extremely low, as compared with most of the other politicians that exist on this planet. As compared to most other politicians, he has very few "skeletons" to be discovered; therefore blackmail (by the cabal) will not be an issue.

I was not even planning to watch Obama's acceptance speech because of my extreme bias. But then, I received a very strong telepathic message that my "Friends Upstairs wanted me to watch his speech with an "open mind." Because I have learned to listen to them and to follow their "suggestions," I felt that I had better watch. Furthermore, I had to admit that this was indeed a historical moment with an African-American actually running for President. Knowing what I knew about the cabal choosing all the past Presidential candidates, I figured this would not be any different. I wondered if for some reason the cabal had changed their minds and decided to choose Obama rather than Hillary.

For many years, I have been able to tune-in and see individual's auric fields. As I was watching Obama deliver his speech on television, I noticed a couple of very significant things about his energy. First, I could see his beautiful golden-colored auric field and I also saw intense Light shooting out of his eyes, which increased more and more as he became animated with his speech. It was then that I knew that he was a highly-evolved soul, a fellow Light Worker, and a Star Person. I sensed much more "substance" to his words and Inner Spirit.

A few days later, Ashtar shared some very important things with me about Obama. He wanted to "set the record straight" because of some untrue "psychic rumors" that were, obviously, created by negative astral forces.

Greetings In the Light of Our Radiant One, this is Lord Ashtar of the Ashtar Command of the Intergalactic Confederation of Worlds. I want to give more insight into the soul you all know now in this life as Barack Obama, a little about his background, of his soul's origins, and his Mission for being here as a Volunteer in Earth embodiment from a far more evolved world and star system. Though he has lived on many other worlds of our Federation and is also a key member of the Ashtar Command and other Commands of the Federation, his true soul's origins are from my own star system, that of Sirius.

As a fellow Sirian Brother of Light, Obama is a very "old soul" who has, as I often used the phrase, "been around the Intergalactic block many times," and as a fellow Elohim, has held a key membership within numerous Higher Councils. As a great Intergalactic Diplomat on our Higher levels, he chose to take Earth embodiment this final time to fulfill his Destiny of becoming the leader of the United States of America and to do this despite the attempts of the cabal to block his actual candidacy. Though the cabal thought they would just let him "attempt" to win the nomination, as they had "intended" and planned for Hillary to win by manipulating the votes. They knew that she was more likely to be controlled and they were not sure if he would allow himself to be totally controlled and be just another one of their puppets. In fact, Obama actually received a far greater number of votes in these earlier primaries than the "official tally." Even though the cabal manipulated the votes like they normally do, because we (at the Higher level) neutralized most of their manipulation, Obama still came out ahead of the number of votes for Hillary.

I would also like to confirm what this channel heard earlier from more than one "alternative Earth source." Already, there have been at least two major attempts [three, already as of now] by the cabal to assassinate Barack Obama, but we helped block and neutralize these attempts. He is being protected from any attempts that the cabal may try. Because they sense that he will (with our help, of course) expose their conspiracy and the many evil things they have done, they are desperate to try to get rid of him.

President Kennedy initially had contact with the Federation, but, unfortunately, ignored our warning about going to Dallas, Texas that day in '63 or he would not have been assassinated by the cabal. Obama will be more alert and not let himself be distracted from our guidance. He will "awaken" to his soul's original Higher extraterrestrial origins, and, in so doing, will be a powerful and inspiring leader and diplomat for planet Earth, who will help bring peace to the planet and help prepare the population for our First Contact scenario. One of this Channel's friends made the comment that he perceived Obama as a "black JFK," who will, once he becomes President, set in motion all the things that President Kennedy had planned to do, before he was stopped by the cabal. This time, though, they will not be successful and we will help him usher in a true Golden Age in which these forces of darkness will loss their power and influence.

So, we of the Federation want you all to tune-in, to go within, and to sense all that I am sharing with you. Not only is Obama the better choice for President of the United States of America, partly because of his Inner strength of character at this challenging and epic time of human history, it is also, in fact, his Destiny and his Mission to fulfill this. A part of his Mission includes how he will influence and help transform this planet, politically and spiritually, as his wisdom and love for all humanity shines forth and as a healing force for the challenges that have to be faced. With our help, we of the Federation of Light look forward to meeting openly with him, and all of you, in these next few years as First Contact finally takes place, as well as NESARA finally being officially activated. Blessings to you all, and "keep your Eyes on the Skies," as more and more off our ships are sighted on a mass level in preparation for this most wondrous and glorious event. Adonai Vassu Berogus!

I must say, this was a most interesting and insightful communication from Ashtar and it helped clear up some of my confusion and concern. Now, I understand why Obama appeared to have "wobbled" a bit on his initial positions to actually fool the power-elite (such as those at that Bilderberg meeting he met with a few months ago with Hillary) into thinking that he could be controlled like most Earth politicians. And, I have a much clearer understanding of what has been going on for the last year or so as Obama gained more momentum (of Destiny). In fact, like the analogy of a football game, I also got an impression that Obama is like the quarterback for a team with Dennis Kucinich and Ron Paul blocking for him along the way, while he chooses a strategy and follows a secret path past the oncoming team to get to the end-zone.

Confirmations from Other Sources

After receiving this Channeling about Obama, I received four confirmations from other sources. One of my friends who participates in a teleconference Channeling group called "Ashtar on the Road" told me that in their most recent Channeling session Ashtar and other fellow Cosmic Beings of Light shared very similar things about Obama. They stated Obama had experienced the "Walk-in" of a very powerful Cosmic Being of Light whose soul merged with his soul in July 2008. This was done to help strengthen him for his Mission and to help protect him from further assassination attempts. Another friend told me that she had read a Channeling in the Sedona Journal publication over a year ago that stated that the next President of the U.S. would be a highly-evolved spiritual Being of Light and would definitely be a man--which is significant also, considering the timing of Hillary Clinton running in the Presidential Primary. The third confirmation came from another friend who told me that David Wilcock, who is supposedly the reincarnation of Edgar Cayce and who is also a very gifted psychic in this lifetime, had Channeled (over a year ago) that he saw that the next President would be a man who would be highly-evolved and would be able to help spiritually guide this planet into the upcoming Golden Age.

Then, Marcia, the editor of this book, who was finishing up her work for the final copy, told me that she remembered a very significant statement from Ruth Montgomery. Ruth Montgomery was famous for having first presented the concept of "Walk-ins" to the Earth in her two books Strangers Among Us and Aliens Among Us. In the early '80's, Ruth's Spiritual Guides Channeled through her that the man who would be elected President in the last election before 2012 (obviously, the 2008 election) would be a "Walk-in"! From her more recent book The World to Come (1999), she says: "The Guides have long predicted that a Walk-in would become president of the United States and would be of inestimable value in preparing us for the cataclysmic shift of the Earth."

A Reading from the Universal Akashic Records (The Cherubim through Carolyn Evers)

Isis asked about reports that Barack Obama has healed people through touch. What is the truth of this?

You know Mr. Obama as a Presidential candidate, but he is an elevated soul who has been sent here to unwind the decadent society which is embroiled in a struggle between the light and the dark.

This soul is rather new to the circling experiences of this planet. He has come from another planet and has little experience on the Earth plane. He was sent here to be one who would change the evolution of the political scene. We see the possibility of being elected as President, whereby he will be supported by those from his home planet who will work very diligently to bring forth the equal playing field of peace and prosperity for the world view of equality.

He will be a hardworking soul for peace and cooperation as these are his two goals for this lifetime. What he says will be direct and if one stops to weigh his words, they will be easy to understand without the subterfuge of deceit.

Mr. Obama is not aware of his abilities on a conscious level, but his spiritual practices and abilities are evolving. What you see as healing individuals is really just a preparation for something much greater in his life; the healing of a nation and in it the intent to begin healing the world.

This may sound like a grandiose mission, but it must start somewhere. We see that there is a very great possibility of his election to be the leader of your nation as president. The possibilities are moving towards that realm of probability. The turning point will be soon as there is still much division between the candidates. Know that this is a struggle between the light and the dark and the dark is not ready to concede.

Mr. Obama's real mission is to heal the nation as we said. However, in his many lifetimes he has been a healer on many different levels. He would have bound the nation's wounds and united the North and South as **Abraham Lincoln** before he was assassinated by the dark. He has come again because he loves this country and also loves humanity. He understands the struggle between two rival sides and understands how to bring forth cooperation.

That is his main mission. His ability to heal physical bodies is just beginning to surface. These are abilities that he worked upon while he journeyed in Egypt. He was an adept then and was incarnating in the Pharaohic line. He built pyramids and understands the vibration of sound. Of course, this is contained in his data banks of past memories which are only now starting to surface.

As you are aware Isis, he is closely aligned with the planet of **Sirius** and he is being followed by that hierarchy and is being protected by that authority. We see that you will hear more about this ability as it will become main-stream when the time is right to bring it forth.

Gordon-Michael Scallion (Edgar Cayce Conference - May 2007)

In a Higher state of consciousness Gordon-Michael Scallion was asked, "Who will be the next U.S. President?" He responded, "Lincoln will once again occupy the White House." He was then asked, "Who is Lincoln?" The response was "Obama.

Other Information about Barack Obama

Barack Obama was born under a master number: 8+4+1+9+6+1=29/11. His birth date and time was: 7:11 pm; Aug. 4, 1961, Honolulu Hawaii. He has a Leo sun; Aquarius rising, and moon in Gemini.

Messages from Matthew (Channeled by Suzie Ward)

Attention is being given around the globe to the United States presidential candidates. Despite the rigged primary elections to favor Hillary Clinton and John McCain's supporters waffling because he himself waffles, soon it will be glaringly apparent that Barack Obama's greater popularity among voters will be sustained. Thus free will choices of the majority have been made and now, without influencing those choices one whit, we can reveal that in the energy field of potential, Obama's momentum always was unstoppable, and we can tell you that this highly evolved soul with many lifetimes as a wise and just leader came from a spiritually and intellectually advanced civilization specifically to rise to his current prominence. At soul level he knows this is his mission, but consciously he is aware only of his innate leadership abilities and genuine intent to serve his nation as he so states; in time he will become consciously aware of his origin and purpose for embodying in this lifetime. Once he is in office, some darkly-intentioned persons expect to control him just as they and others before them have controlled a succession of U.S. presidents and many members of Congress. However, that vicious kind of governing is at an end, and contrary to the protestations of Hillary Clinton that this race is not over, she and other top Illuminati know they are witnessing the demise of their "secret government," therefore, the Obama family members are among the most intensely light-protected persons on Earth.

From Sylvia Brown's Newsletter (September 16th, 2008)

I recently spoke to a friend who receives a Bimonthly newsletter from the well-known Psychic Sylvia Brown. In the Question and Answer section of her most recent newsletter (which, obviously, was asked before Obama chose Joe Biden as his Vice Presidential running mate), she was asked: "Do you have any predictions on who the Democratic presidential front runner Barack Obama will choose as his running mate?" Sylvia responded: "No, but I feel that Obama will be our next President."

Another Message from Mathew (Channeled by Suzie Ward -September 24, 2008)

To the even greater number of questions, with Palin as his running mate, will McCain win the election? First I repeat: We are apolitical. We neither endorse nor favor one soul over another, but rather objectively report what we see in Earth's energy field of potential and what exists in the continuum. So then, ever since McCain's announcement of Palin as his selection, the energy field has been quite astir! But even if her popularity within specific groups of voters were to continue instead of wane, and wane it will, it could not change the outcome of the election. Earth, a sentient soul, cried out in her death throes sixty-some years ago for other civilizations' help to save her planetary body; she chose to have no more terrorism like "9/11;" she has been ridding herself of negativity so she can rise to vibratory levels where her original health and vibrancy will be restored and the Higher consciousness of her humankind will glory in spiritual renewal. The energetic force that has been propelling her ascension out of third density's darkness has been leading naturally to a spiritually evolved visionary as President of what you consider your world's most powerful nation.

Thus, in line with Earth's own vision, Barack Obama will accomplish his mission to bring wisdom, justness, and integrity to the United States government and his example of governing with compassion and reconciliation to unify a divided nation will resound around the world. He is not the only highly evolved soul who will lead Earth into the Golden Age—many others also came to fill influential positions, some to support Obama and some as leaders of other nations. Be aware that mainstream "news" in the United States is falsely portraying some leaders as posing a danger to democracy or destabilizing their nations, whereas they are light beings distancing their countries from the Illuminati's empire-building, which in large part has grown through two centuries or more of the US government's covert intrusion into other countries' affairs. Foremost among these leaders vilified by the Bush administration is Vladimir Putin, and another is Hugo Chavez. In countries long involved in violent conflicts, negotiations seesaw from pessimistic to optimistic to pessimistic, but eventually there will be stability under wise, benevolent leadership throughout the world. As the consciousness of Earth humankind continues to rise and truths continue to emerge, all light receptive peoples will rejoice—so will all lighted beings throughout this universe!

The suicide bombing in Islamabad was a CIA "black ops" undertaking with the intent to create more turmoil and fear in Pakistan and hopefully unseat the leader, who is not under the Illuminati thumb. That incident also was intended to divert attention from the crisis in the global economy and the outrage about bail-out shenanigans. If you suspected as much and also thought that the bombing may indicate the Illuminati's growing concern that they won't be able to control Obama, so they are beefing up voter support for McCain's war-like stance on Terror, you are indeed connecting the dots.

Telephone Conference Interview with David Wilcock

On the same day, I received another very insightful e-mail of a telephone conference interview that David Wilcock had with Kerry Cassidy and Bill Ryan, who helped start "Project Camelot" (support@projectcamelot.org), which took place on September 9, 2008. During the interview, they discussed Richard Hoagland's research regarding NASA cover-ups, Benjamin Fulford's revelations of what is occurring to stop the illuminati, and other subjects related to the conspiracy of the illuminati and New World Order forces and their plan for total control. The entire interview was quite lengthy and I would recommend reading the entire transcript because of the many interesting things that were discussed.

I will only quote portions from this text that relate directly to Obama. As you will see, what Richard Hoagland states in regard to his own feelings & intuition about Obama, specifically confirms what Ashtar telepathically conveyed to me around the same time. I channeled this "Intergalactic Commentary" concerning Obama on September 3rd, 2008, which was a historically quoted statement that Ashtar had repeated to me, because of the **SIGNIFICANCE** of why Obama had Brzezinski as one of his "top" advisors, since Brzezinski is not aligned with Higher Forces. This was one of the reasons that many unenlightened people have mistakenly and falsely assumed that Obama is not really aligned with Higher Forces and that he is not a Higher Being in Earth embodiment. However, Ashtar specifically repeated this famous statement to me: **"Keep your friends close, and keep your enemies closer!"**

Here is the section where Hoagland repeated this famous quote:

Brzezinski and Obama

Kerry Cassidy: OK. But you have to get around to Brzezinski and the fact that his whole M.O. is to bring down Russia.

David Wilcock: Sure.

K: But his candidate is Obama. And they're actually at war, within the Rockefeller side, with the, you know, McCain, you know, Neo-con faction.

D: Right. I agree. Now, the Brzezinski thing is a very interesting and controversial angle. And I've had extensive conversation on the phone with Richard Hoagland about this. Because, as I've said before and I'll say again, I've had extensive dream data telling me that Obama is one of the good guys. And then you'd say to yourself, OK if he's a good guy, then why in the world would he bring in Brzezinski? And Richard and I have talked about this. And Richard's opinion, which I agree with, is: "You keep your friends close, and you keep your enemies closer!!!"

What better way to know what they're planning and what they want to do, than to have the guy there in your cabinet? You hear his side of things, and you hear what he wants to do, because you're smart enough not to be manipulated by him. Now, granted, he's taken a lot of heat for it. And a lot of people think that he buys into Brzezinski's beliefs, but I don't believe that at all.

And again, I think when he picked Joe Biden as his V.P.; it's a political decision that was made because he's trying to win an American election. And it's a dirty game, it's not easy, and it's ugly.

But I honestly don't think that, just because he's got his enemy in the camp that means that he's agreeing with everything his enemy says at all. I think Richard and I are unanimous in this, in agreeing that the extent of change that Obama actually wants to create is much more than he's actually been saying so far. And, from what I can tell, the insiders are terrified about Obama ever becoming president.

And you're seeing a massive media effort to try to frame this election as if it's an even run between McCain and Obama, which is ludicrous. It's ludicrous. And we know for a fact, from the TBRNews source, that these polls are faked, that they've been faked for a long, long time. You call up 700 people in the reddest Republican state, who you know are the most likely to be brainwashed fundamentalists. And, even in those cases, only, like, 50% of 'em are saying they're going to vote for McCain. And that's where you're getting your 50/50 dead-heat from.

Letter from Michael Moore

On September 29, 2008, Michael Moore sent a letter via the Internet that summed up the major points about the recent attempt by the power-elite to cause a "financial bailout of the economic system." This economic mess, that the citizens of this country are presently experiencing, was started when these corrupt "puppet-masters" created the illegal Federal Reserve banking system so they would be able to openly and covertly manipulate our economy in any way they wanted. Recently, their karma finally caught up with them and now they want us to bail them out.

This particular letter was actually sent to the "Star Doves" who are a very dedicated New Age couple who help enlighten Light Workers by sharing information (i.e. many of my channelings) with them over the Internet.

Here is part of Michael Moore's letter:

"My Dear Star Dove Friends,

Let me cut to the chase. The biggest robbery in the history of this country is taking place as you read this. Though no guns are being used, 300 million hostages are being taken. Make no mistake about it: After stealing a half trillion dollars to line the pockets of their war-profiteering backers for the past five years, after lining the pockets of their fellow oil men to the tune of over a hundred billion dollars in just the last two years, Bush and his cronies--who must soon vacate the White House--are looting the U.S. Treasury of every dollar they can grab. They are swiping as much of the silverware as they can on their way out the door.

No matter what they say, no matter how many scare words they use, they are up to their old tricks of creating fear and confusion in order to make and keep themselves and the upper one percent filthy rich. Just read the first four paragraphs of the lead story in last Monday's New York Times and you can see what the real deal is: "Even as policy makers worked on details of a $700 billion bailout of the financial industry, Wall Street began looking for ways to profit from it. Financial firms were lobbying to have all manner of troubled investments covered, not just those related to mortgages. At the same time, investment firms were jockeying to oversee all the assets that Treasury plans to take off the books of financial institutions, a role that could earn them hundreds of millions of dollars a year in fees. Nobody wants to be left out of the Treasury's proposal to buy up bad assets of financial institutions."

Unbelievable! Wall Street and its backers created this mess and now they are going to clean up like bandits. Even Rudy Giuliani is lobbying for his firm to be hired (and paid) to "consult" in the bailout.

The problem is nobody truly knows what this "collapse" is all about. Even Treasury Secretary Paulson admitted he doesn't know the exact amount that is needed (he just picked the $700 billion number out of his head!). The head of the congressional budget office said he can't figure it out nor can he explain it to anyone.

And yet, they are screeching about how the end is near! Panic! Recession! The Great Depression! Y2K! Bird flu! Killer bees! We must pass the bailout bill today!! The sky is falling! The sky is falling! Falling for whom? NOTHING in this "bailout" package will lower the price of the gas you have to put in your car to get to work. NOTHING in this bill will protect you from losing your home. NOTHING in this bill will give you health insurance.

Health insurance? Mike, why are you bringing this up? What's this got to do with the Wall Street collapse? It has everything to do with it. This so-called "collapse" was triggered by the massive defaulting and foreclosures going on with people's home mortgages. Do you know why so many Americans are losing their homes? To hear the Republicans describe it, it's because too many working class idiots were given mortgages that they really couldn't afford. Here's the truth: The number one cause of people declaring bankruptcy is because of medical bills. Let me state this simply: If we had had universal health coverage, this mortgage "crisis" may never have happened.

This bailout's mission is to protect the obscene amount of wealth that has been accumulated in the last eight years. It's to protect the top shareholders who own and control corporate America. It's to

make sure their yachts and mansions and "way of life" go uninter-
rupted while the rest of America suffers and struggles to pay the
bills. Let the rich suffer for once. Let them pay for the bailout.
We are spending 400 million dollars a day on the war in Iraq. Let
them end the war immediately and save us all another half-trillion
dollars!

When you screw up in life, there is hell to pay. Each and every
one of you reading this knows that basic lesson and has paid the
consequences of your actions at some point. In this great democracy, we cannot let there be one set of rules for the vast majority of
hardworking citizens, and another set of rules for the elite, who,
when they screw up, are handed one more gift on a silver platter.
No more! Not again!

Yours,
Michael Moore
MMFlint@aol.com
MichaelMoore.com

PS Having read further the details of this bailout bill, you need to
know you are being lied to. They talk about how they will prevent
golden parachutes. It says NOTHING about what these executives
and fat cats will make in SALARY. According to Rep. Brad
Sherman of California, these top managers will continue to receive
million-dollar-a-month paychecks under this new bill. There is no
direct ownership given to the American people for the money being handed over. Foreign banks and investors will be allowed to
receive billion-dollar handouts. A large chunk of this $700 billion
is going to be given directly to Chinese and Middle Eastern banks.
There is NO guarantee of ever seeing that money again.

PPS From talking to people I know in DC, they say the reason so
many Dems are behind this is because Wall Street this weekend
put a gun to their heads and said either turn over the $700 billion or
the first thing we'll start blowing up are the pension funds and
401(k)s of your middle class constituents. The Dems are scared
they may make good on their threat. But this is not the time to
back down or act like the typical Democrat we have witnessed for

124

the last eight years. The Dems handed a stolen election over to Bush. The Dems gave Bush the votes he needed to invade a sovereign country. Once they took over Congress in 2007, they refused to pull the plug on the war. And now they have been cowered into being accomplices in the crime of the century. You have to call them now and say "NO!" If we let them do this, just imagine how hard it will be to get anything good done when President Obama is in the White House. THESE DEMOCRATS ARE ONLY AS STRONG AS THE BACKBONE WE GIVE THEM. CALL CONGRESS NOW.

Obama's Achilles Heel

I wish to state one more thing about Obama, which is perhaps his "Achilles Heel." I believe that he will change his mind about this next subject once he has a chance to examine the facts. This is in relation to what I term our "health freedoms" and, specifically, in regard to the "vaccination scam." Big Pharma, that is the multi-billion dollar pharmaceutical cartel, is in league with the AMA, as well as many politicians. These bureaucrats have passed unconstitutional laws which force mandatory (and EXTREMELY TOXIC AND DANGEROUS!!) vaccinations upon the entire population which is extremely profitable for them. This is an utter tragedy and a conspiracy of the worse kind which will destroy both our health and our consciousness. There is plenty of evidence that is based on research by thousands of holistic doctors and health professionals that backs up what I am stating here.

For decades, there has been a huge "Vaccination-Compensation Program" in which parents have been paid literally billions of dollars because of the numerous deadly and toxic side effects from vaccinations, which has caused thousands of young children to die or be horribly injured from the side effects. And, yet, despite this program, the medical establishment is planning to force even more mandatory and toxic vaccinations on children so they can go to public schools. These laws and plans for such mandatory vaccinations should definitely be challenged legally, not only because of the extreme questionable nature of the ingredients that are in these vaccinations, but also because of the unconstitutionality of such "mandatory" requirements, which contradicts our constitutional guaranteed Rights and Freedoms. Parents and citizens should demand to see the list of ingredients contained in every vaccination, for once they know what is in these toxic vaccinations they will never take a vaccination again.

I brought up this subject because I was confronted with some information that suggested that while Obama has a lot of great qualities and abilities that we need in a President, he may not have a complete understanding of this problem. As a part of the universal health care system that he wants to establish, it is important that he recognize the health freedoms of the citizens and the dangers of having mandatory vaccinations forced upon the population. People should have the right to choose whether or not they want to receive vaccination shots; it should not be forced upon them.

What Really Happened Between Georgia and Russia

The other important topic to mention is how our corporate-controlled media manipulated the facts regarding the recent events that transpired between the countries of Georgia and Russia. The real facts are that the Georgian military, with support and backing from the U.S. and Israel, attacked and killed hundreds of Russian citizens and peacekeepers. This even involved brutally killing a lot of women and children by throwing grenades into basements of homes where they were hiding to try to escape this massacre.

Russia responded very quickly to stop this horrible tragedy and then was accused by the U.S. of being the aggressor and was blamed as the ones who supposedly did the killing. But, as a result of Russia responding so fast, certain U.S. special forces were forced to leave so fast that they accidentally left behind some very important classified documents, which the Russian troops found. These documents described plans by the U. S. and Israel (in the very near future) to use Georgia as a base to launch a nuclear war on Iran and the Middle East. Other documents that were found described plans to establish martial law and the activation of the 800 concentration camps (that already exist in the U.S.) before the Presidential elections in November of 2008.

When the Russians found these documents, they shared this information with some individuals in the U.S. military who are opposed to these evil plans and who want to uphold the U.S. Constitution and do the "right" thing. As a result of these plans being exposed, the information has produced massive upheavals in the military and intelligence agencies. And, since the dark forces work best when there is "surprise, stealth and F.E.A.R.," these plans became disempowered very quickly.

I also know that our "Friends Upstairs" helped bring about this discovery, which helped expose the plans of the cabal from behind the scenes. This is just another instance of Divine Intervention from the Spiritual Hierarchy in which they use "subtle" ways of Overshadowing people to be sure that whatever needs to be done gets accomplished.

A Final Word about the 2008 Presidential Election

On the "Cosmic Connection" Internet show that I hosted on November 1, 2008, I talked about "Discernment and the 2008 Presidential Election. The discussion centered on how critical this election was and how much was at stake, not only for the U. S., but also for the entire planet. "This election is the most important election that this country has had in many decades, and, perhaps, even since this Republic was first founded by our Forefathers. Voters must use their abilities to discern the best choice for our country. This choice must not be based on 'old paradigms' of whether one is 'liberal' or 'conservative' or whether one is 'democrat,' 'republican' or 'independent.' We must identify the 'real issues' that the candidates must deal with and, especially, examine the level of consciousness that they each possess. This election is actually a type of 'Planetary Consciousness Discernment Rorschach Test' by the Higher Forces which will determine the person's ability to handle the intense planetary frequency changes that are forth-coming. (Note: The Rorschach test is a type of personality test which uses inkblot designs for individuals to describe what they see.) The new President must be able to meet the real and exciting challenges, such as planetary Divine Intervention (mass landings of Federation Lightships). Citizens must choose wisely in order to be as prepared as possible for what we are about to experience. Are you ready?"

CHAPTER 8

STEPS LEADING UP TO WORLD EVACUATION

First Contact

From the time that I was born into this present 3rd-dimensional Earth life, I have always known (on every level of my being) that it was the Destiny of this planet to ultimately experience overt mass Divine Intervention during my lifetime. This glorious event is now imminent and most likely will occur by the year 2012. I have also known the specific plan that the Higher Cosmic Forces of Light will use to carry out this dramatic event for the entire planet.

The details of this plan for Worldwide Evacuation have recently been referred to by many channels and contactees as "First Contact." Within this chapter, I will be sharing this in-depth information, which is based on numerous sources including: UFO sightings and contactee experiences, channeled information (both personal and from other books that have been published in the last two to three decades), and strong conscious memories that I have brought with me into embodiment from the Higher Galactic realms (where I served as a part of the commands of the Intergalactic Confederation).

This information about the upcoming plan was strongly reverified in this present life, not only through numerous channelings from these same Higher forces that I had personally known prior to this Earth life, but also in the presence of the benevolent human-appearing ETs whom I met when I was physically aboard the Merkabah Lightships. Both times that I was aboard the Lightship, I was reminded of the sacred promise of the definite plan for Divine Intervention. I was given another major confirmation of this information in 1981, when I was physically contacted by a human-appearing ET from the Galactic Council (of the Higher dimensions) who was specifically sent to Earth to reconfirm these facts to me. The point of this was so that I would in turn share this with other Volunteers with whom I would be meeting.

Many millions of Volunteers whom I have never met, and, perhaps, even those who are reading this book, have received telepathic communications, visionary experiences, and/or visitations from some Higher spiritual or extraterrestrial presence. Through these experiences, individuals have been informed of this imminent First Contact (Worldwide Evacuation), which is a conscious reminder of this promise that they were given prior to taking Earth embodiment. For some people, these final chapters will be very comforting and will help confirm their inner "knowing" which, until now, may have merely been based on faith. However, it is now "Officially & Cosmically" reconfirmed!

One of the books which helps verify this information is one of the most significant books ever to be published on this subject. <u>Project: World Evacuation by the Ashtar Command</u> was first compiled and published by Tuella in 1982. It was republished numerous times through her organization, Guardian Action International. In the early 1990's, Tuella made her own "Spiritual Ascension" back to the Higher realms from where her soul originated.

Tuella was a fellow Volunteer, a contactee, and a beautiful "old soul." She was very dedicated to her work as a "Cosmic Messenger" and was a very clear channel for the Federation of Light (specifically the Ashtar Command). A lot of the work that she did was to help prepare souls for the ultimate plan of the Spiritual Hierarchy. This plan allows for this dramatic event to occur when the planet has reached the "Cosmic saturation point" where it absolutely cannot sustain any more suffering and where the negative forces are just about to destroy the entire planet. At the present time, Mother Earth cannot sustain any more suffering. Due to very recent developments, including the positive energy consciousness shift and the mass planetary awakening, the Transition will not be as turbulent as was originally predicted.

I was privileged to get to know Tuella many years before she had passed from this realm of reality. In fact in 1982, during one of the visits that Aurora and I had with Tuella, we discussed that we would be eventually publishing one or more books. At that time, she gave us permission to quote specific passages from her books. So, it was no surprise when in 2000 I received a sudden, unexpected, and very strong telepathic communication from her from the Higher Dimensional Intergalactic Realms. She returned to remind me of her earlier verbal permission and gave me a "Cosmic OK" from her present existence to quote from her books. So, I feel honored to have been given this opportunity to reveal many wonderful revelations concerning this specific plan that she introduced in her significant and insightful writings.

I know that some of what she received in her own channeling experiences (with her own space contacts), in regard to the time-frame and intensity of certain geological Earth disasters and negative climate changes, has not occurred as she had originally predicted. The reason that this did **not** happen is because, as the Higher realms have communicated, there are a number of factors that have altered these particular predictions. Possible factors that have affected these predictions include: humans' free will, secret manipulations by the cabal, and recent developments of more advanced consciousness technology from the Higher forces that is being used to alter these conditions for the better.

An even more important fact is that the Higher Forces have recently reported (especially during 2007 and 2008) that there are very powerful Cosmic energies hitting the Earth. These Cosmic energies, coming from the Great Central Sun, have literally never existed in the Universe before and even the Elohim have never experienced them. These energies are drastically altering the outcome of what will be happening on Earth over the next few years. Some of the changes are for the better, as compared to what were originally foreseen a few years ago by the Elohim. This may include how soon changes will occur and even help in totally transmuting some of the original predictions.

So, some aspects of what Tuella reported have been postponed or transmuted, however about 90-95% of what she published about the Worldwide Evacuation is still going to occur, as was always predicted. It is mostly the timeframe that was delayed. In all due respect to Tuella, she, as are all Volunteers, was "only human" and had same "flaws" along with her mostly positive qualities. Unfortunately, her critics have tended to blow her "negative flaws" out of proportion and ignore the majority of what she accomplished for humanity, just as they have done with many of the other famous contactees of the '50's.

Overall, I consider Tuella to have been one of the clearest and most-attuned channels of her time and the Spiritual Hierarchy is extremely proud of her and the work she accomplished while she was here on her Mission. Her sincere desire to assist humanity through helping Volunteers awaken is evident in the "Dedication" in her book Evacuation: "This book is lovingly dedicated to all of the members of the 'Intergalactic Legion of Special Volunteers' now present upon this planet."

As quoted from Evacuation:

I was told that this book will **(as will this book!!)** trigger into action many yet outside of this awareness and that the Intergalactic Fleets would take up the work from that momentum in establishing these key souls on their pathway and personal mission. Further, that "all emissaries now in embodiment will be assisted immediately to fulfill the divine plan for their lives." Many who will read the book are "Ambassadors" from far-flung vistas of outer space, having volunteered to endure the limitations of fleshly existence that they might in some way aid the coming of Light upon this planet. It was explained to me that within the vast army of volunteers, there is an inner circle of souls on very special missions of

130

great responsibility to the others, like a circle within a circle. In Cosmic circles, these are referred to as the "Intergalactic Legion of Special Volunteers.

It seems that mankind must make a new adjustment of attitude toward these intermediaries between Earth and Heaven. The Commands plead for mankind to accept them, their existence, their presence, their dedication and loyalty to the Confederation and devotion to Earth, that the Kingdom of God shall come and that Earth shall become a beautiful sun and part of the united heavens. They are telling us now that, "our special representatives must be lifted, taught, and prepared to fulfill their part in the plan for rescuing the planet and its people."

Much of what Tuella expressed and channeled (from the benevolent human-appearing ETs) has been almost word for word like many of the channelings that I have received through the years from the same Higher Beings. This information is about the upcoming events and the many implications of its ultimate effect upon this planet and all its inhabitants. For this reason, I am quoting a number of segments and passages from the Evacuation book as I have been Divinely Directed (Spiritually Overshadowed) by Tuella to do so, as well as told by her in 1982.

In the "Preface" of Evacuation, Tuella writes:

Just as many are called and few are chosen, likewise, many who read this book will neither understand nor receive the information. But those special souls for whom it is intended will rejoice in its guidance and accept its timely and imperative revelation.

This information is not entertainment! It is comparable to "sealed orders" given to dedicated volunteers on a strategic mission. It is dispersed to them, compiled for them and will be cherished by them. It is neither defended nor justified. It is data recorded as given and passed on to those for whom it is intended.

If your inner truth identifies you as a volunteer from another realm or world on an assignment to Earth, these words are for you! If you are persuaded you are one of the "Star People," you will read this volume with awareness and clarity. If you are a disciple or initiate of the Higher Revelation, you will discern and perceive the purpose of this message from other dimensions of being. If you are a growing, glowing Christian (or of any of the other major religions upon this planet), just beginning to look up and outward beyond the walls of manmade divisions of earthly ecclesiastical hierarchies, your heart will witness to these things. If you are not consciously any of these, read not to scoff, but to hold these revelations in your heart while you "wait and see."

As Elisha prayed that other eyes might be opened to see - and eyes were opened, "to behold the mountains filled with horses and chariots of fire all around Elisha" - so do I fervently call that your vision, as well, be lifted up and expanded, as if by a miracle, to perceive that our planet is "compassed about with such a great cloud of witnesses". Mission completed, TUELLA.

Tuella Channeling Jesus

In the FOREWORD from Evacuation, Tuella shares a channeling from Jesus the Christ:

There must be peace on Earth. There must be an end to wars and hatred between brothers. The millions that come from other worlds, from far-off galaxies to assist in bringing Peace upon Earth, have my staunch support and backing for all of their endeavors. They have come IN MY NAME and they serve under My Banner, as Lord of this planet. They come neither as intruders nor usurpers of My Authority, but in loving subjection to the Spiritual Hierarchy of this Solar System, and the Divine Plan for mankind, the deliverance from bondage that has long held humanity in subjection to darkness and sorrow.

This shall be no more, for these come as My Angels, to reap that which has been sown, to divide and set asunder the tares from the wheat, to gather the wheat into My Barn. For I AM the householder who cometh at the end of the day for an account from His Servants, and to give to all men justly in the manner given by them to Me. So judgment must come; divisions and sorrows must come, but the Earth shall survive all of its totterings. The Just shall inherit the New Earth and the Meek shall know the joy therein.

I AM SANANDA, KNOWN TO YOU AS JESUS THE CHRIST. I speak in the Authority of My Name and My Office, and I say to you that in the multitudes of the people of the Earth there shall be found that remnant that can steadfastly be faithful to those right principles of My teaching. Those who come In My Name go from heart to heart, sealing them against that day and marking them for deliverance and safety from all that would destroy. But you shall NOT be taken out of your physical forms, but you shall be spared to live on in those days that follow. So, I shall call unto them who follow Me, to listen to the voices of these who come from other worlds, and harden not your hearts against their words or practices. Rather, lift up LOVE unto them and desire for their coming, for THEY ARE THE ANGELS OF THE HARVEST! I AM SANANDA AND THIS IS MY MESSAGE TO THE WORLD.

Tuella Channeling Ashtar

In another channeling by Tuella, she channels Commander Ashtar of the Ashtar Command:

I am Ashtar, the Commander of ten million men surrounding this hemisphere in the protective force within the Alliance for Peace in the Intergalactic Council. We have called upon this messenger to compile this book for this point in earth time that mankind might consider and understand the details of those things that could come to pass, for our Father doeth nothing except first He warneth His prophets. There is method and great organization in a detailed plan already near completion for the purpose of removing souls from this planet, in the event of catastrophic events making a rescue necessary.

This book is not intended to frighten anyone, but on the contrary, to hold out the hope and confidence of our presence with you for any time of trouble. The dangers to the planet are very real. The resulting tragedy to humanity would be unavoidable. However, our presence surrounding you thirty-five million strong will assist you, lift you up and rescue you, and hold you in safety.

Inner disturbances taking place within the planet itself are direct reflections of the aspirations and the attitudes and vibrations of those who dwell upon it. We have repeatedly attempted to turn the thoughts of humanity toward the reality of Divine Truth and Principles. We have dared to lower our craft into your frequencies in a visible way. We have dared to expose ourselves in vulnerable situations in order to convince souls of Earth of our presence.

Now we take further steps, because of the shortness of time and the dangers that beset you and the pressure of coming events. We come to you once again with our call and our warning, but this time WE DARE to expose our most secret strategy to sound the alarm that this indeed is the midnight hour. Now is the time to inventory the inner values. Therefore, we dare to expose within the pages of this book, our plans to come out into the open and send proof of our presence and existence back to Earth to silence forever arguments and denials of our Overshadowing protection.

This is the new strategy unveiled to you at this time in exposing our proposed gatherings of those who have come to walk among you as our representatives. They have to work in service to you, and we dare to reveal them and their identities, for no harm can come to them. We would simply remove them from your midst if you were to attempt to harm them in any way.

They are citizens of your planet, who have lived with you, suffered with you, walked with you and truly been one of you. Now we call them forth to admit their identity, to be gathered together to spend a brief time with us that they might return to you and share with you the facts and the proofs of our existence and the truth of our words.

The Ashtar Command now sends forth this book, that you, oh men of Earth, might be forewarned that these things shall take place. As these are gathered with us and returned once again into your midst, you will know that the events described in these councils are also true. You will know that global evacuation will take place. You will be helped and you will be rescued and by the proofs that are given our representatives who return to you, you will know that our promises are true.

We leave this book upon the planet for the few who will accept it. These words are not for the many, but for those to whom they are sent; more importantly, that later, those who remain behind will know why they have not been taken. Let all read and be quickened in the inner levels of being!

Tuella Channeling Kuthumi

Next, Kuthumi, one of the many famous Ascended Masters of Earth (who are also "Honorary Members" of the Ashtar Command) stated:

Those who have come to your world and taken upon themselves the garment of flesh to serve the planet in Our Name are approaching a time of crisis. These have chosen to be present upon Terra to serve in the great harvest of souls that now comes. To these, many instructions must be given, and many discussions sent to them to be assimilated within their guidance systems. Now is the hour when these special emissaries are to be temporarily removed from Terra for a brief moment of time, to receive specialized training instructions and personal directives that they may be clothed in preparedness for the times that are at hand!

Planetary changes have already taken place on inner levels within the auric field and the astral belt and surrounding regions. Soon, these emanations will penetrate the physical octave and those who dwell thereon. We have prepared the hearts and souls of incarnate humanity in our own manner, for the coming events. It is imperative that our special emissaries under Hierarchal authority to participate in planetary evacuation now receive our attention, by focusing our efforts toward their thorough preparation for the mission ahead.

Several million universal (conscious, core group) volunteers now walk the Earth! They are filled with Light, complete in their dedication and consecration to serve the Celestial Government, the Solar Hierarchy and the Intergalactic Confederation, in the salvation of a planet. The Highest Celestial Councils have decreed that these chosen ones shall be personally removed from Earth, to be temporarily placed in a higher frequency, within our domain, and there be prepared spiritually for the mission to be completed.

The planet Earth is tottering upon a crisis of many changes. The input of direct energies from many sources, now whirling in clockwise fashion around the globe, has been set into motion to offset a multitude of inner earth actions now racing toward chaos on the outer crust of the sphere. Because of these inner convulsions of energy within the orb of Terra that now press toward their destiny upon the crust; we must immediately organize our special training efforts for those assigned to these emergencies.

Therefore, I send forth this alert and summons to our Elect, to be ready for a sudden removal for a brief time to be spent in the presence of those who guard the planet. They will receive special instruction and directives to hide within their being. Many have been called, but few have been chosen, and to those a very special training now awaits. It is true that much teaching and preparation has taken place before entering the human manifestation. It is also true that these have proven their loyalty and love to the Father many times over. Every chosen disciple and initiate participating in this great rescue program must now consciously imbibe details, directions, and specifics through the human consciousness. The summons may come through personal guidance, through the word of another, through this book **(or this more recent book!!),** or through a lecture perhaps **(or through experiencing a personal empowering Transformational channeled reading!!!),** but be assured your call will be given and heard. Then you must organize the details of your lives to be ready for withdrawal from your personal situations for a period of approximately 14 to 21 days for purposes I have outlined.

The interim of "waiting" for your summons should (also) be a time of personal discipline, assimilating information, and bypassing worldly activities which rob one's spiritual strength and power. Saturate your inner being with the spiritual vibrations that interact with your own energy field. Meditate upon the needs of humanity and the power of the Light of God to meet those needs. Let this interim be a time of great expectations, of deep soul searching and counting the cost.

You remain free to withdraw your original commitment to this mission, under the concept of free will. Beloved sons and daughters of the Light, the choice is still your own. You will receive reward and gratitude for work accomplished thus far. If that mind be in you to carry on and continue the battle against darkness through your dedication to the Legions of Light, your blessings shall be unlimited. You shall be highly protected and specially anointed with gifts such as are necessary for your personal service to mankind.

I am Kuthumi, World Teacher, and my own emanations and vibrations surround every world volunteer at this hour. I cover you with my Golden Cloak, and I charge your being on inner levels to hold fast to your crown and to steadfastly remain faithful to your pledge. Realize that a great cloud of powerful Beings surrounds you and exalts your calling and giveth you grace equal to the task. Others who speak after me will introduce the details of our plan. I shed forth my love and blessings to all who have determined to serve as "ground forces" in this tremendous undertaking. My beloved brothers and sisters, initiates of the Golden Light, not one of you shall fail; not one of you shall be lost; not one of you will be touched by the Destroyer! None shall fail in your choice to complete the Mission, and not one of you shall be plucked from the Father's Hand! Beloved ones, you are the Light of the World in its darkest hour for this cycle of time. Stand in our places. Stand firm in your consecration until the hour is come. Blessings be upon you in the Name of Our Radiant One. So be it.

Tuella Channeling Andromeda Rex

Continuing on, Tuella next wrote:

Further insight into the new strategy of the Space Confederation came in a message from Andromeda Rex, one who will become a very familiar Ambassador of Light on television and radio (and over the Internet, of course!), broadcasting warnings to the people. He states: "The gathering of our ground Commanders for these 'secret' council meetings will begin a new way of doing things by the Confederation. Hitherto, we have had to be coy and careful and subdued on our activities. But now we are prepared to be more outward in manifestation and bolder in our efforts to win the hearts of mankind to our cause and purpose, which is really their own. This is why those who are taken up to these seven gatherings will be permitted to bring back with them so much evidential material. We will allow our participants to be interviewed and quizzed by the curious, because only in this way can we be heard and vindicated. This is a brave thing we ask of all of you. We are aware of the temptations involved to vaunt the self for such widespread attention. Yet we have chosen you well, and we believe none shall be spoiled by any of these developments but shall hold steady in the consecration previously made. All of you have been thoroughly scrutinized and monitored, down to the minutest detail of your inner being and personality traits. This was done before our final choices were made, to carry on and complete this program which began one hundred years ago.

Soon, now, with much joy in our hearts, we will once again send back down into Earth those whom we have, by their own election, chosen to prepare the planet for its initiation into a new field of expression with the rest of the solar system. In the anointing that is to be given at the inaugural ceremony (also known as 'The Earth Alumni Party"), signs and wonders will be bestowed for convincing the world, each receiving in accordance with the mission, whatever is needed to complete it. We have designated certain areas of the ships where your cameras will operate successfully. Your tape recorders will also operate normally with batteries only. Primarily there will be many items of interest which can be brought back with you as evidences. THESE COUNCILS, OR GATHERINGS, AS YOU HAVE BEGUN TO CALL THEM, ARE PRIMARILY FOR THIS PURPOSE OF SENDING BACK TO EARTH THE CONCRETE EVIDENCE WHICH EARTH AS SO LONG CLAMOURED FOR. You will also have photographs to return with you which will show the views of the Earth taken

from our ships, taken upon our highly evolved technical equip-
ment--photos which cannot be denied.

All of those who are summoned to these briefings will in some
manner all be linked together to assist each other in the overall project of evidential presentation. Thus, there will be those from the
media, from commerce, from messenger work, and from church
groups. Each will be a coordinated group, who will be made
known to each other for coordinating your efforts toward convincing unbelievers of our existence and our good intentions. This
program is designed for the purpose of convincing mankind, as
well as the training of those who attend. Thus with the books that
will be written and the efforts of higher echelons to protect those
books and those writers, this will be an all-out onslaught against
ignorance and bigotry as it pertains to us, our presence, and our
mission.

The ranks of the officers will be revealed, specific missions will be
assigned as this last phase of the transition period will be underway
and soon to be completed. This 'legion of special volunteers' will
be the most active on inner levels to initiate the preparedness for
our coming into Earth's atmosphere. Commander Ashtar and many
others will address the groups and explain the mission of each one
present so that all can hear and know the direction that each individual will take. This program is a crucial step in our gearing
down. All details for each personal life and its related problems or
complications will be clearly discussed and dealt with in private
council. Some of our guests will need much calming, for many
will be lifted up rather suddenly from the midst of their affairs,
creating some internal anxiety. It will be the work of all of you
and us to calm such as these.

We are naturally tremendously thrilled over this coming fellowship, as well as our new policy and program. Our last effort of
fifty years and later did not succeed as we had hoped. It was to
have culminated with our full and open appearance in your skies.
This should have occurred in the sixties had our program proceeded as planned, but the hindrances and hostility of the governments of Earth totally thwarted our original plans."

This is putting it "mildly." In fact, in the next book of The Divine Blueprint Series, <u>The Cover-Up on Human-Appearing ETs</u>, I will address the reasons for what Andromeda Rex is referring to here. This includes not only how the early emissaries (the famous contactees of the '50's, such as George Adamski and the others) were horribly treated by the "agents of disinformation" of the UFO community, but also the numerous instances where the contactee's lives were destroyed (by character assassination) or in jeopardy (by physical or psychic assassination) from the cabal. These courageous men and women were only attempting to share the real life experiences that they have had with the highly evolved beings from the Confederation.

Other information that I will be sharing in the following book includes information about President Kennedy and the little-known fact that he was going to announce (to the public) the truth in regard to these benevolent ETs. About two weeks before he was assassinated, he had already mentioned that he was going to do this when he made a presentation at Columbia University. Just recently, some very interesting information surfaced which documented the fact that at the time when President Kennedy was assassinated and Connolly was wounded; Connolly was actually carrying the speech (in his coat pocket) that Kennedy planned to give after leaving Dallas. When Kennedy got into the car, he had handed the handwritten speech to Connolly. As Connolly was being rushed to the hospital, he handed it to his personal aid with instructions to put the paper in a safety deposit box and not to release it until after he died. So, just recently (over 45 years later), this aid released this document to the world which confirms that President Kennedy actually was planning to officially announce not only the existence of the ETs, but also his plan was to officially prepare humanity for their mass appearance over this planet.

More Information from Andromeda Rex

We do not desire to force our presence upon you, and thereby feed the negative nature of those who would oppose us. This would gain us nothing toward Interplanetary Fellowship. We CANNOT, we WILL NOT make our appearance (in normal times) unless it is accepted by the military and higher branches of your governments.

Things have changed considerably in the last couple of decades since this book by Tuella was published in 1982, especially considering how corrupt most governments have become. The aspect of caring what the government and military thinks really does not matter, since it will be the citizens (the masses) who are the ones that will benefit from this ultimate mass appearance and open-mass landings. And, this will cause an end to the cabal that controls all levels of the government anyway.

> Therefore, this new policy of inner penetration into human hearts will hopefully achieve that necessary change in the policies of mankind which will build us a platform of goodwill upon which we may make our approach to uplift your way of life.
>
> It must be done peacefully and lovingly, while it CAN be done in that manner. If circumstances develop danger to the Elect and danger to the solar system before these negotiations are completed, then we will be forced circumstantially to intrude ourselves into Earth's forcefield for evacuation and intervention in the name of the Intergalactic Council governing the Universal Peace agreement.
>
> I am Andromeda Rex, and I speak this message on behalf of the entire Space Confederation and the Council of Universal Masters who serve the Divine Government.

Lyara Channeling Lytton

From another section of Tuella's book: "As we think together of a vast army of volunteers to Earth for this crucial time, our understanding is penetrated by these words of Cosmic Being, LYTTON, which came to spiritual messenger 'Lyara'."

> Each of you who are attuned to this material has a mission of service to mankind. Each of you, as sparks of God, is a divine and unique ray of the Father. Cosmic family members have already achieved mastery and forms of advancement in other dimensions, realms and/or realities and are reawakening this dormant knowledge. You each agreed, in coming here, to be veiled, that you could adjust and understand the people of this planet to better serve them....All of you have awakened, or will, to the realization that the home you are most clearly attuned to is not resemblant of Earth. Planets where you have spent the most time and call home

are Higher vibrating and have all-pervading auras of Christ Love. All of you belong to the Intergalactic Fleet. At Debriefing Time before embarking on this **(FINAL!!!!)** mission (right before coming into Earth physical embodiment, either moments before biological birth, or years later as a "Walk-in"), you realized only to some degree the hazards that you would experience on this planet. The most serious was not preparing yourself to wake up, by getting involved and caught up with Earth's activities and pleasures and forgetting your identity. Many brothers and sisters have not yet awakened sufficiently to fulfill their missions in the remaining time allotted. It has made for many adjustments in plans, and many others of you will be asked to assume greater responsibilities than originally contracted for. We realize it will cause some hardships and extra burdens, but by staying attuned to your guidance, these new assignments which are being asked of you in the Father's name can still be expressions of joy. Allow your spirits to soar while your feet are on the ground for planetary functioning.

Three Waves of the Evacuation

Tuella next relayed that the "Cosmic Veils" (Cosmic Amnesia) will totally be lifted during the initial Secret Wave of the Evacuation. This wave is also referred to as the "Gathering of the Eagles" or "First Contact." Following this smaller wave will be three major waves of Evacuation (Great Exoduses). This is what has always been planned by the Federation of Light and the Universal Christ Forces. I will be describing more about this later on in conjunction with the in-depth confirmations that I and other channels and contactees have received.

Tuella's ET Encounters

As quoted from Evacuation:

As we present the messages coming to several others within this revelation on the various topics covered, it is hoped that the children of Light will realize this is not something coming to just one source, but that the same trend of information is coming to us now through many different space channels, like the rush of a mighty river. I have spoken with too many to quote all of them here, but

142

as I present the same questions for reasons of confirmation, the answers all correlate in a remarkable way.

Tuella, as with myself and other channels and contactees, had numerous physical encounters with the benevolent human-appearing ETs, as well as contacts that occurred first in the physical, and, then, a short time later in the etheric or astral (O.B.E.), that confirmed the many things that are soon to occur with the Evacuation

For example, as Tuella shared in her book:

Many years ago at my home deep in the woods of southern Pennsylvania, my two daughters and I had been in a meditative moment together, when three Space Brothers (physically) appeared in the front yard. They preferred to remain outside when invited in, because of their height and my normal sized doors and ceilings. We were asked if we would enjoy visiting their ship (in the etheric state), and we responded with a joyous affirmative. The appointment was made for the following evening at 8:00 and we were instructed to relax in a reclining position on the floor for meditation and an escort would come for us.

The following evening we relaxed as instructed, and set out upon our three separate meditation experiences. I (etherically) left my (physical) body and rested my hands upon the forearms of my two escorts, and experienced the tremendous motion as we ascended at incredible speed upward to the waiting ship. I was immediately standing in the great ship and control room looking at Athena, with tears streaming down my face. She also wept, and we embraced. Athena (a Lady Commander) began showing me the various maps.

She goes on to share what she experienced aboard the Merkabah Lightship while in the etheric state, which (in many ways) was just as real as being there in the physical state. She also expressed that many hours passed in that Higher-dimensional state, while here on the physical level only a few minutes transpired.

At the end of her book, Tuella shares her uplifting, inspiring, and exhilarating experience of first observing a huge Merkabah Lightship as it appeared to her in the physical. She described how this was only one of several physical confirmations and manifestations from the Space Brothers that confirmed all that she had telepathically received from them about the upcoming Worldwide Evacuation:

The compilation (of Evacuation) was nearing completion. Necessary housework haunted me. Friends were thinking I had withdrawn from the human race! Dinner invitations went begging. My public life had almost ceased. During these busy days, while attempting to meet a publishing deadline given by my Space Friends, I had been arising about an hour before sunrise, when first light appeared in the eastern sky.

One morning as I turned to silence the alarm, my gaze fell on the eastern bedroom window. There, beyond the left corner, I beheld the largest, most brilliant ship I had ever seen. A long groan escaped as I thrilled with peace and love, watching it beautify the clear and otherwise empty sky. Stars were no longer visible. Much light had already spread across the horizon. The edge of the magnificent craft sparkled as if rimmed in diamonds strategically spaced at certain points. The distance was great; nevertheless, I realized its tremendous size, and thought surely this must be one of those etheric cities they speak of.

My window is five feet wide, but two feet are obscured by drapes. In the remaining viewing area, I watched this stately craft majestically move very slowly in a diagonal path toward the upper right hand corner area of my observation point. With great joy and amazement, I carefully observed as its slow-moving brilliance silently disappeared behind a nearby telephone pole and then gradually slipped out beyond the other side. Again, I traced its sparkling points as they hid, one by one, behind the leafy limbs of a small tree, to reappear within my vision beyond each limb. While my eyes were fixed upon the awesome wonder of it all, on the ceiling just above the window a sparkling flash of light exploded, (an "energy beam" from the ship was sent to bounce against her ceiling to help confirm the definite physical nature of this sighting) and in a second, was gone again. I wanted to phone a nearby friend, but I was rooted to the spot.

Its deliberate, easy pace across the sky seemed to be saying, "Hey! Look us over!" In fact, it moved so slowly that had I not been taking position marks by the panes of the window and the nearby telephone pole in its relationship to the little tree, I might have missed its movement. At first observance, I ran to the east end of the house for a better look, but found the ship to be totally obscured by the mulberry trees. I flew back to my observation window, and it was then I discovered it had moved from my former position marks. I decided to watch it intently, in position with the pole, and discovered the slow, steady, easterly upward movement. To a casual passerby just glancing at the sky, movement would have been unnoticeable.

As the great ship gradually climbed higher and traveled into the east away from me, it became smaller and smaller in appearance until it remained only about one-fifth its first appearance in diameter. I had been too enraptured by the scene to attempt communication, but as I relaxed in the moments following, I was (telepathically) told they would appear each morning at six. I began to wonder if the incident was related to their book. It had first appeared low and large at about 5:45 a.m. and had taken forty minutes to negotiate diagonally the observation area up and across my window. I was determined to be ready the next morning....

For hours afterwards I could not discipline my mind to remain long on anything else. My eyes filled with tears again and again. It was as if they were saying, "We want YOU to see and know that we are real, that we ARE here...and then...TELL THEM....

At 11:30 a.m. the overhead electric light in my dark study blinked three times, quickly, but the other lights did not. I entered the alert (to begin to receive her telepathic transmission).

Tuella Channeling Anton

Tuella, this is Anton, of the Silver Fleet at Cook mountain headquarters. I am interrupting your day to bring you this information. The ship that you saw this morning is the one on which this sector Gathering (Evacuation) will take place and the one into which evacuees will be brought. It was much farther away than you think. It was far beyond the end of our mountains. It is the same ship which positioned above you two years ago and it is a city-size ship, being almost one-hundred miles in diameter. Your mind cannot grasp the significance of these dimensions (mentally, I quickly agreed). The ship has come to remain in this general area throughout October. It has Andromeda Rex and Ashtar both aboard, and it will appear THREE TIMES AS A SIGN. Watch for it each morning faithfully, and they will respond to your love and appear.

Though you have received a beam from it earlier, the beam was strengthened this morning as you gazed upon it. I have felt the necessity to intrude to give you these answers, understanding how curious you are concerning the appearance. The ship did NOT come up out of our installation here. It is MUCH too large to be based here. This ship does not land, but remains in a cruise pattern. Its appearance IS related to our book. As it departed, it did not leave your sector, but positioned itself in the higher atmosphere. You were permitted to see it for reasons that will be shared by them soon.

Messages from Andromeda Rex through Tuella

Tuella: That evening at my regular 9:00 p.m. appointment with them, Andromeda Rex was the first to speak:

Greetings in the Light of Our Beloved, I am speaking to you directly from the Command Ship you saw this morning. We have permitted you this experience for specific reasons. We will appear to you two more times when the skies are clear, to seal the vision and complete the testimony for others. Then the sightings will end. (That is, for these consecutive sightings to confirm Tuella's book.) This is the purpose and confirmation, as well as for your infilling of faith and confidence. You cannot convince them if the trumpet gives an uncertain sound. You must see and be convinced beyond any shadow of a doubt that the words we speak are true and your experience is real. This experience will soften and humanize the impact of the messages we have sent like a final exclamation point. We request that you write this account to be shared at the close of the book, to linger in the memory of the readers.

Be posted at dawn for the next several days until the three sightings are fulfilled. Then they will be concluded. I am Andromeda, and it is I who will speak at the dawn vigil with a brief message to the people. I am the Commander responsible for this western sector, sharing my mission with Monka, who will oversee the central sector, and Alphon, who heads up the leadership for the eastern sector. Communication was withheld this morning to allow the emotional impact upon your being to have its full sway for the moment. Whenever the eyes are closed, you may recapture, visualize and completely relive that intense moment when you followed our path across the eastern sky.

Tuella's Experience Continues

Tuella: The following morning I was stationed in my car by 5:00 a.m. I parked at the eastern edge of the farm, away from all structures, for good observation. A dense cloud cover lingered listlessly across the east, without the slightest breeze to encourage its departure. Any sighting was impossible under these conditions. They had specified "clear morning."

On Sunday morning which followed, I turned off the alarm at 5:00, but from extreme overtiredness, it took twenty minutes to maneuver myself into a sitting-up posture. I regretted the delay immediately. The Star Ship was already at "half-window" position. It was early! Perhaps because of the dense black cloud rift that covered the upper half of the eastern heaven.

I bounded out the screen door and leaned motionless against the car. I chose a distant telephone pole as a marker to track its movement. The illuminated edge points of its outline were still discernible. Very slowly, it resolutely closed the gap left of the pole, as I remained unmoving in my observation. In its ascension it was taking on the appearance of a star. In fixed pace, it finally disappeared behind the pole. As I watched for its gleam to slide into view on the right side of the pole, the lower edge of the black cloud density touched that point on the pole, and I didn't see it again. Nevertheless, I experienced great joy because they had kept the promise to appear twice again. One more to go!

The next dawn I awakened long before the alarm was to sound. By then I was settled into my vigil amid the clutter of recorder, camera, binoculars and notebook. The sky was clear. The stars overhead gleamed like diamonds in a jewel case. It was still too dark to select position markers. I waited. I knew, with an inner knowing, this would be the final morning of my vigil. I knew they would come, and I knew there would be a final word. Not for me...but for those who would read their book.

For a considerable time I slumped in the car seat, leaning against the door...just waiting. Low on the very horizon line I noticed a very bright light. I assumed it was a street light in yonder Deming (Tuella was living then near Deming, New Mexico). Then, on second thought, I decided to get out of the car to be certain. Focusing the light in my inadequate binoculars, I realized with a start, it was not a street light, for it was already arisen above the horizon line. Its size and its glow compared to the city limits at my lower right. They had come! They had kept their word! This was the third appearance, in the trinity of completion, the law of the triangle. I immediately greeted them in my mind, hoping, they might courteously blink the lights or something spectacular, but nothing happened. I focused the beautiful ship between two tall stalks of a yucca plant, and waited. They held to the location for about ten minutes, and then slowly began to slip away to the right of my vision barricade. The time was 5:58.

I wondered why the yucca plant stood so motionless, and the fence posts remained so indifferent. Couldn't they hear the pounding of my heart? Why didn't the rocks cry out? Why didn't the Earth tremble as I did? The promised sunrise was spreading a strip of deep peach tones across the horizon. A low elongated cloud was absorbing hues of yellow, as the dawn silently invaded the slumbering desert scene. The great ship had now ascended the length of a "telephone pole" above the pole. I traced its pathway between the yucca stalks, across three fence posts, toward a distant telephone pole. In this awe-inspiring moment I had followed its climb through the telephone wires to the cross bars of the pole. I waited in peaceful confidence, knowing it would appear beyond each crossbar at the top of the pole, to adorn the uppermost tip like a jewel atop a royal scepter.

Andromeda Rex Speaks To Tuella

I was warmed within my being, when according to his promise, Andromeda presented (telepathically) his credentials and spoke, while I was locked into a great love vibration:

WE HAVE COME TO YOU IN THE FATHER'S NAME AND IN HIS LOVE. THIS SIGN IN THE HEAVENS WHICH WE HAVE GIVEN OUR MESSENGER IS A SIGN TO MANKIND THAT OUR WORDS ARE TRUE. THIS VISITATION COMES, THAT OUR WORDS WILL HAVE IMPACT, FOR THIS IS THE WITNESS TO ALL THAT WE ARE PRESENT WITH YOU. THIS IS THE VITAL MEANING OF OUR MORNING RUNS ACROSS THE EASTERN SKY. IT IS THE FINAL MESSAGE AND THE LAST ACT **(For Tuella, but not for myself and other channels and contactees who continue to get many more confirmations of what is about to happen at long last!!!!)** BEFORE THE CURTAIN IS DRAWN UPON THIS, ANOTHER EFFORT OF THE SPACE ALLIANCE TO CONVINCE MANKIND.

WE ARE YOUR BROTHERS AND SISTERS FROM OTHER WORLDS AND MEMBERS OF THE ASHTAR COMMAND. PEACE AND BLESSINGS BE YOURS, AND THE LOVE OF THE HIGHEST LORD GOD OF HOSTS BE UPON ALL OF YOU.

The Spaceship Disappears

Tuella: Then slowly, it escaped! Totally free from markers of any kind or any earthly thing, it escaped high into the clear blue of the morning sky. Its movement still appeared to be incredibly slow, and while its appearance diminished in size as it pulled away to the east, its brilliance in my little binoculars continued to thrill the very soul of me. In my thought world, I projected to that time when we of this world would be on and in that Great City, that Great Shining City that pulled away from me after its third visitation. A sense of peace settled around me and within me, beyond anything I have ever experienced.

The sun had not yet arisen, but the great light beginning to fill the sky heralds its coming. I wondered if others had watched this brilliant "star" that continued to shine so long after all others had yielded to the advancing dawn. It had now become very small in the distance, and I felt that a part of me had gone with it. Finally, my little opera glasses could scarcely retain the pinpoint of light and the tears didn't help, but I watched until it dissolved into the etheric.

Goodbye, dear friends, thank you for coming. I promise... to TELL THEM!

Then, into the cathedral dome of heaven, above the glowing footlights of nature, came the bursting beauty of a grand finale, as the golden sun arose before me! I watched in mute inspiration this exquisite symbology:

OF A NEW DAWN FOR MANKIND; A NEW EXPERIENCE FOR THE BEAUTIFUL EARTH; A NEW DAY FOR MANKIND!

Information from Lt. Colonel Wendelle C. Stevens

I shall return to Tuella's book later on, but now I want to refer to another very important book by a well-known UFO researcher Retired Lt. Colonel Wendelle C. Stevens: UFO: Contact From Angels In Starships. This wonderful and inspiring book also strongly confirms the imminent Divine Intervention and Worldwide Evacuation. The book is about the spiritual experiences of an Italian contactee, Giorgio Dibitonto, which took place almost 30 years ago. One of the remarkable things about Mr. Dibitonto's real life encounters was the fact that he met (and got to know) the same benevolent angelic human-appearing ETs that the famous '50's contactee George Adamski met. These beings confirmed their earlier encounters with George Adamski (Adamski described these encounters in-depth in his two famous books, <u>Flying Saucers Have Landed</u> [Co-author Desmond Leslie]and <u>Inside The Spaceships</u>, as well as Mr. Dibitonto's brief meeting with George Adamski in his Higher dimensional body.). Lt. Colonel Stevens states the following in his book:

> My interest and my convictions about the validity of George Adamski's UFO contacts had been growing steadily since late 1979 when Swiss journalist Lou Zinsstag had given me her original manuscript on Adamski who stayed with her on his trips to Europe. She was personally acquainted with George almost from the time he came to the attention of the press in 1953, and they corresponded and met when possible since that time. Modified parts of that manuscript were used in <u>GEORGE ADAMSKI, The Untold Story</u> by Lou Zinsstag and Timothy Good. The gold Papal medal given Adamski by Pope John XXIII is kept today in the safe in Lou's brother's jewelry store in Basel, Switzerland.

It was very interesting, though not surprising, when in May 2008, the Vatican astronomer publicly stated "believing in aliens is OK and does not contradict one's faith in God." He even used the phrase, "They are our Brothers." This is interesting because I have a very unique perspective regarding this whole reality. I am very aware of numerous events connected with UFOs and ETs and I have reason to believe that the Vatican and the Catholic Church have always known of this reality.

I have spoken to two people that have very seriously stated to me that they were allowed to go through the Vatican Libraries and Records. Normally, no outsiders are allowed to visit the libraries. Both of them basically told me the same thing: "The Vatican Records contain the biggest UFO and metaphysical library in the entire world." The collection consists of numerous historical records from very ancient to more modern day events, which have been kept from the masses. For example, when Mother Mary appeared to the three small children at Fatima evidence suggests that part of the phenomena that was seen in the sky that day involved very spiritually-evolved human-appearing "angelic" ETs and their Lightships (in other words, UFOs). In fact, for many years the Vatican has sent their own investigators out around the world to personally scrutinize these types of events, and they have stored their findings in the Vatican Libraries, along with all the other things they have discovered.

Also, a couple of specific incidents occurred in which the Catholic Church had direct personal involvement relating to UFOs and extraterrestrial contact. I have investigated these incidents and I am truly convinced that they did occur and both of the individuals, that I referred to earlier, were also given confirmation of this when they explored the Vatican Library.

One of these events occurred on February 20-21, 1954. (This event is thoroughly documented at this website: www.exopolitics.org/Study-paper-8.htm.). This historical event, which was covered up for "National Security" reasons, happened when President Eisenhower, members of his staff, and a delegation of community leaders representing religious, spiritual, economic, and newspaper reporters, actually met with extraterrestrials at Edward's Air Force Base (previously known as Muroc Field). The official explanation for President Eisenhower's sudden absence was that he had an "emergency visit to the dentist because he had broken a tooth cap." However, the facts have been verified from more than one source by those who were actually there and others who knew some of those who were there. So, I believe that this event did, in fact, take place.

One of the individuals that represented the religious part of the delegation that day was a well-known Cardinal of the Roman Catholic Church. The following is a quote from a research paper that was listed on this website: "Cardinal James Francis MacIntyre was the Bishop and head of the Catholic Church in Los Angeles at the time (1948-1970), for it was theorized that he would have been an important gauge for the possible reaction from religious leaders generally, and in particular from the most influential and powerful religious institutions on the planet - the Roman Catholic Church. In particular, Cardinal MacIntyre would have been a good choice as a representative for the Vatican since he was appointed the first Cardinal of the Western United States by Pope Pius XII in 1952."

The second incident involved a visit to the Vatican by George Adamski whom I believe, both through my own research, as well as having been given strong confirmation in communication from my own space contacts, was another authentic "contactee" who had many contacts with the ETs, just as I have. These benevolent and spiritually-evolved human-appearing ETs were the same type of ETs who landed at Edward's Air Force Base. George Adamski actually met with Pope John XXIII at the Vatican on May 31, 1963, a few days before the Pope's death. Adamski gave the Pope a "sealed package" from his space contacts, that he had been instructed to "specifically give to the Pope."

Two books that describe and document this historical event are George Adamski, The Untold Story by Lou Zinsstag and Timothy Good, and UFO... George Adamski, Their Man On Earth, also by Lou Zinsstag. In the first book, there is a photograph of the specific medallion which was given to Adamski by Pope John XXIII. This medallion, by the way, is a very special medallion that is very rare and has only been given to a few people throughout the years. It is known as the Ecumenical Council medallion. Zinsstag, who also happened to be the niece of the famous Swiss psychiatrist Carl Jung, helped sponsor Adamski for over 10 years. She was in Rome, along with another witness, and watched as Adamski went through a special entrance into the Vatican for the private audience with the Pope and then watched him return after his meeting with the Pope.

In final analysis, it is my opinion that one of the reasons the Vatican's chief astronomer is coming out openly now to make the statement that "believing in aliens is OK and does not contradict one's faith in God," and the fact that the governments on Earth (as even mentioned on Fox and CNN) have recently been releasing vast amounts of formerly-classified documents about UFOs and extraterrestrial contacts, is that they now believe that this planet will soon be experiencing much more open UFO sightings and what some have traditionally termed "Divine Intervention."

My convictions were reinforced after reading Bruce Cathie's report on Mr. Adamski following his personal investigations in March of 1979, the only recognized UFO researcher ever to go to that trouble. He published a report on his findings in the last pages of his book THE BRIDGE TO INFINITY.

An unusual twist to the Adamski story came out of a UFO landing in England on 24 April 1965, near Scoriton, in Devonshire, where three space-beings in "light-body" got out of a bell-shaped ship and made contact with Mr. Arthur Bryant, a gardener there, and one of the ETs indicated association with the former George Adamski, who left his physical body the day before in death in the United States of America. That report and its investigation fill an entire book titled THE SCORITON MYSTERY by Eileen Buckle.

We picked up other confirmations of the Adamski story in our loop through Europe during the next two weeks, including his private audience with the King and Queen of the Netherlands in 1959 and his private meeting with Pope John XXIII in the Vatican a few years later. We spoke to witnesses to both events and find them to be highly credible.

Giorgio Dibitonto's First ET Experience

As quoted from Giorgio Dibitonto's, this is the contactee's own personal account of his first physical meeting and interaction with these Higher dimensional benevolent human-appearing ETs:

I turned around and saw three men coming toward us. I was afraid that Tina would become panic-stricken, but on the contrary, she got out of the car and went toward them as if she was greeting old friends. I followed after and found myself directly facing Raphael, who was wearing a loose-fitting, silver colored space suit.

He greeted us joyfully, as did also the other two, who were dressed more or less the same way as Raphael, except that their space suits were tighter fitting and darker in color. They were of normal size, and their beautiful features expressed great beneficence and an inner depth of spirit.

They introduced themselves, and said that their names were pseudonyms that were given to them by an Earth brother, George Adamski, who had met them some years ago. "I am Orthon," said the larger of the two. "My name is Firkon," said the other.

Raphael took me gently by the arm and led me to a small overlook. There he sat down on the grass, and I sat down beside him. The other two space brothers remained a short distance away from us and talked with Tina. I could see their hair moving in the wind, and also Tina's long hair, and her clothing. Great clouds scudded across the darkening skies. Raphael and the others seemed to pay them little heed.

"I, too, was given a pseudonym," said Raphael. "I was named Ramu, but it is well that it should now be known who I really am. What Earth brothers must know is the role that the Heavenly Father has entrusted to us from the dawn of time, in order that their salvation on this planet might be brought about."

A little later on, after Giorgio and Tina are allowed to physically meet many of the other Space Brothers who were on board one of the light ships, it was then that he finally, though very briefly, had a chance to meet George Adamski, himself (in his Higher density E.T. body) along with a few other beings who were introduced to them by Raphael, who had also been some of the same, exact beings that Adamski had first met and interacted with, as described in his book, Inside The Spaceships:

> We greeted Raphael, and with him, Orthon and Firkon, whom we had already met. Orthon was distinguished by his erect bearing and noble demeanor. Firkon again displayed that heartiness of manner which had so impressed us before. We shook hands all around. Their looks bespoke sincerity and good will; their gestures, an unpretentiousness that was calming and reassuring.
>
> Then another brother was introduced to us. He was dark-haired. He impressed us as one whose talents were along practical lines. He was no less handsome in appearance than the others, and his behavior was marked by that same harmonious calmness. "This is our brother, Zuhl," said Raphael, by way of introduction. "He is greatly valued for his knowledge and ability."
>
> Then another man was introduced to us, who impressed us immediately with his kindliness and amiability. He smiled like one who had much to say, but would not speak. "His name is George," said Raphael, nodding in my direction, "the same as yours. This, our brother, lived for a while on Earth, where he chose to come on an assignment. Now he has returned to us." We greeted one another with a warm handclasp.
>
> Then four young women came up to us. We were struck by their gracious charm. The smallest one had blue eyes and light blond hair. "I am Kalna," she said, "and I am happy to be here with you." "I am Ilmuth," said the second, as she warmly extended her hand. "This meeting brings me great joy." She was taller than Kalna, and her hair, as black as ebony, fell freely over her shoulders. Her dark eyes looked at us penetratingly. She was beautiful, but along with that, modest and unpretentious, as one could tell by her manner, and by her words, as she spoke to us.
>
> Then two more young women were introduced to us, and they were dark complexioned. We were not told their names. They, too, were a clear example of other-worldly beauty, and of amiabil-

ity, grace and goodness. The men and women were all wearing space suits with rather full sleeves and trousers. From all, there seemed to radiate a soft glow.

Later Encounters by Giorgio and Tina Dibitonto

This account of Giorgio Dibitonto meeting George Adamski (in his Higher dimensional body) among the Space Brothers, and The Scoriton Mystery (mentioned by Wendelle C. Stevens) which relates Adamski's ET experiences on Earth, indirectly, confirm another account that was described in a newsletter (published by Saucerian Publications, Clarksburg, West Virginia). This particular issue of Spacecraft News (#1, November, 1965) which was printed a few months after Adamski's death was titled "In And Out of Saucers." It stated: "We mourn the passing of George Adamski, who died this summer. Surely he made an impact upon the study of flying saucers greater than any other individual."

THE INTERPLANETARY NEWS edited by Jim Wales, stated in a recent issue that "during a memorial service held for George Adamski, some in the audience witnessed his apparition appear briefly, dressed in a white robe."

During Giorgio's and Tina's series of physical ET encounters, several of their friends also witnessed the ships at a distance, while waiting for them. Some of these friends also reported receiving strong telepathic confirmation (of their own) about what Giorgio and Tina experienced while with the Space Brothers. More of their experience follows:

Tina waved goodbye, and the brothers turned and again signaled a friendly farewell. Then we saw the disc rise up over the green countryside in a tremendous burst of velocity. It ascended to the clouds in an instant, and disappeared in their midst.

When we arrived at the place in the valley below, where our friends were waiting for us, they told us they had seen the flying discs, and they repeated to us certain parts of our conversation that we had had with the brothers, which they received telepathically.

Another example verified, once again, the telepathic communication that their friends were receiving:

With warm embraces, we bade a fond farewell. The three boarded the waiting disc, which disappeared inside the starship a moment later. From the huge craft a humming sound could be heard, and the light around it grew stronger, changing from pearl-white to orange-gold. Then it quickly lifted starward, streaked like a flash of lightning, and disappeared from sight.

Our friends had remained near the spot where we had left them. Robert had recorded the images that came into his mind telepathically, and had sketched exactly the starship and the four disks. Nico had seen, from a nearby knoll, a light moving erratically in the sky. Its zigzag course left no doubt of its identity. Anna and Paul had followed parts of the conversation by means of Cosmic contact, mentally. Each one had received a sign that confirmed the reality of the direct contact with the space brothers that Tina and I had experienced.

Ray Stanford's Account

This incident was very similar to an account that Ray Stanford ('50's flying saucer researcher) shared in an old issue of <u>FATE</u> magazine. While attempting telepathic contact with a saucer in Texas, Ray and his fellow researchers were able to telepathically tell what movements that it was going to do. They knew this before it actually appeared to them and they also knew what movements it would make after they actually saw it.

Suddenly, we saw a white light coming across from the sea, from the direction of San Fruttose. In his excitement, Paolo shouted out loudly and I had to urge him to regain control of himself.

The light came nearer, until it was about fifty meters from the shore which our walkway bordered. Now the flying disc was there, where it could be easily seen by all, and Paolo and Gianna called out excitedly, "It is really them! It is the brothers!"

Paolo had a clear Cosmic (telepathic) contact, and he could tell us exactly what was about to happen throughout the various phases of the encounter. "Now they are switching on the white light on the underside," he said. And the light really did go on. "Now they are making the light brighter!" And the light would grow brighter.

"Now they are about to dim the lights!" And the lights would grow dimmer.

And so it continued. Paolo announced in a loud voice when the red, green and blue lights would go on, and they promptly did so. The flying disc changed many different (rainbow) colors, and then flew off in a southwest direction and disappeared over the horizon.

More Information from Giorgio and Tina

Several times, the Beings that were in contact with Giorgio and Tina, made very strong statements about how the "scientific, researcher types" (spin doctors) within the UFO community constantly demand "concrete proof" of the existence of ETs in order to "believe" in their reality, but, at the same time, they will never be satisfied regardless of the proof, partly because of their level of consciousness. However, it is not just because of their lower consciousness level, it is also, primarily, because these "agents of disinformation" have a hidden agenda.

Most of these individuals are well-known names within the UFO community, who refer to themselves as "professional UFO investigators". Even though for the last two to three decades, they have basically had this covert agenda, I was specifically informed by my own space contacts about their true intent. They chose to ignore and suppress the true evidence about UFOs and ridiculed the authentic '50's contactees, while stuffing the "grey alien abduction cases down everyone's throats." The true version is that these positive contacts with benevolent human-appearing ETs were and are always inspiring, uplifting, and **EMPOWERING**. On the other hand, the negative encounters, which I refer to as "Cosmic Civil Rights Violation Cases," create F.E.A.R. (False Evidence Appearing Real) and unnecessary trauma, and are very disempowering. These particular beings are not members of the Federation, but instead are considered renegades because it is totally against Federation policy to allow these abductions to occur. It is only because of a secret (unconstitutionally illegal and immoral) treaty that was set up with the cabal, that these abductions were allowed by the power elite of Earth in exchange for ET technology. This will be fully examined and exposed in my next book: **The Cover-Up On Human-Appearing ETs**.

Their account continues:

"We work by every means that we have," said Raphael, "in order that the good will eventually blossom on the earth. This necessitates on our side a choice of action, always in harmony with the universal laws which are the Heavenly Father's will. Many times these are scarcely understandable to you, because you (the masses of Earth humanity) follow logic of human might which is opposed to universal love. As a consequence of the limitation of your human understanding, you err when you judge us. Therefore it has been said and written, 'Judge not.' And yet you do pass judgment on God, on us, and on your brothers. Your judgment is in measure to your prejudice. When you have arrived at a true understanding, the error of having been judgmental will be revealed to you. For in love lies the true understanding. The planet Earth has less love than the air which the inhabitants breathe."

Another quote: "The inhabitants of planet Earth," began Raphael, sitting relaxed in the center of the group, his legs lightly crossed, "are ready to spend enormous sums of money to join us in space. And yet, we are already everywhere on Earth. We are among you, both visibly, as you see us now, and also in ways unknown to you. Many know of our existence and our presence, yet deny any knowledge of us. Many of those who have seen us insist that we behave in a strange and senseless manner, yes even that we appear to act contemptuously toward them. Yet they don't want to take that small step that would lead to an understanding of the whole picture and answer your longing to know the 'whence, where and whither?'"

There followed a period of silence. I rejoiced inwardly over this amazing meeting with these "pilgrims of the light," in the stillness of the night. I remembered the words that Raphael had spoken at our meeting at Zosgil, and in my mind compared them with what he was now saying. I was convinced that the Garden of Eden (Earth) had been desecrated beyond recognition by mankind who had rebelled against the Creator-Father's love. Just being in the presence of these brothers enabled me to sense and to comprehend so many things. I wished that this night could continue without ever ending.

"Some people," Raphael began again, "ask themselves whether we exist at all, and they think, 'if the extraterrestrials really exist, why then do they not show themselves to, and cooperate with, us in an open manner?' However, many people of Earth know very well that we do exist, and that we do not share their egoistic outlook or warlike tendency. In reality, they would like to have us in their power, in order to gain knowledge from us which would give them greater opportunities for power and domination. That is the reason why we must act in such a way as to avoid this danger, and why we are waiting for the time when it will be possible to bring knowledge to Earth brothers from the children of God, in conformance with universal law."

The man with my name (George Adamski) looked at me with love and compassion. My feeling toward him was one of gratitude and awe (because of what he went through at the hands of those earlier, as well as modern-day agents of disinformation, those 'spin doctors' of the UFO community, whose job it has been for the cabal to destroy and defame his character, and similar to Jesus [Sananda], he was symbolically 'crucified' by them to cover-up the truths that he attempted to share with the masses, of the reality of these beautiful and benevolent Space Brothers, who Giorgio and Tina, and myself and other contactees have had the privilege of physically meeting)."

Later on: "Why is it," asked Tina, hesitatingly, "that you don't give this message to the people with influence and power? It is surely much more likely that such persons would be believed. They could accomplish much toward bringing about the understanding of those words of scripture that are about to be fulfilled."

It was Orthon who replied. "We have always chosen ordinary people for our message," he said, "who would not distort the real meaning of our words through the influence of their own thoughts and training. Only a receptive mind without the preconceived ideas is qualified to convey with fidelity a message from Higher realms. The fact that Earth people will not believe what is told by a common person (such as the contactees of the '50's and today!) is proof of nothing but a discrimination based on arrogance. Nevertheless, we know that those who want to hear this message, and who love the truth, will not have this difficulty. Each one will feel the truth of the message within his own heart. Scripture provides the touchstone, or test of reality, for that which is coming upon your world. We speak to all men of good will."

This was brought up later on by Giorgio:

I thought about the fact that Earth men seem to conduct their lives as though this was the only one. So I put the question to Raphael: "Isn't it possible to give some concrete evidence to Earthmen as proof that there are other worlds where beings like you are living? That would surely bring more certainty to their thinking; for they live in error on maintaining that after life on Earth, there can be no other."

Raphael looked at me with loving kindness, but in his eyes was a half-veiled sadness, which seemed to me almost like a reproach. "You still do not understand," he said after a pause, "that it is not the outward proof that will cause many to turn from error and wrong-doing. So many proofs have been given to man over the many thousands of years of history full of blood and injustice. But these were rejected, and so, for many, the responsibility and blame grew greater. Jesus gave many proofs during His public life, also as He died on the cross, and even after His death. Few, however, have accepted them. Today, many people are seeing things which would make it possible to accept the reality of what we have told you, yet they have given them a misleading explanation. And when they are persuaded to give up their skepticism, they console themselves by saying that one day these facts will be explained by conventional science. Your world will not be saved by proofs, but by love, patience and belief of those on Earth who are already spiritually progressed, namely men and women of good will. The unlimited power of love will triumph over evil, which is ultimately limited in its nature. So your way of death and rule by force will come to an end. The love of the Father, and His children, who are true to Him, will be the irresistible power that moves the stubborn-hearted; then will their minds be opened. Of what use is it to appropriate new truths without first having gotten rid of the errors in one's way of thinking? It would only increase the burden of blame. You must understand," he said, "that the light that is given mankind is just that which is most useful, not more, for too much would harm the eyes of your understanding, so accustomed to the darkness."

Eufemio del Buono Speaks

Finally, in the "Concluding Remarks" of UFO - Contact from Angels in Starships, (by Lt. Col. Wendelle C. Stevens) Eufemio del Buono has this to say:

The attentive reader may ask, having learned the identity of Ramu, if the extraterrestrials act only for the benefit of those who accept the Old and New Testaments. The answer was given by the appearance of a great Cosmic space fleet on November 4, 1954. On that day, forty flying discs came in delta formation from the four directions of the compass over Rome, and then over the Vatican City, the center of Christendom, and formed an immense Greek cross, the symbol of the universal brotherhood.

After reading this book, it would be useful to read again about the glory of the Lord as revealed to Ezekiel, about the burning bush from which the Lord spoke to Moses before He led His people with fiery discs and column-like space ships, and so many evidences of that sort that are to be found in the Bible. In this way one can understand that all that Georgio Dibitonto, Tina, and their friends, and other contactees of different nations and religions have experienced is part of a great operation of rescue and homecoming for all mankind that is being carried out on a grand scale over the whole planet by this extraterrestrial space fleet.

It is not surprising that the "contactees" are not chosen from the ranks of the educated or scientific elite, although there are exceptions; the extraterrestrials do as Jesus did, who befriended simple fishermen. They trust their message to humble persons, who are gifted with spiritual receptivity and strength of soul.

Relying on these inner resources and guidance from above, one can learn the significant message this book has for us without the encumbrance of tedious detail, which most people would probably find unbelievable anyway. Ramu spoke with great insight when he told Georgio: "The confusion which reigns over Earth today serves to convince but a few persons that all the prophecies which have been given to mankind to lead them toward a better life are about to be fulfilled. They have been ridiculed, misunderstood, despised and even repudiated. And yet, their words have always been fulfilled. So much sorrow that earth brothers could be spared if they could set aside their pride and their reliance on destructive force. If you would renounce the use of evil to fight evil, then your way would be shortened, and you would make enormous strides toward the good."

For George Adamski, life was full of bitter disappointment (because of all that the agents of disinformation within the UFO community in years past have done to attempt to destroy his character and suppress the real facts about his historical contacts). Georgio Dibitonto is well aware of this, and gives the message which he likewise received sorely on the basis of his love and good faith. It is up to the reader to allow himself the spiritual receptivity necessary to embody it and let its light shine through his soul and manifest through his actions.

At Fatima, thousands of persons saw a light or luminous object come from the heavens to earth where Luzia spoke with the apparition of the Virgin Mary. This was witnessed even by non-believers who were there at the time to observe the promised wonder from the skies. I believe this object and these realities were the same as those experienced by Giorgio, Tina, and their friends, and the same as those experienced, each in a different way, by George Adamski and many other people all over the Earth, as well as the prophets of former times. Ezekiel is perhaps the most striking illustration of the latter, with his description of discs and vehicles.

Giorgio & Tina Meet Mother Mary & Sananda

Among the wonderful experiences aboard the Lightships that Giorgio and Tina had, included meeting Mother Mary and Jesus (Sananda). They learned that the space ships participated in the Fatima appearances. Their experience continues:

The gracious Lady from the universe (Mother Mary) arose, and we all did the same. The sun was now lower and lightly veiled in misty clouds, which painted the sky with reddish strokes. We walked through the wheat fields, and the young woman stroked the heads of grain. Then she stood still and turned to us: "Fear not! No person of goodwill should allow anxiety or fear to touch his or her heart. Whoever loves peace and truth, for them there will soon be great celebration. Not a hair of your head will be touched, except there is a redeeming purpose, known only to the great Universal Father."

She went a few steps in the direction of the disc-shaped craft, which one could now see behind the stalks of grain. Majestically it rested there and reflected the colors of the sky from the surfaces of the round dome, which appeared to be a crystalline meld of metal and glass. No lights were visible inside it, yet the gleam of reflection was such that one might expect it to burst forth with light at any moment. With majestic dignity, the young woman raised her gracious, all-loving eyes to mine; from them, there seemed to emanate a powerful radiance that penetrated deep into my soul and granted me unspeakable joy and inner peace.

"In the appearances at Fatima," she said, "thousands of people witnessed the great apocalyptic sign in the sun. Two great wars were unequivocal proofs of the truth of that message, which is the same message I have given you, and is nothing other than a clarification of the scriptures for your times. You are living in the days that immediately precede the thousand year kingdom foreseen by John. Soon you will understand what he meant by his prophesy of this kingdom and the first resurrection. You will experience what it means for the survivors to be taken up into the 'clouds' to meet the Lord of the air. Very soon the new day will come," she added in a firm voice, "in which a new humanity will dwell on the Earth. The animals will no longer be wild, neither poisonous nor harmful. Your fears (for those of us who are Volunteers and all souls who are "Graduating off the endless wheel of karma") about the sad events that are anticipated will change to unimaginable joy. We will be with you during the time this is coming to fulfillment, and after that, in the New Age of universal love on your planet."

A few days later, Giorgia, Tina and their friends experienced the same type of phenomena that was experienced and observed during the Fatima Miracles:

Suddenly, Gianna shouted, "Look--the sun!" The light all around us had grown noticeably dimmer. In front of the sun a large globe or disc circled in undulating fashion, creating the impression that the sun itself was beginning to rotate. At first, I was afraid, but then I watched with calm fascination while the light rays seemed to dance and play over all the surroundings.

"If you had looked toward the sun earlier," said Raphael in Cosmic (telepathic) contact, "you could have seen us sooner. But now, we wish to bring you greetings of God the Father, The Creator of the sun, which gives life to the Earth, in accordance with His will."

In utter amazement we watched the dramatic spectacle before us, comparing observations excitedly from time to time. Nico had his sun glasses with him, so we all tried using them to observe the rotating globe. In that way, one could see more clearly how the object moved over the sun's disc with a circular motion. It gave the impression of seeing the sun itself wobbling on its axis.

This phenomenon continued for some time, and I sat down on the grass to rest....Suddenly Nico cried out, "Look up by the sun!" The sun seemed to still be turning, but now the disc had moved off to the side, just within a fiery circle surrounding the sun. It was not as easy to look at as before, because of the brightness of the sun. But we could see the sun and the discs as two objects now, and gradually everything returned to normalcy again, including the light over the surrounding landscape where we were.

Messages from Raphael

There is also a reference by Raphael to those of us who are Volunteers in Earth embodiment:

"Many of us have come down to earth since the earliest days, and sometimes have been born in earthly bodies in order to fulfill some particularly difficult assignment, and to confront evil directly. One must first save oneself, before one can carry out the work for which one was born on Earth."

I was astonished at what I had just learned. "Tell me," I asked him, "do people come to earth from the Higher worlds in order to learn how to become good, or to help those who must learn? For it is as if one went into the trenches; first, one must take care not to lose his own life, and then one can fight the enemy, in order to help save one's comrades-in-arms."

"Yes," said Raphael, "but in this battle the weapons are love and wisdom, which require God's grace and patience, and the confidence that the Father's plan for salvation, which is set forth in the Holy Scriptures, will be perfectly fulfilled, in spite of the growing disbelief of mankind. God is called Lord of Hosts. The Bible tells you of a battle between the heavenly hosts and the powers of evil. It is good that the Hosts of the Lord are always present, working diligently for the triumph of the good on Earth,--an invited army in a 'battle' of love and salvation against evil. Our numbers grow ever larger now in this time of our coming to Earth for this great mission. We are many."

"And are they all aware that they are here on a mission?" I asked.

"Many are not," he answered, "for a veil of forgetting comes over them so that they have no clear memory of their past. This forgetting is necessary, in order that the lifetime they spend on the planet is not too difficult for them to bear. But afterwards, any soul that belongs to Universal Love and has completed his time on Earth has full knowledge of who he is, what his work was, and the never failing help we gave him from our side."

"I asked, "Does the Scripture speak of this also?"

"Certainly," replied Raphael. "The Book of Genesis relates that the sons of God were born on Earth to bring healing to the society of that time, which was already full of evil, and took unto themselves wives from the daughters of men of Earth that pleased them. Great efforts toward purification were made in those days in order that the good might gain the upper hand over evil."

There were several specific references made in regard to the imminent Divine Intervention and Evacuation. This included information regarding the clouds (Lightships) and information about the event traditionally referred to as the "Rapture" and "Second Coming." This was a confirmation of what Tuella, I, and numerous other contactees and channels have received.

"It has all been written," said Raphael, as he resumed walking. "Everything that might eventuate from the freedom of choice of earthman was foreseen, and his salvation was provided for through a great plan of love, corresponding to the justice and goodness of universal law. Rebellious man will never be abandoned; rather, he will be given support; he will be led, he will be chastened and comforted. There will come a time when the One to whom is given power in Heaven and on Earth will come with His own, and then the rule of evil will be ended, as has been ordained. God the Father will know how best to deal with those who are not yet ready for salvation. We will then not be able to do anything further. We will carry out the new plan of the Father, which He has carefully prepared, but for those concerned, there will be great sorrow and anguish that they did not understand how to make use of such a great opportunity of being rescued."

He was silent for a while. Then he added, "We are the cherubim of the scriptures. We were appointed by God Himself to be Guardians of Eden. Now, when no clouds were there, that might have brought rain, of what was the Father-God speaking? The word 'cloud' meant flying ships, spaceships and starships; in other words, God's covenant would be assigned to us, and, above all, to the one who is in our midst, and who was sent to Earth, even this new Moses, who now will lead Earth in its exodus from evil to the promised land of Eden."

"Isaiah spoke of us when he asked, 'Who are those who fly like clouds, like doves to their dovecotes?' He spoke of our flying discs, which fly to the mother ships, as you saw this night. The expression 'clouds' is found throughout the Bible. Ezekiel found himself confronted by a great cloud, and he described the starship. Read again what he recorded. And what were the pillars of cloud by day and pillars of fire by night that led the Hebrew people through the wilderness? The Cosmic majesty of the Lord God is revealed in His heavenly hosts. He, the Lord of Hosts, has acted through the ages through us with these signs of His presence. I already told you," Raphael said with emphasis, "that the Lord spoke from the clouds, as is stated in the Psalms."

"Do you not think that the appearance of our craft in your skies becomes more frequent? We assure you, God, the Father has told us, that the time is now at hand, in which He has determined to call forth the flagships of the true children of Earth and soon the rainbow will be seen above them, in order that the covenant between us and the father may be known to all, a covenant which will also be extended to the children of Earth. On these ships from the heavens we will be found, and there will be before all, the one who promised to come in the clouds of heaven in glory and power. He will take you with us back to Eden, to dwell in His garden again."

Mother Mary Speaks of the End Times

During the time when Giorgio and Tina meet Mother Mary and Lord Sananda aboard the Lightship, Mother Mary telepathically projected (to Giorgio) a vivid vision of some of the upcoming events of the End Times. Then, she verbally communicated the following information to him:

"Some people who lived where my city is now, had gone aboard a starship. These pictures, which were being shown me, ran quickly through my mind, in vivid accompaniment to the words just spoken by the Lady (Mother Mary) from the Higher realms. Again, I saw what was impressed on my mind a short time before: people were fleeing to the hills....

I saw thousands of flying discs and starships arrive. Men, women and children were entering open doors, others were sucked up and lifted off the ground, for there was not even time for a landing, the rescue work was so urgent. Again I saw these things, and found that the words of this wonderful Lady had described the true circumstances of humanity's plight in the greatest detail."

She waited until my thoughts and great agitation had calmed down somewhat, and then continued, "Unfortunately, Earth people today think the scriptures are only fairy tales, and take great pains to convince others like themselves that all that stands written is merely symbolic. That is a great evil, which serves to spread the delusion still more. Noah was laughed at when he foretold the flood (last great cataclysm or axis shift of the Earth), which then really did come. It is written that that came about as a result of corruption of the souls of that time. When the force of one's very spirit becomes corrupt, then the material and Cosmic life, which are in very close union with the spiritual, must share the burden of all the consequences. All spiritual pollution causes pollution in other dimensions, which maintain a living interdependency with the spirit. Your planet is becoming ever more impure because you are impure in your hearts. The wickedness, and therefore impurity, of the people of Noah's time brought about the catastrophe that came to them. Today a much greater one faces you, in view of the consequences for the whole Earth. We give you this last warning in the hope that you will come to realize the true situation you are in, but we have no intentions of putting our brothers in the dangerous position of those at the time of Sodom and Gomorrah, when the inhabitants of those cities sought to take our emissaries by force."

"Sodom and Gomorrah were, in fact, destroyed by fire, in order that they might be saved by a different destiny than is provided by the material form of manifestation, which they had so abused. We are here for the sake of all Earth children, to warn you of an impending holocaust. If we were to show ourselves today (openly), as in former times, we would fare no better that did those brothers who were sent to tell them of imminent doom. The corrupt people of that city wanted to use force against our messengers. Today, we would be treated even more disrespectfully; at best, with indifference or with condescending smiles." (This information was written in the 1970's, and, fortunately since that time, we have had a tremendous positive Global shift of Higher Consciousness [especially from 2007 on], which has created a much less destructive outcome and which allows for more open mass sightings and landings to occur.)

Messages from Raphael, Firkon, & Kalna

The tactics used by the "agents of disinformation" within the UFO community includes: suppressing references in regard to the reality of these benevolent human-appearing ETs, ridiculing the contactees of the '50's and '60's who attempted to spread the message of their own contacts with these beings from the Higher realms, and distorting the facts about such contacts.

Raphael indicated that he had something to say. "It is written," he commenced, "that, in that moment, of two men working in the field, one will be taken and the other left behind; of two women grinding the mill, one will be taken and the other left behind. Whoever meets the prerequisites to be rescued will be rescued. We cannot force anyone, not even for the purpose of rescuing them. Brothers cannot be brought to other worlds against their wishes. The Father never uses force to compel one to come to Him. Each one does it freely, on his or her own volition. Since the hour is nigh, it is necessary to think carefully about this, so that the time, which has been prepared by the insanity of men, will not come as a surprise."

Firkon gestured with his hand, to indicate that he, too, wished to speak. "The scriptures tell you," he said, "to be conscientious in your devotion, but today hypocrisy and denial abound. It was said that signs in the heavens will herald the new age of love on Earth, although this would be preceded by great tribulation. Does it not seem to you that these are the signs foretold? Our starships and flying discs are seen by people of Earth in ever greater numbers. There are lights that move in the heavens, and signs in the sun, the moon and the stars. Many persons are witnesses to these extraordinary occurrences. Haven't you begun to realize that for some time now we have been signaling to you the approaching fulfillment of all prophesies? The signs already are seen in the heavens. Strange things are happening, as foretold in the writings of John; for example, the waters that turned red in the rivers and seas. The mighty rulers of Earth now have the means to kill the people and leave the material things undisturbed. These and other things, when you consider them thoughtfully, confirm that you are in the times that were foretold."

We continued in conversation until Raphael again requested our attention, saying: "The scriptures tell you that when the time of Tribulation comes, all the people of the earth will see the Son of man coming in the clouds with great power and glory. 'He will,' the Bible says literally, 'send His angels with a great sound of a trumpet, and they shall gather together His elect from the four winds, from one end of Heaven to the other....' Now you know what it means, to be taken from the Earth, or lifted up, or evacuated. You have seen, and we have explained in what manner this may be accomplished.

"Picture in your mind," Raphael began again, "the situation on your planet...as we showed it to you once in Cosmic contact. In such a case, we would immediately evacuate the Earth brothers from the surface of the Earth, but we could not do this for the enemies of love, even if we wanted to. The life-energy of their bodies, as a result of their state of consciousness and the disordered and impure condition of their finer bodies, would not allow us to evacuate them from the Earth. And even if it were possible for us to do so, it would be a greater evil than for them to be left behind on Earth. For this reason, Jesus spoke to you about the fires of Gehenna, and of a hell, which perpetrators of evil, death, and all wicked thoughts and deeds will experience unless they are purified through deep-felt, honest repentance. This works to cleanse and restore balance, and so creates the conditions of life-energy for a reconstruction of the life-expression at an appropriate level. These brothers would see us as something terrifying or monstrous, for their consciousness is sadly deformed, and, in addition to that, they would suffer harm from the energies of our flying discs and starships, as their mode of life would seem to be so completely turned upside down, it would not be able to accommodate the harmonious and unchangeable order which is the rule with us. The inner torment of one who is so out of harmony with the universal laws of the Father, is in itself a means of salvation and a reminder, in spite of all impenitence, that true freedom is found in goodness and in love for the Creator and the brothers."

"In any case, even if, through the Creator's forbearance and our intervention, Earth humanity were to escape the tragic moment foretold in the Scriptures, the Lord would still come, and we with Him, to prepare for the final victory over evil in the world, and the evacuation from the Earth for all who can be saved will follow, before the end comes."

"It is also written," said Kalna, "that this was to be the first resurrection. Truly, those who are lifted from the Earth will experience this in their material bodies, which will have undergone a process of dematerialization, and will be like ours, with the capability of rematerializing when it is needed." The Scriptures say further: 'Blessed and holy are those that take part in the first resurrection (the first wave of the Evacuation). Over such, the second death hath no power. They shall be priests of God and of Christ, and shall reign with Him...." "Therefore," explained Kalna, "whoever is transported from the Earth will be one of our own, somewhat as Elijah was, who was taken away in one of our starships, and ten years later could return to bring a message to the Earth-dwellers of that time. Those who will rule with Christ...will be able to live on Earth, and He will be in the midst of them, and we will also be there. And they will be able to ascend with Him, and with us, into the Higher worlds of the limitless universe. The Earth will once more take its rightful place in the brotherhood of universal love, and will again, as already told you, become a true Garden of Eden. We will no longer have to turn you away from entering Eden, that unspoiled region which has remained true to the Father and His universal laws. We, the cherubim with the drawn, flaming sword, will be among you, and you will be with us. Also, you will undertake missions on behalf of Him who has power in Heaven and on Earth, in accord with the Father's will, and His loving kindness will be the foundation of His sovereign government. Truly, the resurrected shall be priests of God and Christ,--a priesthood that proceeds directly from Him, according to the promise made by one of our ambassadors to Earth, the great priest-king Melchizedek. And then you will know no other death. In any event, the word which was delivered to you, in accordance with the truth, will be ful-filled."

I noticed that Raphael joined the group who were seated. Now we were shown a scene which was so dreadful that I would rather not describe it. A man's voice spoke the words of the prophet Joel: "The sun shall be turned into darkness, and the moon into blood, before the great and terrible day of the Lord has come."

Then a woman's voice spoke the following words of hope: "Whomever shall call on the Name of the Lord shall be delivered; for in Mount Zion and in the spiritual Jerusalem shall be deliverance of the remnant, as the Lord hath said, and of those whom the Lord hath called."

We saw innumerable men, women, and children, who had been evacuated from Earth and brought up to one of the starships, which were assembled in large numbers over the devastated planet. It was as if everyone who was rescued carried a sign of recognition on them, for they seemed to radiate with the same white glow as the starships.

Raphael sat down, and after a short pause, continued, "We will **first evacuate** the brothers who have always sought after goodness and justice; **after that**, the repentant, and, **finally**, those who came to acknowledge and worship God the Father only at the last minute. There will be deliverance for all, except for those who have become enslaved by their own hardness of heart. He, who has ears to hear, let him hear!"

I added the **bold** type in the preceding paragraph to emphasis important words. While this entire particular account by Giorgio tends to be of a more "religious-Biblical" orientation, the essence of what these Higher beings are expressing is basically true. Although the **masses** will desire to be rescued, in order for this to happen they must be on a Higher consciousness level or at least they must be making an **attempt** (through their **intent** and **motive**) to be of this Higher consciousness. The three (distinctly different) waves of the Evacuation are also confirmed here, and this is referred to as the "Tribulation Period."

He was silent, then spoke in a gentle manner: "We invite all brothers of the Earth to open their hearts to the good, and we pray that they turn to God the Father and to us, who are His agents on Earth. All your longings will always be answered, as has been the case through all time. We are in a position to know your thoughts and the needs of your hearts. And this is infinitely truer of God the Father. We beseech and implore you, good and righteous people of Earth; to root out, once and for all, this brother-murdering pride that so poisons the spirit of mankind today. Not one syllable of your prayer will be lost, not one sigh of your soul for truth and justice will be in vain **(Ultimately, this will soon be true!).**"

At one point in Giorgio's narration of his experiences aboard the Light-ships, he describes the type of "consciousness technology," used for the intense column of light and the glowing walls that I also observed aboard the Merkabah Lightship in 1979.

The control room and the larger inner room were separated by softly glowing partitions. In the middle of the main room was a large column of light, which reached from the floor to the apex of the domed ceiling.

Lord Jesus the Christ Speaks

At one point, the 'Commander-In-Chief' of the Intergalactic Confederation, Lord Jesus the Christ (Sananda) appeared before Giorgio, Tina, and all the other beings present and spoke:

"Soon," He said, "I will come, brothers of Earth, yes; we will come in the 'clouds' to bind the power of hatred and death. Then you will see virtues of humility and integrity shine forth. Service in love and learning will replace the grip of might. It will be the end of the beast that wanted to put itself in the place of God. Man is symbolized by the number six, whereas the number three is the symbol for God. Six-sixty-six is three sixes, and therefore represents the man who would put himself in the place of God the Father. That is the number of the beast that will be defeated, and with it the false prophet, who has given his own false word, a word which is not mine, nor yours, nor that of the only true universal Father."

"When all has been brought to fulfillment, then you, the cherubim of the scriptures, will take up your guardianship duties, and ensure that all my Earth children can travel throughout the numberless realms of space created through the Father's love. I can testify to the joyous, creative power of the Father's love. No one knows the Father as I do. His children have the right to explore the immense reaches of space, to visit innumerable created worlds, and to pluck the abundant fruits of His love, but they do not have the right to abuse His great love, or to betray themselves, their own lives, or those of their brothers."

"We sent Noah, Moses, Elijah, Enoch, and many others. The brother Elijah, a great son of the Father, cried out, 'I am consumed with eagerness for God, the Lord of Hosts!' And, like him, so have others we have sent out prayed to Him who sent His heavenly host to Earth before Him. We carried Elijah and many others to our starships, and thus occurred an instance of the first resurrection of the body, of which all the prophets have spoken, and of which John also spoke in the book of Revelation, in connection with the millennium."

CHAPTER 9

WORLD EVACUATION

Time Travel

Throughout the years, I have found many sources (written and through meeting with other contactees) that provide definite confirmation of the World-wide Evacuation of those souls whose intent, motive, and consciousness levels are suitable. From a personal standpoint, I have retained **conscious memories** of events that happened prior to this life which have proved (to me) to be the most important confirmation of this Evacuation plan and I know that it is not a matter of "**if**" it is going to happen, but rather it is only a matter of "**when**" it will happen.

I have also had confirmation of this (in this lifetime) due to a prophecy that was given to me during a specific Cosmic event. In Chapter One, I shared that I have had conscious memory of much of what transpired prior to this present life. One thing that I intensely remember is that the Evacuation is Destined to occur and is a SACRED PROMISE for all of us Volunteers. This also includes the souls of the Laggards who are now in this final Earth lifetime Graduating off the old Wheel of Karma. The following is my conscious recollection of the event that I experienced.

The particular event I am describing occurred in the Galactic Council on a Higher dimensional level, approximately in the mid- to late-1940's. I say "approximately" because there is really not an accurate word to describe the concept of "chronological time" on the Higher dimensional realms, because time does not really exist there. In some sense, based upon this Higher vibrational state of consciousness, one could say that to exist in this Higher dimensional realm one actually exists in the future. From this standpoint, when Volunteers or Star Persons come down to Earth on their individual and/or collective mission(s), they have come from the future into our present timeline.

So, the theory of time travel is correct because in order to come down to Earth one must travel through a time-space portal (i.e. stargate or wormhole) from a Higher vibrational level to this lower vibrational level of (past) existence. The "normal" person has trouble grasping this concept. However, it is basically correct, because everything in this universe is actually in a state of constant evolutionary change. Theoretically, everything in the universe is in a form of a "Holographic Projection" from the Godhead and is symbolically like "reality molding clay" on this and all levels of existence. By that I mean that it can be "molded" or reshaped by beings with the right combination of consciousness and technology and this allows for it to be changed or altered on specific energy levels.

The "Elohim" (Creator Sons and Daughters) who are on this Higher Cosmic level and are working under the direction of God (the Great I Am That I Am) can affect or change this timeline, so that future realities are thereby altered. The Elohem were also known as "Eagle Commmanders and Commandresses" prior to coming into Earth embodiment. These "Secret Agents of God" have come to the planet on "Cosmic Spiritual Espionage Missions of Light." They (literally) have come back into the past--which is now--to change SOME of this past timeline. This means that some of the upcoming End-Time Tribulation Transition will not be as "intense" or destructive as was originally Foreseen and Prophesied. The concept is that God (the Divine Creator) can change His/Her own created reality any time and as many times as wanted (without resulting chaos)--as long as Divine Will and the Holy Spirit and Trinity are involved in the process. So, one's reality and, even, the entire universe (as a gigantic hologram) can be altered, if one visualizes enough Light, love, and consciousness in the process.

The Divine Creator's Message

Now, let's get back to the event that took place within the Galactic Council meeting during the early 1940's which involved an energy level link-up through the Stargates of consciousness. All of a sudden, there was an overwhelming and awe-inspiring manifestation of the Divine Creator and the very Essence of Divine Creation merged into and through all of us that were present at that Galactic Council meeting.

There are no human words to adequately describe the intensity and beauty of this Cosmic experience, but one of the main things that I wish to express is the topic on which the Divine Creator specifically focused. The subject of the Divine Creator's message was about the imminent Divine Intervention and Worldwide Evacuation of planet Earth. And, the purpose of His/Her message was to potently convey and confirm to our "I Am Presence" (our very souls) and all levels of reality that this message is real.

In briefly summarizing a part of what was powerfully projected through our consciousness, I would state that some of what I learned directly was parallel to the experiences conveyed in two other books. Norman Paulsen shares a similar experience in his fascinating book, Christ Consciousness (formerly titled Return of the Ancients), as does Dr. J.J. Hurtek in YAEH: The Book of Knowledge, the

64 Keys of Enoch. If you have not had the privilege of reading these wonderful books, I strongly suggest that you do so.

The specific aspect of Direct Knowledge that was given to us during this sublime mergence, was the Divine Plan (God's Divine Will)--which would (or could) not be changed, no matter what. This is unlike a number of other timelines that have been slightly altered or changed.

The only aspect that was not given to us during this all-powerful mergence was the specific date and time of the Divine Intervention and Worldwide Evacuation. However, it was definitely conveyed that this is the Divine Will, Plan, and Promise of God (our Divine Creator) and that it would occur sometime within an approximate 40-year period of 3rd-dimensional Earth time.

The feeling of the first probable "time slot" (as there were quite a few possibilities) of when this might occur was that it would begin sometime in the early 1980's and one of the last probable "time slots" would be toward the end of the second decade of the New Millennium. The reason it was not specific was to help throw off any interference from the dark forces that have been operating on the planet.

In other words, God purposely was not giving us the exact date, but was making a PROMISE that the Higher Councils of the Federation of Light and Spiritual Hierarchy would definitely fulfill Divine Intervention and Worldwide Evacuation.

Atlantis and Lemuria are examples of Divine Intervention (over 12,000 years ago) where the Confederation had to make a last minute emergency-style evacuation. This involved physically beaming up a few million souls just moments before the Earth shifted on its axis. During this evacuation, there were many other souls who might have made it (Graduated off the Wheel of Karma) if they would have had another chance.

During the present time, the Plan and Will of God is to give the masses of humanity (at the end of this present Age) more than one chance to be evacuated. This includes a plan of being prepared ahead of time and, specifically, calls for three major Waves of Evacuation (Exoduses) over several years of Earth time. This scenario provides more opportunities for as many souls as possible to be saved before the shift of the axis (cataclysm/final planetary cleansing).

We were also told of a smaller "Secret Wave" (a Gathering of the Eagles) which would "officially" begin this series of Evacuation Waves. This initial Wave is ordained, scheduled, and mandated by God to allow His/Her "Chosen Ones" to make their Spiritual Ascension by being beamed aboard the millions of Merkabah Lightships of the Ashtar and Jerusalem Commands and other Commands of the Intergalactic Confederation. These Lightships are presently hovering in mass right over the planet in the 3rd or Higher dimensions in Guardian Action. Because of this aspect, I thought of naming this book Prepare for the Hoverings! but decided Prepare for the Landings! was more appropriate. The truth is that most people will be beamed aboard ships that are hovering overhead, but there will be many ships that will also land to pick up other individuals. This will certainly be accurate in regard to ships that "come and go" from the numerous "rainbow-domed cities of refuge and sanctuary" that will suddenly manifest during the Tribulation Period (as later described).

There were many other specific things and events that were relayed to and through us during that incredible moment of emergence with God. Besides for the collective message that we received about Divine Intervention, which included Worldwide Evacuation, what was also conveyed were personal sacred messages from God to each of us who were present in the Council. I was specifically told (by God) that it was His Will that when I reincarnated for the final time on Earth that I would have conscious memories of this experience of God speaking to us at the Council.

I was also told that my specific mission would be to PREPARE the Volunteers (and any of the masses who are ready to "Graduate off the endless Wheel of Karma") and remind them of God's PROMISE of the imminent Evacuation and Divine Intervention, so they will not "give up hope." This is not just a plan by the Intergalactic Confederation and Spiritual Hierarchy, but, more importantly, it is a sacred PROMISE and the WILL of God. I was reminded that our individual choices and behavior (intent and motive) do, indeed, count and are monitored by our "Friends Upstairs."

As I sometimes convey, when referring to those potent and sacred memories, that "I read the 'small print' in this sacred Cosmic Agreement." One of the PROMISES in this agreement is that if the Volunteers in Earth embodiment (who [indirectly] "technically," still represent the Higher Councils) can no longer freely travel or openly speak out against the injustices of the cabal, and if the corrupt forces of the New World Order attempt to stop us from being able to fulfill our Missions, then, Divine Intervention and Worldwide Evacuation would occur.

As many may have noticed in the last couple of decades, we have watched as many of our freedoms have been taken away. Under "Bush fraud's" war on terror, Big Brother has encroached more into our lives under the disguise of making us safer. Part of this intrusion through advanced biometric technologies, gave the cabal the ability to totally track and monitor everyone anywhere in the world, so that individuals have become more controlled by the "beast system."

Another thing that was shown to me (by God) was that, after I reincarnated in this final lifetime, as a child I would have the physical encounters that I have had with the beings onboard the Merkabah Lightships as Preparation for Divine Intervention and Worldwide Evacuation. I was also told that while I was young, I would meet Lord Jesus the Christ (Sananda), who is our Commander-In-Chief. I understood that He would appear to me on this 3rd-dimensional level of existence for the purpose of inspiration and as a confirmation of who He truly is. His appearance was also a sign that He will be returning as was prophesied over 2,000 years ago. Additionally, it would be for the purpose of establishing His "Consciousness Technology" and how both Old and New Testaments (as well as in other sacred and ancient religious writing of all the major religions) describe encounters with the benevolent human-appearing extraterrestrials and their starships.

Part of the PLAN to reconfirm these memories to me, was that while I was still young, I would receive very strong telepathic messages from my "Friends Upstairs," and, then, when I got older (and was more mature) I would be physically contacted by a Space Brother (or member of the Galactic Council). This Space Brother would be dressed incognito in Earth clothes and would physically approach me. Once he was in my presence, he would telepathically reverify all that I had experienced and was told by God when He merged with us in the Galactic Council. What was most important about this was to confirm God's Promise and Plan for all of us, whether it be Volunteers or others who are attempting through the Cosmic Law of Grace to "Graduate off the Wheel of Karma."

Important Note to Readers

Note: Some of the following scenario about martial law and activating the 800 U. S. Concentration Camps will not now be allowed to occur. This was information that was communicated to me from the ET at Squaw Peak Park in 1981. I was told very recently that this has changed because of the powerful increase in the planetary frequency and the mass shift in consciousness that has occurred on the planet during 2007 and 2008 and, particularly, right before the Presidential Election of 2008.

This was highlighted by the transformational election of Barack Obama as the 44th U. S. President. It is wonderful to know that Obama is a Higher Cosmic Being of Light in Earth embodiment who is being guided by the Federation. This time during the election, the Higher Forces prevented the manipulation of our votes. This election also symbolizes the end of the cabal's power upon the Earth. For the first time in the history of this coun-

try, an African-American was elected to the Presidency which effectively ended the reign of the elitist, "good 'ol boys" white-man's network.

The information herein was included because it is important for readers to understand the difference in the scenarios of the "Old Time Line" verses what is presently occurring. Keep in mind that the "Old Time Line" would have definitely occurred except for the recent planetary consciousness shift, but now with the "New Time Line" the evacuation waves are no longer seen as an emergency scenario. Instead these evacuation waves may now be viewed entirely as wonderful "Cosmic R & R" opportunities that will allow a greater number of Earth individuals to experience an open intergalactic cultural exchange.

It is important to understand how the cabal historically manipulated events from behind the scenes. Just days prior to the election, Bush had almost everything in place to create a national emergency which would have allowed for martial law to be activated. He was literally stopped by Higher Forces and many courageous patriotic heroes within the military who decided to stop his plan of turning the U. S. into a fascist dictatorship. Most people have no idea just how close we actually were to martial law being activated. However, it was miraculously averted by these forces intervening at the last moment in late October 2008. But, now, the mass population has awakened and is demanding a change for the better, an end to the fear, and more accountability from our governmental leaders.

My Confirmation

So, sure enough, as I was growing up, I had that first physical encounter (as detailed in Chapter One) and, then, a couple of years later Lord Jesus the Christ (Sananda) materialized before me. (This experience will be described in detail in the fourth book of The Divine Blueprint Series: Who's Who in the Cosmic Directory). About another two years went by when one day, I received a very strong telepathic message that was a reminder that someday in the future (when I grew older and more mature) I would be approached by a Galactic Being dressed incognito in Earth clothes, and would confirm to me, telepathically, about the eventual Divine Intervention and Worldwide Evacuation that would occur later in this life.

The final confirmation occurred in February of 1981, during a New Age event called "The Festival of Light." This special event was organized by a woman named Norma Graham and was held at Squaw Peak Park, in Phoenix, Arizona. When I first heard about this event, I assumed it would be similar to other New Age events that I had attended in the past, with people networking, doing psychic readings, or selling alternative or holistic products and services at a number of booths and tables.

Then, I suddenly received a very potent telepathic message from my "Friends Upstairs" that I must definitely go to this event as I would be making a very special and important connection there and that I needed to be there "no matter what!" The intensity of this telepathic message, surprised me at the time, but, of course, later on it was very obvious why it was projected that way.

I had learned through the years to always follow this Higher Guidance, especially since my Inner Guidance gave me a strong confirmation of this. So, off I went that afternoon, not consciously knowing what was about to occur. When I arrived at Squaw Peak Park on that sunny, warm afternoon, I leisurely strolled around waiting for this "very important, special connection" to take place. After walking around for awhile, I found myself wondering if this was actually going to happen, since I had not met anyone with whom I had a special connection.

At one point, I got into an animated conversation with another person who was also there just visiting and networking. I had no conscious plan of going there and doing an "impromptu" lecture, but as I continued to talk to this person I suddenly felt a familiar sensation. The sensation was what happens when I am about to receive a telepathic message (channeling) or when I am strongly "Overshadowed" (when a specific type of energy-consciousness beam from a Merkabah's consciousness computer is placed over me). I began to speak in a louder, more powerful voice, and a small crowd gathered to listen to what I was being Guided to share. Within a few minutes, the crowd had grown to about 20 to 30 people as I continued to speak about my own UFO and channeling experiences. Then, as I was speaking, I noticed a man walking toward us, and the moment I laid eyes on him I inwardly knew that this was the special and important connection that I was supposed to make. I knew deep-down who he was, why he was there, and what he was about to share with me.

As he approached me, I had this inner realization; I discovered that I could not stop talking. It was as if this Higher consciousness energy beam from the ship's computer was inducing me to continue giving this impromptu presentation.

As I observed this Higher Galactic being, who by now was standing about 15 feet away from me; I saw that he was dressed in a short-sleeved shirt, white shorts, and sandals. I knew that he looked like a "normal good-looking Earth human." Yet, at the same time, I had a very powerful vision of him dressed in a metallic silver-blue jumpsuit aboard a lightship. I knew that he had been sent by the Galactic Tribunal Council aboard the Merkabah that was now hovering overhead on the 12th dimensional level. The powerful beam that was prompting me to do this presentation was coming from this Lightship. I also had a vision of this spaceman being beamed down from the ship and I knew for sure that he was here to confirm to me what was coming up in the future.

Although I wanted to approach him to say hello and to shake his hand, the energy beam that was influencing me made it impossible for me to do anything but continue the lecture. When he walked up toward me, I noticed that the people who were standing by me (with their backs toward him) starting moving around as if they sensed his Higher vibrational presence. I also noticed with my inner-sight, the huge, brilliant golden-colored auric field that surrounded him. I had great respect for him, knowing that these Higher Galactic beings make a great sacrifice by coming down (from a purer setting) into the harsh environment on Earth with all the horrible environmental pollutants and the negative thought-forms surrounding us.

I watched him as I continued my presentation and observed that he was looking straight at me with very intense eyes (as though he was looking right through me). Then, he telepathically communicated with me: "Michael, as you know, since you have telepathically picked up on this, I am from the Galactic Council and I was sent here to give you this final confirmation of the upcoming Worldwide Evacuation and Divine Intervention."

I must say, despite the numerous physical and telepathic experiences that I had had prior to this final manifestation, it still was totally "mind-blowing" to have this happen, even though I had been told that it would. But, what was most important now was the in-depth message that he shared with me, as I continued to lecture. He sent me a "compressed" mental message, along with very colorful "holographic-3-D" mental images of the upcoming events. Part of the message that he gave me was that I would be meeting others who were receiving the same information about the number of waves of the Evacuation, as well as other such details. (In fact, later on, I did hear from other channels and contactees who received basically the same information that I did).

During his telepathic transfer of information, he made a reference to some kind of "legislation" that had passed that would classify those of us who were in contact with the Space Brothers as criminals. I could not possibly understand what he was referring to at the time, but about a year and a-half later the major newspapers reported that in 1982 General Westmoreland actually had been physically taken aboard a UFO. Because of this, government officials reinstated the "ET Ruling" that Congress originally passed into law in 1969 (unbeknownst to the general public). This law states that anyone having contact with extraterrestri-als will be taken by armed-guards and quarantined for an indefinite period of time, and that not even a court hearing can overturn it; so, basically, our civil rights and the rite of habeas corpus no longer exist. Of course, since President George W. Bush has been President, the rite of habeas corpus has been taken away anyway by him and Vice President Cheney.

According to many military intelligence people that I have connected with since 1982, this ruling has been totally forced upon all military personnel. It has not, yet, been enforced upon the civilian population. Of course, once the initial Secret Wave of the Evacuations has occurred, at that point the forces of New World Order (the cabal) may attempt to enforce this rule. Basically, under this law, anyone connected with these waves of Evacuation could be considered to be a "criminal," and may be arrested and thrown into one of the 800 "concentration camps" that have already been built by Blackwater mercenaries in numerous locations throughout the U.S.

Tuella Speaks of Cosmic Protection

If not for the great amount of Higher protection from our "Friends Up-stairs," all of us Volunteers would be arrested or eliminated. Tuella specifically received a number of strong channelings about this Cosmic protection for all the Volunteers and, especially, for those of us who will be taken up in the Secret Wave and then "boldly" return after two or three weeks of Earth time. In this particular channeling, Kuthumi is speaking:

> As these things (planetary-social upheavals) come to pass, many voices will be raised, and many great works will be seen, such as have never been seen. These will be the works of these who have been lifted into our midst, from whom the veils have been re-moved, and whose chakras have been fully opened. Souls who see and hear them will know that these anointed ones have truly been with us and returned with a witness and the evidence that cannot be denied. For a "brief moment of time" their ministries will be blessed and protected, and they shall no longer be secluded away without freedom of service. They shall stand boldly in many places, witnessing to the experiences that came to them in Higher realms, where they were given a full insight to the events that are just before the world.
>
> When they have been raised in your midst, listen to these voices! These are the chosen and Elect Leaders, placed upon the planet by collaboration of our beloved brothers from other dimensions and

other worlds. These witnesses will return to you with the unction of authority upon their words and their deeds that will convince and prepare many for the evacuation that is to follow.

Their words shall remove fear and heal unbelief and expose the reality of that great invisible army of the Legions of Light that surround you. Every moment of the day, they monitor thoughts, words and deeds, and planetary responses, conditions and affairs. But a time will come when they are no longer able to contain the planetary action destined to come to pass. When those hours are upon you, many of you shall be prepared in your hearts, by those who return to you to give you our message. They have come as Volunteers to serve the Earth in her hour of trial. They shall be the spokesmen on the physical octave for those who remain in the Higher dimensions. You shall know them by their fruits and by the evidence which they bring with them.

We give warning to the world that ye seek not to destroy them, for that is not possible, and such an intention will precipitate grave results in your own lives. This inner circle of incarnated ones will walk amongst you when we have returned them to you. You will be electrified by their words and the story they have to tell the world. Since the creation of time, there has never been a time such as this, when the chosen and Elect Volunteers to Earth shall be gathered together to receive their credentials and their authority and sent back to bring these things before humanity. Hear my words, O beloved ones; take heed that you touch not a hair of their heads, for they also are emissaries of the Golden Light from other worlds. I am Kuthumi, and I bring you my blessing, my Love to all of you. My Light shines upon each and every one of you who read these words and handles this book.

At another time, Tuella telepathically asked her space contacts an important question for them to answer for her book, regarding the status of those of us who are representing these Higher councils and worlds. Technically, this makes us a major threat to those in (present) positions of power and threatens our "legitimate status" as Earth citizens, etc.:

Sir, you have stated that upon returning, we are to become open witnesses to the fact of our representation of your Commands above. Is there not some sort of illegality to be reckoned with in being the representative of an alien government?

Answer: That is a good question, Tuella. Let's discuss the matter. It is true in a certain sense that to an alien from another Earth government this would apply. And of course, considering the hostility of your Earth governments, this would probably also apply in the present. However, I wish to point out to all of you involved that you do not represent an alien helpless government. You will be backed by all of our enabling intervention in any problem that might arise. So often your own CIA personnel are required to enter into missions in which they can do no calling upon those who have sent them. They cannot in any way reveal their identity of their source of authority. In the case of our representatives, such is not the case. On the contrary, you will have full and open access to all of our abilities to protect you, to work with you in confusing those who would harm you, and convincing them of the truth of your ambassadorship....

However, if the powers that be indeed wanted to become belligerent and unduly ugly, then they could stress obscure technicalities as grounds for incarceration. But a few visits and occurrences from us would soon end all such. And if necessary, we would simply remove or transport our faithful who were so treated.

Have no fear of any of these earthly reverberations, for we will have all things in hand. This will be easier to believe and understand once you have seen our equipment (consciousness technology) in operation with your own eyes. Then fear will be impossible within you.

Here is another reference to this protection and help:

The bringing in of these Earth volunteers to a state of fellowship under these extraordinary circumstances will vitalize all of you to such an intense state of energy and enthusiasm that you will never forget it, never get over it, never lose the vision for it until all

things are come to pass! This will be the firing of your personal
momentum in a most spectacular way and will bring into all of
you, the inner level awakening you need. No one will leave these
briefings without all chakras attended to, all physical problems removed, and all obstacles removed from the pathway of your mission. You will be equipped with every kind of gadgetry assistance,
as well as spiritual weapons for all challenges to your ministry.

Another thing which was referred to several times in Tuella's book was
that as each Volunteer is lifted up during the Secret Wave, each person will
receive a special crystal pendant that is to be worn at all times that totally protects
them and gives them special powers and abilities:

Basically, the communication devices we have proposed are to be
fairly identical in all seven divisions. They need not be the same in
appearance, but in function they must be the same. As the needs
were presented to each group quite some time ago, it has been in-
genious the diversity of designs that have been brought forth, yet
all do indeed coordinate with all others in the functions performed
and the vital needs fulfilled. There will be an identifying crystal of
certain color for each, which immediately indicates the group to
which that person is assigned, as well as the Sector Commander.
This central stone will also be the crystal that is in attunement with
the body vibrations of the one who wears it and who is in direct
contact with his Commander craft. The device will also have a
factor incorporated into its design which will serve as levitating or
traveling (teleportation) device for any emergency, as well as another built-in deposit of crystalline energy functioning as the
means of producing invisibility as needed in times of danger. Of
all the equipment with which we will arm our Earthean Eagles, the
greatest will be the unveiling of their memories and the revelation
of their identities and missions to the planet Earth.

I send a special dispensation of anointing for this task upon all
these whom you will take into your midst. They shall carry within
their inner being great power and perseverance in this ongoing battle for the minds of men. They shall not be left unequipped without the proper spiritual weapons with which to carry forward this

encounter. All shall be filled with spiritual power and anointed to meet every need from the overflow of their inward blessings.

They will have constant attunement with those of you who guard them and guide their ministries. The mystical objects you have prepared for them represent a great contribution for their behalf, and this will secure for them all of the remaining protection that is necessary. When the days of evacuation are upon us, these will be the ones to whom you will turn for help that is needed upon Terra. Those few moments of feverish action will bring about the gathering of the wheat into My barn for the eternal harvest.

Since you Earthly Light Commanders will have a closer and even a bodily contact with us over the next few years, or whenever evacuation must be executed (it is absolutely dependent upon Mankind's Free Will), at this very moment we are preparing for each of you a pendant. This is no ordinary pendant, but one similar to those worn in Atlantis by those working in the strong electromagnetic fields around the crystals. In the center of the pendant is a small body crystal which we are attuning to the vibrational frequencies of each Commander. Preparation of the crystals is going on at a feverish pace aboard the host Command ship.

As each person is welcomed aboard, he or she will have a pendant slipped around the neck, never to be removed again in bodily form....The body crystal attuned to each one's vibrational pattern will help each to tolerate changes in frequencies on the Earth plane as well as when aboard the Command ships. Each will receive a special assignment and report to that specific Mother Ship involved with a particular area of Command. We need use of caution here, that not all be revealed at this stage.

Communication will also be greatly enhanced through mental telepathy, as by wearing the body crystal, one's vibrations will be stepped up and a more synchronous match can be established between the realms. A matter of vibration is all that defines dimensions. We cannot give anymore information at this time without divulging classified information to the public. Not everyone who will read your forthcoming book, Tuella, will be of the Light **(nor**

this book, either!). Therefore, we are not permitted to go any further, just as you will not be permitted to give out time, dates and what not.

The Rejuvenation Chamber

One of the major aspects of being physically beamed up aboard the Merkabah Vehicles of Light is that this is definitely a Spiritual Ascension, just as Jesus the Christ (Sananda) experienced over 2,000 years ago. The difference is that what is coming is a mass ascension of millions of Light souls experiencing this all together. (Earlier, when this was telepathically communicated to me by the being at Squaw Peak Park, I was shown that we would first be lifted aboard smaller "scout craft" and, then, taken to the fleets of the much larger Mother Ships [city ships] hovering above the planet on the Higher dimensions. Then, once we are aboard the Mother Ships, the first thing we would go through would be to step into Rejuvenation Chambers, which will create for us totally transformed, rejuvenated, and perfect bodies.)

Tuella received part of this information (just like I received from the Being) that confirms what one will experience at that time:

I asked if there would be medical treatments or physical examinations given while on board. Andromeda Rex was in contact at the time:

Yes. All who enter must undergo a physical examination to determine the exact status of the physical form. (This is in no way to be confused with the crude, rough, and backward-type of physical "examinations" [violations!] of the traumatized abductees that the negative grays have kidnapped for their weird genetic experiments!) This will be for the purpose of personal adjustment when entering into the cubicle (rejuvenation chamber) in which the Light Body is rejuvenated. Just as many of your own medical profession would require an examination before diagnosis and procedures. Any medical treatment that is necessary will be immediately disposed of by our electronic equipment and technology. Then, we will proceed to the body change into Light Force. None will return with less than a perfect body. It is ordained as one of the necessities of service of this nature. (Just one of many "Cosmic fringe benefits" too numerous to list!) There will be built-in energy responses which will guarantee energy drive at all times, with alertness and above-average abilities in quick mental response and telepathic qualities. Vision (as well as hearing) will be strengthened and made keen beyond the usual nature of human vision (and sound). This is a most-needed tool. We intend to equip our representatives with all of the best in every way possible. We also intend to flow to all of you all that is needed in the way of capital for carrying out what must be done (that is if the new economic gold-backed system referred to as NESARA has not been Officially Announced and activated by the time that the Secret Wave has occurred!). None shall know want or deprivation, but all shall live in what is termed a comfortable manner according to their choice. As they desire, they shall have, in keeping with a dedicated motivation for service.

The Being gave me in-depth information, regarding the exact nature of this rejuvenation process. It included: People, who are physically older in appearance, will see themselves being transformed into younger bodies; they will literally watch as rainbow-colored rays, frequencies, and harmonics pass through their bodies. These rays, which will be projected out from the surface of the surrounding walls, the ceiling, and the floor, will cause their cells and molecules to reverse themselves, becoming more elastic and firm once again (no more face lifts, liposuctions, plastic surgery, etc.). In actuality, this chamber is not only used for "rejuvenation," but, it also acts as a "decontamination" chamber in which negative viruses, bacteria, and pathogens of any kind are instantly eliminated.

In these wonderfully uplifting telepathic visions from the Being, I saw this same scene repeated (simultaneously) on the hundreds of Mother Ships high above the planet, where those of us (who were taken up suddenly) stepped into the chambers and, then, soon emerged from the chambers appearing as "perfect" as one could imagine. Keep in mind that the reason for doing this is not for some vain purpose, but this is in total harmony with the Divine Will and Plan of God to restore one's physical and spiritual beauty. The cultivation of physical and spiritual beauty, harmony, and esthetics is something that has always been emphasized on the Higher worlds, where the women, literally, are gorgeous goddesses and the men are handsome gods, whose physical beauty is the same as their inner beauty.

The Vibrational-Frequency Scale

Further information that was given was that some people will receive tele-pathic messages only moments before the Secret Wave (First Contact) occurs. This is in keeping with the prophecy in Revelation (of the Bible) that "No one knows the exact hour or day" (Cosmically top secret). This is so that the organized dark forces will have no time to stop it or to endanger those individuals involved. This is why it is Biblically explained that it will happen "in a twinkling of an eye."

It is important to know the aspects or qualities that will influence or hinder one's ability to be effortlessly beamed up aboard the ships when these waves of Evacuation begin. This also relates to a channeling that another channel and contactee received from the Space Brother Monka, back in the 1950's. This person asked Monka about what conditions or factors could make this experience easier or what might hinder or stop it from occurring when being rescued from the planet in a mass Evacuation. Monka's response to this question is most significant. Keep in mind that Monka used a type of "vibrational-frequency scale" of harmonics from zero to 500 on this particular type of consciousness scale. He stated that 500 on this scale roughly represented the "average-higher conscious-ness" of the Space Brothers and Sisters and the Ascended Masters in their Higher Ascended Cosmic Consciousness. He revealed that in order to be physically beamed aboard a Lightship, one would have to (at a "bare minimum") be able to vibrate at about 200 on this scale, and that there are several key factors that determine exactly where one would be on this vibrational scale. Those lifestyle factors include:

(a) One's intent, motive, and one's choices of free will (the most important aspect)
(b) How pure and healthy one's diet is (a very close second in importance)
(c) Whether one meditates, does Light decrees and invocations, and prays
(d) The use of quartz crystals and gemstones worn as pendants.

This last one is very important, because the quality of natural crystals and gemstones is used to amplify all the positive qualities, and, synergistically, allows all aspects of this "energy recipe of life" to be amplified and transformed. Aurora Light was guided by the Higher Forces to design beautiful Rainbow-crystal pendants and to make them available **only** to Light Workers. For more informa-tion and photographs of these stunning custom-designed Rainbow pendants, go to the web site listed in the products at the back of the book.

The Detox Ionic Footbath is a recent invention that is available to assist Light Workers in raising their vibrations. This technology is an ionic-detox footbath that removes the accumulative toxins, heavy metals, and pollutants from the body. Individuals place their bare feet in warm water and are hooked up to a special ionozer device that pulls these pollutants out of the cells and organs of their bodies. The machine also charges up the individuals' auric fields which kill viruses and pathogens within their bodies. It is awesome to see how dark the water gets as all these toxins are being released by the body. As a result of this procedure, the vibrational level of the person will be more in harmonic attunement and, thus, more prepared for being beamed up during the Evacuation. As with the Rainbow Crystal Pendants, information about this machine is located at Health-Galleria.com. (Further information about this will follow in a later book of The Divine Blueprint Series: Cosmic Insights for Survival until Divine Intervention.)

Back to discussing Monka's scale, it was estimated that most Volunteers are slightly above the 200 level, whereas those Volunteers, who follow very strict guidelines adhering to the listed criteria (above) and who follow the highest ideals and quality of life, are probably way over 300 on the scale, and, in a few instances, some may be up near the 400 level. By the same token, most of the mundane masses of humanity who have been stuck on the "Wheel of karma" (Earth life after Earth life) and have no awareness of these Higher realities are definitely below the 200 level and many are even around 100. In the case of **very** negative people (those who murder, etc.), they are most likely way below the 100 level (or even near zero!) on the chart.

There are infinite combinations of this "synergy-energy recipe" that will cause one's vibrational level to fluctuate either up or down. For example, someone may have very high ideals and principals, but have a diet that is basically "garbage." In this case, the level would be much lower than it would be if they had taken better care of their "Temple" (physical body).

There may be many cases of Volunteers who spiritually desire to "Graduate" and make their Spiritual Ascension when the Evacuation waves begin. However, these individuals may be totally "ignorant" of how they should treat their physical bodies, and, therefore their bodies are very toxic and full of disease. In other words, "the soul is willing, but the body is not." In order for them to be able to take their physical body with them in this Spiritual Ascension, they will have to spend time in one of the numerous Rainbow bubble (sanctuary-refuge) cities (discussed later) where they will go through an advanced "holistic crash-course" to change their bad diets and unhealthy lifestyles. A part of this change would include adding colonics to their routine. (Colonics is the cleansing of the compacted undigested food products in the intestines that may have been accumulating for many years.) This course will quickly detoxify them, as well as raise

192

their lower life-force (chi) energy to at least the 200 level mark, so their bodies will be capable of being taken aboard the Merkabah.

How will it be determined who will be the ones to Ascend in the First Wave? There is an "automatic" harmonic sequence of the waves of Evacuation. Individuals will not be "picked and chosen," except according to their levels of intensity of responsibilities and the "authority" bestrode upon them as leaders amongst those who are taken aboard (this denotes a certain level of "required consciousness" and vibrational-frequency-harmonics).

To roughly explain why the first one million souls will be a part of this "automatic sequence" (verses the other souls who will be taken up in later waves); I will use the following analogy. If you take a container and put numerous "different" types of substances in that container (pieces of paper, wood, plastic, glass, metal filings, etc.) and, then, you move a magnet closely over it, the only thing that will be lifted up will be the metal fillings. When the Word from On High is given to "go ahead" with the Divine Plan (a Cosmic green light), it will be as if a "giant magnet" draws the souls upward who are in alignment (attuned) with the magnet (as "the wheat is separated from the chafe") and so it will continue, likewise, for the following waves afterwards. Most people have probably seen the bumper stickers that say, "CAUTION: In case of the Rapture, this car will be unmanned."

It is important for Volunteers, regardless of how high they are on the harmonic scale, to always strive to improve their vibrational level prior to the Evacuation occurring, because when they report back to the Council and their lives are examined, they want to be proud of their accomplishments and to know that they did everything they possibly could to help humanity by making the Transition (Tribulation) period less severe for others. They will want to be more loving and positive in their attitudes and to live their lives as responsible and empowered Guardians and Emissaries, because, "technically" they still represent the Higher Councils and the Federation of Light. The importance of this is so they can bring more Light and love and a higher quality of life to this planet. It is also so they are capable of channeling Higher, more intense Cosmic energies and helping to transmute the lower energies off the planet. Volunteers need to keep in mind that it is extremely important for them to take total responsibility in everything they think, say, and do, including purifying their diet, for they do not want to "blow their chance" of being rescued. So, the most important aspect of this is the Volunteer's intent and motive and the qualities of honesty, personal integrity, and "self-sacrifice" that they display.

Will Pets Be Taken?

One of the questions I have been asked many times at my lectures and workshops has been whether those who are taken aboard the ships will be allowed to take their pets with them, and the answer is (usually) yes! What one needs to understand about this is that the animal kingdom (like the human species) also has more advanced (Volunteer) souls and less advanced (laggard) souls who can build up a type of "good" or "bad" karma. Normally, animals tend to be "innocent" group souls, especially those that are pets who are more "individualized" and tend to be more evolved than other animal species. Most Volunteers (Star People and "Walk-ins") tend to draw to them certain types of more evolved animal souls from other worlds.

The plan of the Confederation is to evacuate as many animals as possible during the years of Tribulation, so they will not have to suffer any more from mistreatment of mankind. As a matter of fact, I have been informed by the Federation, that some of the species that supposedly have became "extent" (because of the horrible environmental conditions that Mother Earth has been experiencing) have actually been taken off the planet, and they will be reintroduced to repopulate the Earth again, at the beginning of the Golden Age of Peace.

Rex 84 & Martial Law

[Note: As previously noted, there has been a powerful frequency consciousness shift on the planet. As a result of this shift, many of the potential negative scenarios have changed for the better. This section of the book was left in to show the seriousness of what could have occurred in the "old timeline," which has <u>NOW</u> been replaced with a "Positive Reality Timeline."]

Most of the other information that this Being telepathically told me that day in 1981, correlated with what Tuella shared in her book. The one exception is that I also mention the possible threats that the cabal may attempt after the Secret Wave occurs and during the time frame of the other three Waves. The cabal has had a plan referred to as "Rex 84" (which includes FEMA) that allows martial law to be declared and the U. S. Constitution to be suspended, if any type of large-scale state of national emergency is declared (like another "9-11" type "false-flag" event). Of course, George W. Bush, during his tenure as President, "suspended" the Constitution in various ways, including many of the Executive Orders that he wrote following "9-11."

Establishing martial law for this situation could create chaos. As a result, many thousands of people might end up in one of the 800 government "detention facilities" (concentration camps) that have been built across the U. S. Much of this information has been confirmed to me by intelligence agents and undercover operatives in the years since 1981. These courageous patriots wanted the public to know what the cabal had secretly been planning under their New World Order policies and conspiracies. Furthermore, there is some very accurate information available on the internet that addresses this topic.

According to recent reputable sources, there have been numerous "military training exercises" (suburban-guerrilla style warfare) all over the country that involve mercenaries from many foreign countries that are a part of Blackwater. This has been done in preparation for the upcoming "insurrection" that the cabal has covertly planned in conjunction with the potential "chaos" that could be generated by a so-called "state of national emergency." Part of their plan is to conduct "house to house searches and seizure," which could be instigated under the numerous "directives" of FEMA that allows these mercenaries to march right in and take over as many places as they want to.

If these "emergency plans" of FEMA and Rex-84 are put into motion, Blackwater mercenaries plan to round up large numbers of the population (totally against their will and constitutional rights) for transport and processing. Part of these illegal plans is to transport people in horrible cattle-cars where they are, literally, shackled to the cattle-car to keep them from escaping. In the last couple of decades, I have actually spoken to more than one person who have told me that they have personally seen hundreds of these particular-type cattle-cars (parked in numerous locations in Texas and other Midwest states) which have human shackles in them.

In the very clear telepathic transfer of information that I received, the seriousness of our situation was emphasized. It was pointed out that if not for Divine Intervention and the Waves of Evacuation, most of the Volunteers would either be killed or arrested as "criminals" under the "ET Ruling" and thrown into these concentration camps. But, Thank God, because of the Secret Wave, the Confederation and Spiritual Hierarchy would be "one step ahead," of these organized negative forces. Also, the Light Workers (who are picked up in the Secret Wave) will receive "special training and conditioning" aboard the Lightships (as previously mentioned) and will come back to Earth as "Planetary Liberation Reconnaissance Teams," totally prepared to handle anything that the negative forces of the cabal attempt to use against us.

[Note: There is intense Karma that has built up on this planet, and even though the Cosmic Law of Grace is now more fully manifesting on the Earth, it still appears that some individuals may experience very difficult situations due to their own Karma.]

The Waves of Evacuation

In 1981, when I connected with the ET at Squaw Peak Park, I was initially informed that there would be about 500,000 Volunteers who would be taken up on the Starships for about two to three weeks of Earth time (it may seem like months or years in "Higher dimensional time"). In more recent years, I have been informed that the original amount of people has been increased to about 1,000,000 from what was originally planned.

I was also told that the first major Wave will consist of between two to three million Volunteers, based upon the next level of responsibilities, and they, too, will be gone about two to three weeks of Earth time. In more recent years, I was also informed that this number had increased to between four to five million Volunteers.

For the second major Wave, I was informed that this will include the rest of the Volunteers who have been in Earth embodiment or approximately sixteen to seventeen percent of the world's total population. (This amount has been updated from 10 to 11 percent which was the original percentage in the early 1980's. Now, it has been adjusted to include the increase of "Star Children" [Indigo and Crystal souls] that have since taken embodiment.) This wave will then account for all of the Volunteers that have been on the planet. They too will be gone for about two or three weeks of Earth time, during which time they will experience similar "Cosmic R & R."

Finally, I was told that the third and final Wave will occur at the end of the Tribulation and just before the total planetary cleansing (axis shift) and Cataclysm occurs. According to the Confederation, this Wave will include those "laggard" souls who are "Graduating off the Wheel of Karma" and who will now be able to achieve their individual/collective Spiritual Ascension. In the early 1980's, the number of individuals in this Wave was projected to be approximately one-third or more of the entire world's population. But, in recent years, due to the planetary consciousness awakening this number will now be considerably higher. This Wave will consist of those left on the planet who are able to reach that approxi-mate "200" reading on the harmonic scale (as mentioned earlier).

During this final Wave is when Lord Jesus the Christ (Sananda) officially arrives on the scene. This fulfills the reference made in the Scriptures about the Second Coming of the Christ (our Commander-In-Chief). He will come down from aboard His great Merkabah Lightship, the "City of New Jerusalem," to make sure that all souls who truly want to be free of their karma (at least 51% of their accumulated negative karma must have been transmuted) and who have accepted the Cosmic Law of Grace will "be saved" (evacuated).

There is a reference in scripture that states: "He will gather his 'Elect' from the four winds." To put it another way, these laggards will elect to get off the Wheel of Karma and choose of their own free will to be aligned with God's Divine Will and Plan in order to end their needless suffering. So, now that help has arrived "in mass" and the "hand of Intergalactic friendship" has been extended, they will choose to be rescued and will be taken up "in the twinkling of an eye."

Back in the 1970's, I remember hearing a news story that both Mt. Palomar and Wilson Observatories had detected a gigantic, cube-shaped object (even Carl Sagan mentioned this at one time) which they estimated was about 1,500 miles by 1,500 miles across. The object was estimated to be moving on an exact trajectory toward our solar system from out of what looked like a "black hole" in space. After that initial report, I never heard anything more about it through either the corporate-controlled mainstream media or from NASA. But, my "Friends Upstairs" assured me that what they had seen was the huge "City of New Jerusalem" ship, which is over 1,500 miles across and which is Jesus the Christ's Ship of the Jerusalem Command.

I was later informed that (in the late 1980's) this gigantic Merkabah Ship came into position over this planet (on the Higher dimensions), and that it has been stationed there, off and on, since then. It has gone back and forth to other locations, as well, but when the dimensions have completed merging together and the planet (and all on it) has completed the shift from the 3rd to the 5th dimensional level (most likely by 2012 or after), then this huge city-ship will materialize over the planet. And, believe me, something that large, 1,500 miles across, "every eye will see or behold it!" It is, then, that those souls that are finally "Graduating" will suddenly be "lifted up in the clouds" into HEAVEN (in smaller scout ships which will take these souls up to the City of New Jerusalem) to meet our great Commander-In-Chief, Himself, as has always been promised to all "Believers." This does not have anything to do with any one particular religion on Earth, but, rather, it deals with the intent and motive of individuals and whether they treated others as they wanted to be treated themselves (the Golden Rule). These people are those, referred to as the "Chosen Ones," because they "Choose to be Chosen," just as they have chosen to align their free will with the Divine Will.

After individuals arrive aboard the mother ship they will go through the rejuvenation chambers where they will experience total physical rejuvenation and psychological balancing. Then, they will receive beautiful crystal pendants and either golden-colored robes or jumpsuits to wear (depending on their classification). These will identify them as "Returning Volunteers." Next, they will have the wonderful opportunity of reuniting with their Cosmic Relatives, as well as the Extended Cosmic Family, that they had not seen since taking Earth embodiment. The Hierarchy has always stated, as well, that all of the Volunteers who have been separated from their "Cosmic Other-Half's" (Twin Soul Mates) since taking embodiment on this planet will be reunited during these series of Waves, never to be separated again. This time, the Divine Creator has promised those of us (who have endured the sadness of so many separations in order to fulfill hundreds or even thousands of "Special Missions" to Liberate this planet) that we have earned the right to never be separated again.

When we are reunited, during this sacred Cosmic "Welcome Home" party, we will be serenaded with the harmonious "Celestial Music of the Spheres," which is a combination of the most glorious and inspiring music ever played. The music will burst forth as "Cosmic Trumpets" are blown in our honor, as with the analogy of victorious warriors returning from battle. In this case, it is the "Special Forces of the Confederation" (Secret Agents of God) returning from our Missions for the Federation of Light and Spiritual Hierarchy in the great Spiritual-Consciousness War battling against the dark forces.

This particular scene of total Cosmic Reuniting cannot adequately be expressed in human words. The best I can do is to say that there will be intense joy and ecstasy (like being in HEAVEN, which it is) that all of us will be feeling during those incredible moments--which is why it has been referred to as "The Rapture."

We cannot even imagine the utter bliss of seeing the gigantic crowds of Cosmic Relatives and being able to embrace our own Twin Soul after being separated for so long. Of course, all of these reunitings are happening simultaneously aboard the many ships at the same time. There have been so many serving in "Guardian Action" for so many years (Earth time), waiting patiently for this sublime moment of fulfillment of "welcoming back" so many dedicated and valiant souls of Light.

There are many great parties, celebrations, and ceremonies that are being planned for those of us returning. Some will be large ceremonies with all our Cosmic Relatives, and other celebrations will be very intimate, as Divine Couples have numerous romantic "candlelight dinners" where they may observe the Earth below through crystal clear windows, while sitting in one of many "Light Clubs." These Light Clubs will have the opposite effect on one's essence (compared to the night clubs on Earth that tend to lower one's vibes), so that as one drinks the different types of "nectar of the gods," one's vibes will be spiritually uplifted! The Light Clubs will also have numerous delectable entries for the couples to savor, that even the best gourmet cook on Earth would envy! And, they will be able to meet Galactic beings from all over the universe. Additionally, couples will also enjoy a "Higher dimensional intergalactic sensuality" that is experienced on these Higher worlds.

Due to the "time" differences, there will (appear) be more time on this Higher dimensional realm, so that one has much more time to "catch up on things" that one had to "temporarily go without" while we have been gone on our Missions. This will include things like personal fulfillment and other enjoyments that we "took for granted" while on these Higher realms (in between our individual Earth Missions). Another thing that the ET at Squaw Peak Park reminded me of, and that I also have memory of, is that during this period of "Cosmic R & R," the Light Workers that are beamed up in the Waves of Evacuation, who were previously Eagle Commanders and Commandresses (prior to Earth embodiment) will be allowed to use their own personal Merkabah Lightships (that they had before going to Earth).

Volunteers will have also accumulated a lot of what is termed "Cosmic Hazardous Duty Pay" (not referring to money) while being on our Special Missions on this planet. Since they do not have a economic system on these Higher worlds; it is more like what some refer on Earth as "brownie points," in other words, positive karmic rewards for having done good deeds and for having endured numerous lifetimes of service as Volunteers. These types of service records count especially toward wonderful and beautiful experiences that we have earned--the ecstasies of Heaven! Understand, though, that Volunteers have done the work that they were sent to do, not for the reward, but for compassionate purposes and in order to fulfill their duties.

Cosmic Couples Travel to the Inner Earth

After a few days of this wonderful "Cosmic R & R" time, the millions of Reunited Cosmic Couples will prepare to travel back to Earth, but this time it is to visit the Inner (Hollow) Earth civilization known as Agartha, which is also a member of the Confederation. This is where Admiral Bryd visited in 1947 when he flew through the polar opening. This was documented in his secret log (diary). (This will be presented in book four of The Divine Blueprint Series: Who's Who in the Cosmic Directory.)

There will be several sacred "Cosmic Wedding Ceremonies and Celebrations" that emphasis their Eternal Love and devotion for each other. The first one of these will be held (while within the Earth's interior) at the golden-crystal-domed wedding temple in Shamballah (the Capital City of Agartha, also known as

Arianni, from Admiral Byrd's diary). Lord Eon and Lady Shanna, the High Priest and Priestess, will be conducting these "Celestial-Cosmic-Mystical Wedding Ceremonies" for Divine Couples over many days of Inner Earth time. These ceremonies will not just be inspiring experiences, but they will also serve as Spiritual Initiations that will bring greater Harmony and joy to these Divine Couples.

Then, they will begin their "Cosmic Honeymoons," there in Shamballah and in other prominent Inner-Earth Rainbow crystal cities. These Divine Couples will be the guests in the homes (crystal palaces) of many dignitaries of this Inner Earth kingdom, including a visit for a few days to the magnificent crystal Rainbow palace of Lord Pellular and Lady Virgo, the King and Queen of the Inner Earth civilization. (Lord Pellular is the Master that Admiral Byrd met on his 1947 expedition.)

After a few days on these "Cosmic Honeymoons", the Divine Couples will return back, briefly, to the Mother Ships above the Earth. After which, they will depart for their individual "Cosmic homes amongst the stars" where they will enjoy more Cosmic Ceremonies, which are being planned for these Victorious Cosmic Sons and Daughters, who are returning from their Missions.

Immortal Light Bodies

When we made this "Spiritual Ascension," we brought our physical Earth bodies with us. These bodies were then rejuvenated and our energies and vibrations were raised to a Higher harmonic level in the Rejuvenation Chamber. At this point, we were also allowed to access many of the same mental and spiritual/psychic abilities and powers as we had prior to taking Earth embodiment. While we were on Earth, our "Immortal Light Higher-density etheric-physical" bodies were placed in a type of "Cosmic Suspended Animation." During our time aboard the starships, we will be using this more advanced body that is capable of living forever and never aging. During our Cosmic Honeymoons and the two to three weeks of our Cosmic R & R time, we will use these bodies to experience greater levels of joy and fulfillment. Once we return back to Earth on the 3rd dimension, we will place those bodies (again) in that Suspended Animation where they will remain for several years until the end of the Tribulation (final cleansing period). At that time, our Earth bodies and these Light bodies will be merged together (molecularly/cellularly) and we will then be "Galactic/Earth humans," having retained the positive wisdom of the Earth experience, along with the Cosmic Wisdom from all the Higher worlds of the Confederation. We will be considered very unique in all the Intergalactic realms, and will be Cosmic Teachers to help other souls who still need to make their Spiritual Ascensions back to the Source.

Many channels and contactees have remembered (as I have), that these Cosmic Suspended bodies are laying on flat white crystalline slabs with clear crystal-domed coverings over them. They can only be accessed by one's own unique vibrations, kind of like the ultimate "combination security lock." The individual souls do use these bodies during astral visits aboard these ships while their Earth physical bodies are sleeping at night, even though must individuals do not remember these visits.

The reason we will suspend our Cosmic bodies (again) to return back to Earth is so that our Earth relatives and friends who do not possess "Cosmic Sight" (knowing us by our vibrations and energies while in these more advanced Immortal galactic bodies) will be able to recognize us. We will look somewhat different however, due to the rejuvenation process that we experienced. But, at least we will look more familiar to them than we would have had we appeared in our Light bodies.

When the "Secret Wave" occurs, there will be mass numbers of starships, flashing rainbow-colored lights, which will be hovering briefly overhead, and which will be playing beautiful, awe-inspiring Celestial Music of the Spheres for the millions of witnesses who observe these crafts. At the same time, the first Volunteers will suddenly vanish right before the eyes of their friends and relatives. For most people, it will be pretty obvious that something very beautiful and Celestially uplifting (or bizarre and unusual) has just occurred. How people interpret it will depend on their level of awareness or consciousness.

This aspect has never been clearly defined in the present-day Biblical description of the "Rapture." Part of the confusion surrounding this is based on a couple of things: the "Councils of Nicia" began manipulating the scriptures in the early 2nd Century and, then, later on in the early 4th Century, Constantine, as well as others, altered the scriptures even more. The "Celestial connection-explanation" of the "clouds of heaven" being responsible for all these people suddenly disappearing (vanishing in a blink of the eye) has, in my opinion, confused many. For instance, the more orthodox religious people assume a somewhat different explanation of the exact "removal process" that God and His Celestial Host will use to take all these people up on a mass level.

Biochips & the Second Amendment Right to Bare Arms

The cabal knows very well what these Higher Forces of Light plan to do when they execute their "Cosmic Rescue" plans, so they may attempt to declare martial law, if possible, before the Secret wave occurs. This will be, of course, an attempt to avert the Divine Plan of God, but they are deluded in thinking that God and His Celestial Host would allow His Chosen Ones to become "Planetary Prisoners of War" under a corrupt "New World Order" regime. It is **not** our karma or part of the plan to be "thrown to the wolves." It is our dharma (positive karma) to be lifted up to safety and return as "Planetary Liberation Reconnaissance Teams" to rescue all others who want a better life and the end of all suffering.

The Federation of Light is waiting until the last possible moment. At the present time, the Higher Cosmic Energies of Light are hitting the planet with increasing velocity. Very soon, these organized dark forces will disperse, just like the analogy of cockroaches scattering when the light is suddenly turned on. So, too, these "Earth cockroaches" are about to "flip out" and "lose it." When they see this Secret Wave occur with the dramatic manifestation of so many Rainbow Lightships, they (who are in such denial of the Divine Plan of God) will be so threatened about their power base being destroyed, that they will panic. As a result, they may attempt to instigate some form of martial law, which, in turn, would allow the Blackwater mercenaries to begin their door-to-door "search and seizure" and "patriot assassinations" of those who are a threat to the New World Order (those who want to protect our 2nd Amendment Right to bare arms).

Point of fact: Had the Jews not given up their right to bare arms, there would have been no Holocaust, because they would have defended their homes and fought back. They would have stopped the Nazi's from massacring them and throwing them into the concentration camps. It is also a fact that the "outlaw-all-guns-in-this-country" crowd ignores, that the Swiss, who requires it's citizens (of this Free Country) to own and know how to use personal firearms, have never been attacked in modern times. This is because others (such as Hitler) knew that the Swiss would definitely fight to defend their rights and freedoms, if they attempted to attack them. It is also a fact that the use of firearms to commit a "crime" in Switzerland is extremely low, as compared to other countries where the use of firearms has been mostly or totally outlawed. Crime has actually been reduced somewhat, in a few states in the U. S. that have laws allowing the right to carry "concealed" weapons. In these states, criminals do not know who might be wearing a concealed weapon, so they may be more afraid to attempt a crime.

The New World Order forces of the cabal, who have controlled the main-stream media, would like to disarm this country, so they could then take over without firing a shot. So, they have secretly orchestrated a number of evil plans that have created certain tragedies from "behind the scenes," such as the Columbine High School massacre several years ago. Kurt Billings is a very thorough researcher who has been a guest on the Art Bell national radio program. He has thoroughly documented how the government for many years has been developing the biochip (or transponder microchip) and how large numbers of the unsuspecting public have had this secretly inserted in their bodies through vaccination programs. This biochip is so small (five times smaller than a human hair) that it can easily go threw the head of a vaccination needle. This level of bioengineering and medical technology has actually been around since the late 1980's.

Certain researchers, including Mr. Billings, found out that prior to the Columbine High School massacre, most of the incidences of someone shooting numerous people in a public place "for no reason" were attributed to an "insane" person. These "deranged" individuals were usually former patients from a mental hospital that the CIA had (secret) control over and they were hypnotically programmed through MK-Ultra mind-control programs (like the "Manchurian Candidate"). Then, the biochip vaccination program started. Since it is easy to know who has had one of more vaccinations in recent years, all the cabal has had to do now is to "activate" these biochips in people--as they did at Columbine High School. When these biochips are activated, it can cause some people to (psychotronically) "flip-out" and the general public has no way of knowing what really caused it. The good news is that not everyone can be "triggered" by these biochips. Those who are most susceptible to them are people who have very low consciousness levels and poor health habits.

As a result of these types of mass killings in the past, the public has ignorantly demanded more restrictive gun laws, so that our 2nd Amendment Right to bare arms is again threatened. This has been their secret agenda and objective to totally disarm this country. During the 1930s as Hitler was gaining power, the corrupt German government passed Fascist laws that forced disarmament of their country. (Jay Simkin, head of "Jews for the Preservation of Firearms," has noted that the gun laws that were passed in Nazi Germany are, coincidently, almost exactly like the laws that have been passed in this country and the same propaganda has been used in recent years.) After those laws were passed in Germany, the citizens were powerless to stop the Nazis when they marched in and took over. Many historical scholars see an ominous parallel between Nazi Germany and the most recent U. S. administrations. That parallel is due to the burning down of the Reichstag Parliament Building that was officially blamed on "communist terrorists" and the false-flag inside-job of 911 that was officially blamed on "Middle-Eastern terrorists." Another parallel is that Hitler forced the "Enabling Act" and other fascist (unconstitutional) laws upon the German population and Bush has forced the "Homeland Security Act" and the "Patriot Act" upon American citizens.

The U. S. is almost to the point where, if it was not for Divine Intervention, the New World Order (using Blackwater mercenaries) would be able to totally take over this country in the same way. This is especially true nowadays with their more advanced "black budget technology" and the constant programming of the ignorant public through the corporate-controlled media. But, because the Internet in recent years has become a valuable source of unbiased information there has been an awakening of the general population.

Another example regarding gun control happened in Australia during the late 1990's. Crime shot up by a huge percentage, when the corrupt government there passed laws on gun control. So, we need to pay attention to history and know that we are not going to eliminate crime or terrorist acts by giving up our guns, for if law-abiding citizens give up their guns then "only the criminals will have guns" **(except for the government, of course!!).**

For years now, the CIA and other "alphabet soup agencies" of the government has had this biochip technology and they have had many of their "programmed terrorists" fulfill these "unexplained" mass murders. So, now after many years, society has (in a way) become psychologically conditioned to these massacres and is getting tired of these "senseless killings" of so many innocent victims. This has played right into the cabal's plan of slowly disarming the mass population by passing more and more gun laws and chipping away at everyone's freedoms.

We all want to see an age of total peace, a Golden Age, truly manifesting upon this planet, but not at the sake of losing all our freedoms and sovereignty being taken from us under the pretense of something else. The truth is that until the '08 election our politicians and government officials tended to be very corrupt and were nothing more than "puppets" for the cabal, and the masses were so numbed and dumbed down until the recent "Planetary Frequency Consciousness Shift." In fact, this has been the most dysfunctional planet in the entire Universe.

However, we are <u>NOW</u> headed in a new direction. It is taking the Divine Intervention of a much more-advanced, fair, and humane Galactic civilization to help bring about (and guarantee) the necessary changes for the better. We are also receiving the assistance of the "Cosmic Backup Teams" of the Federation of Light, who are helping the recently awakened population to quickly turn this country, and the entire planet, around for the better.

Once the Secret Wave (First Contact) has happened, suddenly and dramatically, there will be no turning back as far as Divine Intervention is concerned. While those of us (who are taken up in the Secret Wave) are gone, much could be happening upon the surface of the planet that could pose some major "challenges" for us when we return.

The cabal could begin broadcasting a "false-flag" alien invasion scenario through the mainstream media claiming that these people (one million) were abducted (against their will) by gray aliens, who will be returning shortly to kidnap the rest of humanity. They could claim that people were taken to be used for horrible genetic experiments. Then, the cabal could Officially and openly attempt to declare martial law.

Furthermore, the cabal could stress that everyone who is connected with these "abductees" must now protect themselves from being taken also and the cabal could offer a governmental plan that would "guarantee" the safety of individuals by offering them "sanctuary." This plan by "Big Brother" would be used to create F.E.A.R. (False Evidence Appearing Real!!!) and to convince everyone to allow themselves to be taken to one of the "electronically-secure detention facilities" (concentration camps) that the cabal has already prepared just for this type of "fake" emergency.

Through this false "alien invasion" scenario, they would be desperately attempting to convince people to do just that. Although these people might not normally be this gullible, they might be "triggered off" by previous "programming," if they have not allowed themselves to be attuned to the recent "Planetary Consciousness Shift." Such manipulation could be brought about through the use of HAARP and numerous other mind-control procedures, such as the biochips that have been secretly placed in their bodies through vaccination programs. The cabal might also offer to the public a wonderful "product" that would claim to help protect the public from the evil aliens. For those who agree to this, they would then receive an "implant" (biochip/transponder). Of course, there are many of the public that already have one that they are not even aware of it. The propaganda could emphasize that having a biochip implanted will protect them because the aliens would not be able to approach them without being detected. Of course, the true purpose of this "wonderful little implant" would be to allow the cabal to monitor and control them. Unfortunately, the desperate, scared citizens who buy into this would be giving up what little freedoms they still have, because they choose to believe this "outlandish" story.

HAARP

Note: HAARP has been used by the cabal to create powerful artificial hurricanes, such as "Andrew" that hit the Homestead area of Florida in the early '90's. Using the HAARP technology, the cabal artificially created this horrible hurricane from a smaller storm. They have also used HAARP technology to create unnaturally powerful tornadoes that devastated large areas of Oklahoma. It is also very likely that the bridge that collapsed in 2007 in Minnesota was either triggered by HAARP or certainly by a similar type system.

There are millions of us who suspect that not only was hurricane Katrina artificially created by HAARP from a smaller storm and aimed directly at New Orleans by the cabal to destroy the city, but also we know that it was not just the hurricane that destroyed the city. It is a fact that the levees were actually blown up by Blackwater mercenaries. A number of local citizens who lived near the levees testified that they heard explosions going off and moments later the area started flooding. Later on, during the rescue and cleanup process, the crews actually discovered residue from the explosives that was used to blow up the levees.

I was watching on TV when the presiding mayor of New Orleans made the public announcement about ordering the police and local law enforcement to confiscate everyone's guns. When he made this announcement, it appeared as though he was acting the part rather than being himself. It was almost like he was being forced to state this or maybe he was actually being "psychotronically" controlled (like the "Manchurian Candidate") by a powerful psychic beam aimed at him. Or perhaps he had a biochip in him that was suddenly activated, like the "whack jobs" who grab their guns and start shooting in schools and other public places. After the mayor made this statement, they literally forced all the law-abiding citizens to give up their guns or they would have been shot.

I believe this was a "test case" by the cabal to see if they could create a situation in which the local population would be totally disarmed by using a combination of both "normal" means and more "exotic" means. They wanted to see if this could easily be done for any possible future man-made (false-flag) disaster where martial law could be declared, just as they did with Katrina.

However, I believe that their plan backfired, because numerous people, including some local officials, began to put two and two together and it has become obvious how "off the wall" and, definitely, unconstitutional this whole thing was. The fact is that the Mayor ordered local law enforcement to confiscate the guns from thousands of local law-abiding citizens who had licenses to have them. The 2nd Amendment of our constitution specifically states that we, the citizens, have a Right to own guns to protect ourselves. So, what they did was totally unconstitutional, just as numerous other unconstitutional, illegal, and immoral things have been allowed by our corrupt officials. For example during the Bush administration, they suspended Habeas Corpus for prisoners and this was just one of the many *crimes against humanity* that the cabal committed in their insidious attempt to force the fascist-"Fourth Reich" New World Order upon us.

The National Rifle Association came to the aid of the citizens of New Orleans, because they were also aware of this insidious plan to attempt to disarm this country by causing people to react through F.E.A.R. and then outlawing weapons through legislation. Following the disaster, the N.R.A. went to New Orleans and interviewed hundreds of law-abiding citizens, who all basically told the same story that they were forced at gun-point to give up their own licensed guns. And, because of this, they were then at the mercy of the criminal elements who take advantage of such disasters. They further noted that it seemed that none of the criminals were being arrested and it was obvious that the priority of the officials was to focus on confiscating the citizen's guns.

The N.R.A. uncovered these facts and set to work organizing a backlash to this agenda of the cabal. They did this by galvanizing numerous people all over the country, who were in contact with these citizens from New Orleans, and made everyone aware that what happened in New Orleans could happen to them in other areas. Thus, the general public was officially "put on notice" that what had occurred was an unconstitutional act and they should be prepared to confront anyone attempting to take away their guns and their rights. This, of course, was not what the cabal had expected, and, as a result of these actions, other mayors, state governors, and local officials are starting to make a stand against the cabal.

The Cabal & Abductions

Even many of those, who are amongst the ones waiting to be beamed up during the later Evacuation waves, may be fooled into believing (as it was prophesied Biblically that "the Elect will be fooled") that their immortal souls are now in danger on a mass level from these evil "grays." Since the 1970's, the propaganda from the agents of disinformation (cabal) has been presenting evidence about the grays, and their abductions, in an effort to convince the public about these aliens. Initially, this was true (back in the '70's and '80's), but then the Confederation began to capture these renegade aliens and put a stop to these abductions--the "Heavens were being cleansed" in preparation for the "Rapture," as was Prophesied in the Bible.

The truth is that, in the late 1980's and 1990's, most of the abductions that occurred were actually being performed by the cabal, as they had learned how to clone these original gray aliens. The cabal, who had a Treaty with the grays, then began to copy their abductions using "artificial gray alien clones" (manufactured right here on Earth). The reasoning for this "faked alien invasion scenario" was so that if the cabal publicly and Officially attempts to declare that the Earth is being invaded, then some people might believe them!

President Reagan made the following comment (at least six times): "What if we were to suddenly discover that we all on this planet had a threat from beyond earth...wouldn't we all then band together against this common threat?" You see, the cabal has run out of mundane Earth enemies, so now they want to manufacture a new, more-sophisticated enemy, in other words "aliens." It is theorized that the New World Order forces loved this statement, for they have used it to attempt to psychologically gear us all up to accept their ultimate "Official Announcement."

Taking all this into account, one of the reasons that the Federation of Light wanted **this** book to be published ahead of time was to help prepare everyone for what could happen. The hope is that the public will not believe it if the cabal attempts to fool them into believing this "faked alien invasion" scenario, and are then "led to the slaughter," just as the Jews were led to the slaughter and Holocaust. In the past, these evil forces have manipulated the minds of otherwise discerning individuals by their biased presentation of evidence (cramming the grays down everyone's throats and suppressing and debunking authentic benevolent human-appearing ET experiences). Or so the spin doctors of the UFO community like Jeromee Clark, Bud Hopkins, David Jacobs, Stanton Friedman, and all the others would have us believe. Yes, New World Order forces are really proud of these ones who have confused the minds of such gullible people for so long.

It is now time (as I will be documenting in-depth in the 2nd book of The Divine Blueprint Series: The Cover-Up on Human-Appearing ETs) to expose them for what they really are, and to show how they have twisted the facts around to fit their narrow view of reality. They have acted morally unconscionable in fulfilling their individual and collective hidden agendas. But, now "their day is done" and they will be exposed as agents of hopelessness for taking away the dreams and visions of a better world that is free of terror and F.E.A.R. (False-Evidence-Appearing-Real!).

Chemtrails

Another subject, which Mr. Billings has thoroughly documented, is chemical contrails. These "chemtrails" are being released from unmarked, remote-controlled aircraft of all kinds and are observed by millions of people every day over the entire U. S. A "normal" aircraft contrail will dissipate and disappear quickly (usually within one minute), but these "chemtrails" last for an extended period of time (with the planes either going back and forth covering the sky or covering the sky in a grid pattern).. In order to document it, numerous people have filmed these unmarked aircraft. The FAA has assured the public that this is not true, however, these aircraft are flying what is clearly a "grid-pattern" flight path, which (literally) crisscrosses the skies over a particular area--first flying back and forth (such as east and west) and then flying back and forth (north and south)--covering the entire area. As a result, when the sun shines through this "chemtrail grid" area, it looks like "oily" clouds.

There have also been numerous people who have reported seeing strange "gooey" gelatinous material falling out of the sky and when they have handled this unexplained "stuff," they have gotten very sick. In all the areas where this strange grid-pattern has been observed and documented, it was also documented (through medical reports) that there was a great increase in immune system diseases, respiratory illnesses, and health problems, in general. These health problems have "coincidently" been on the increase since this secret spraying has been happening. Both the FCC and military agencies deny that anything "out of the normal" has been going on, and, yet, there are large numbers of people being poisoned from this. Art Bell did a number of shows on this subject that attempted to get to the bottom of it and find out what the officials were hiding, and, if there was anything the average citizen could do to protect themselves from this horrible poisoning of the atmosphere.

One definite fact, that has been well-documented by Kurt Billings (among others) is that (in the late 1990s) the FAA changed the fuel mixture for all commercial flights from "JP-4" to "JP-8." The type of fuel that is now being used contains one or more very poisonous chemical and biological poisons that are known to weaken respiratory and immune functions.

At a "Preparedness Expo" in 1999, Kurt did a very excellent seminar titled "The Biochip and the Contrails: America's Most Thinly Veiled Secrets." In this seminar, he clearly introduced the numerous forms of mind control, such as HAARP that the CIA, NSA, and the cabal have been using on unsuspecting citizens for many years. Until recently, with their more advanced methods (negatively synergistically combined) using the biochip and the advanced tracking capabilities of the Echelon spy satellites, they were able to establish complete control over the average, uninformed, and uneducated persons of society, **however, now with the "Planetary Frequency Consciousness Shift, things have changed.**

[To anyone interested, I highly recommend ordering materials from Kurt Billing's presentations. Refer to product page at the back of the book.]

What he has stated has been confirmed by numerous ex-intelligence and undercover agents that I have met through the years. There were just too many confirmations to ignore or attempt to explain them away. And on top of that, my

"Friends Upstairs" have also confirmed his information from their vantage point of having closely monitored the cabal's evil plans and manipulations. As I have stated many times in recent years, yes, the cabal can monitor us--but guess who is monitoring them! And, as my "Friends Upstairs" have jokingly stated "Big Space Brother" is monitoring them (two can play this game)!

So, Light Workers (Volunteers) have nothing to worry about, since in truth, "there are no secrets in the Universe." If one can monitor anyone or anything, then, what is important is the reason and intent of why someone would want to monitor another. There are completely different reasons why the cabal has monitored people and why the Confederation is monitoring those of us who are their emissaries and why they closely monitor the cabal's negative manipulations. Our "Cosmic Back-Up Teams" (off the planet on these Higher dimensions) are very carefully scrutinizing the plans and activities of these dark forces (24/7) so that they know if we Volunteers are in any kind of life-threatening situation.

Economic Outlook

One of the many things that I was told by the Being at Squaw Peak Park, which now should not occur, was the "666-Mark of the Beast" system that was to have ushered in a total cashless society. The reason that this has changed is that the Higher Forces (since the early 1980's) have "hijacked" the cabal's plan. Now, the entire banking system is being changed into what some have referred to as the "Basil II" system, which leads into the implementation and announcement of N.E.S.A.R.A. (National Economic Security And Reformation Act). This exciting and wonderful development is actually an alteration of the original future timeline by Higher Forces. The result of what has been happening, behind the scenes in the last few years, will create a miraculous economic outcome for the masses and the end of the cabal's economic power over humanity.

The cabal had plans to create "The North American Union" that was to be made up of the U.S., Mexico, and Canada by abolishing the borders between these countries and secretly printing up the "Amerio" bills as their "new" currency. But, now, even these recent plans of the cabal most likely will not be able to be implemented, because of the NESARA (Reformation Act) plan for economic salvation for all humanity. NESARA will put an end to the cabal's economic control and the abolishing of the Federal Reserve banking system and return the monetary system to one that is constitutionally backed by precious metals. All of this has been set in motion "behind the scenes" by the Higher forces, which is throwing off the plans of total world control by the cabal. (More on this in the third book of The Divine Blueprint Series: UFOs, ETs & Divine Intervention.)

I was told by the Being that, originally, (prior to these positive changes) numerous and horrendous economic disasters were being planned. The world "elite power-brokers" had planned to instigate a major economic crash by manipulating the stock market and the economy far worse than even the $700 plus billion "bail out." In desperation, the people would have been open to the government's new "solution" to solving their economic woes. The solution that was originally planned was to usher in a cashless society that would involve having a biochip placed in everyone's arms. So, then, all they had to do was to scan their arms whenever they wanted to purchase something. They would be assured that with this system it was literally impossible for others to steal or duplicate their identity. Plus, this system would also provide for their safety, as they would be monitored 24/7 by the police (or "special security" forces). This was similar to the "Lojack" system that has been placed in cars, so the police can track the vehicle if it is stolen. Then, the evil forces "perfected" the "Lojack" system, so it could be used on humans--this "L.U.C.I.D. Beast 666 system!

This proposed total cashless society that was almost forced upon us, especially with the "Real I.D. system," was recently halted, due to the mass Awakening upon the planet and because the Higher Forces are stepping in to stop these insidious hidden agendas of total control. Initially, before the NESARA system began to be set up behind the scenes, what the Being told me (that day back in the early 1980's) was a very accurate assessment of what would have occurred on that particular timeline, but now, thankfully, this has been altered for the better. At that time, the banks and economic institutions were merging, all privacy was quickly disappearing, everyone was being tracked by the cabal with the Global Positioning System (GPS) and monitored by spy satellites (even more-advanced than what was presented in the movie "Enemy of the State"!!), and numerous people were placing biochips in their pets (and more recently, even in their children) which can be tracked by a GPS System--oh, what security and safety!

The advanced "L.U.C.I.D. 666 Beast system" (referred to by Tex Mars in his book The L.U.C.I.D. Project, the 666 Universal Beast System) was almost totally upon us with only a few steps lacking before it could be fully enforced on everyone (mandatory). That was the situation until the recent "consciousness" shift (planetary wakeup call) occurred. This "666" system might still be partially instigated, if millions allow themselves to be fooled by a "faked alien invasion" scenario and allow the cabal to mislead them into totally being monitored and controlled. This scenario could be enforced by the cabal through the HAARP and other advanced electronic global black-op mind-control technologies. So, hopefully, this book (along with the "Planetary Frequency Consciousness Shift") will succeed in warning many people of this possible scenario before it could be attempted by the cabal.

Communication between Loved Ones

Also, when these first Volunteers are taken up aboard the Merkabah Lightships, they will be telepathically communicating (off and on) with their biological family, relatives, and friends who are still on Earth. This will be done to help counteract the possible blatant misinformation and negative propaganda that could be projected by the mass media. Normally, these family members could be too low in vibrations for someone else to telepathically communicate with them, but with the specific biological-genetic link that we have had with them on Earth, we will be able to clearly and intensely communicate with them.

These conversations (between those on the starships and those on Earth) may be something like: "Hello, this is -----, and yes, you are truly picking up my thoughts. I was not kidnapped against my will; I can assure you that this is so. I chose to go and I went willingly. These Beings are not the evil gray aliens, as the media and government would have you believe. They are truly our Space Brothers and Sisters and are beautiful human-appearing and compassionate Beings who truly care about this planet and everyone on it. Do not let the media persuade you to believe otherwise and do not let them influence you with their negative subliminals. Instead, please quiet your conscious mind and go within to meditate and pray. Ask God and His angels to give you the Inner Truth of what I have just shared with you. Know that this is true--not what the government officials want you to believe. In about two to three weeks time, I will be returning, as will the rest of us who were taken up as well. Then, you will also be given the chance to be taken up to experience the most beautiful, wonderful, and joyous occurrence that you could ever have. This will be similar to the movie "Cocoon," but much better, for **this is real** and includes God, His angels and the Celestial Host! This is the Rapture that was spoken of in the Bible. What has not been fully understood by most people on Earth is that the Rapture involves more than one wave of Evacuation, so that everyone has every opportunity to return to God and Heaven. The Bible also warns Humanity that, "the Elect will be fooled," so do not let this happen to you and become a victim to the government's charade. I plead with you to listen to your heart and Inner Self (the voice of God) and know that what I am telepathically telling you right now is true. Be strong and have Faith and know that I am okay."

Those individuals who are receiving the telepathic messages on Earth will know for sure that this is happening because of the intensity and strength of the message, as well as the love and joy that they will feel as a part of this experience. The one's sending the messages will be using very advanced "Elohim Consciousness Technology" to accomplish this, so we will be very successful with these communications.

Overshadowing & Exposure

This is just one type of communication that will be utilized by the Federation of Light. Communication experts for the Ashtar Command (like the Space Brothers Korton, Raymere, and Andromeda Rex) are specialists in all forms of Intergalactic communication from telepathic (mental/psychic) to telecommunications (with specific computers/machines). Within seconds, they can "Overshadow," totally disrupt, and take control of all forms of Earth's communications facilities (for positive reasons). This has been demonstrated numerous times, such as the famous November 1977 incident in Great Britain. For five and one-half minutes, extraterrestrials broadcast a message without the officials being able to stop them. The officials tried to explain this as "college students somehow pirating their signal." This, of course, was not possible due to the FCC law that requires that all broadcast facilities have "test insertion signals," in case someone should use foul language on the air, etc. These test insertion signals create a few seconds delay of the actual broadcast signal being sent out from the station, so they always have time to "bleep" out whatever they want or to even shut it down, if they so chose. However, in spite of this system being in place, this specific transmission from the Confederation was broadcast anyway.

After these personal telepathic messages to our loved ones, we will then be broadcasting directly from the mother ships through the Earth's T.V. and radio facilities--what was up until now corporate-controlled Fox Network, ABC, CBS, NBC, CNN, UPI, and Associated Press, etc.--without them being able to stop us or shut their systems down while we are transmitting. We will reconfirm what we each personally (telepathically) sent to our Earth family members and friends, emphasizing the same message "not to believe the Earth Officials."

In addition to our personal messages, many of the Higher members of the Ashtar and Jerusalem Commands (and others) of the Federation of Light will be broadcasting special transmissions of their own that will include important messages and offers to help this planet. They will also be broadcasting numerous scenes (from secret films that are stored at the Pentagon and other secret military bases) that were secretly filmed by military film crews that document attempts by the Confederation to diplomatically assist in the positive cultural advancement of this planet (such as President Eisenhower's '54 meeting with members of the

Confederation at Edwards Air Force Base). It will also show that the corrupt government officials turned down the proposals of the Federation of Light and chose, instead, to work with the renegade gray aliens.

They made this choice because they did not want to abide by the ethical and moral standards of conduct that the Confederation required. So, they chose the other alternative of working with the gray aliens. They made an agreement with them that the grays could abduct Earth citizens in exchange for advanced gray alien technology. It was, of course, a very poor choice for many reasons; one being that the Confederation has even more advanced "consciousness technology" than the grays do. Plus, the Confederation would have shared this technology with the general population which would have eliminated all suffering and hardship of any kind from the face of the Earth. They also would have forced the world leaders to answer for their corrupt transgressions and they would have exposed the major governments' cover-up of extraterrestrial contact. The Confederation would then have pleaded for the population to forgive these corrupt leaders, partly because they must be forgiven, if they are willing to take full responsibility and make amends. Part of this would include that these leaders must give full disclosure and officially acknowledge the "cover-ups" and allow the Confederation of Worlds and Universal Alliance of Peace to officially land and have a publicly-open meeting with the world leaders.

This scenario is, in a sense, one final attempt for the Cosmic Forces of Light to create a peaceful transition for this planet into the Golden Age, rather than the One World Dictatorship with a cashless society, and the 666 Beast system that the cabal has been attempting to secretly set up for quite some time. But, considering the "nature of the Beast" and their past record of manipulating humanity, it is most likely that they will not willingly accept this final offer and, instead, they might attempt to instigate martial law throughout the country (as well as in other countries). The Confederation will then release control over the media facilities and everyone will have to use their free will to decide who they believe--the Volunteers and the Confederation (Universal Christ Light forces) or the organized negative New World Order forces of the cabal.

The motion picture "Enemy of the State" was an extremely accurate depiction of the cabal's technological sophistication level and their ability to track and secretly monitor anyone that they have wanted to, no matter where that person happened to be on the planet. It made it easier for them to track someone, when that person had had a vaccination. That is one of the main reasons (besides for destroying the immune system, creating negative health side-effects, and lowering one's consciousness) why government officials tried to force mandatory vaccinations on everyone. People should also be aware that these vaccinations are known to contain very toxic substances.

With these microchips imbedded in everyone, it would be easy to track them 24/7 and individuals could be monitored even more than the actor Will Smith portrayed in this movie. These microchips were designed to have the capability of exposing a person's thoughts and feelings and anyone who attempts to think something contrary to the 666 Beast system, would be taken to the concentration camps or killed, depending upon how much of a threat that person is. This could become real, if mandatory vaccinations are forced upon everyone. Fortunately, Divine Intervention and Worldwide Evacuation provide us with major "guaranteed" hope. Thank God for the Federation of Light and their plan to protect and remove all who want a better way!

Bioengineered Genetic Foods

As hard as this may be to believe, consuming "bioengineered genetic foods" (also known as genetically modified organisms - G.M.O.s) has been negatively, synergistically linked to sophisticated forms of mind-control and the tracking capabilities of the cabal! However, the good news is that this can be changed by developing a new diet routine: (a) Eat only natural, organic foods (and do not consume the "fake" foods that the government has been pushing on us), (b) take plenty of natural vitamins and minerals, and (c) cleanse and detoxify your body (This will dissolve the biochip from your body within a few days, as the PH level in your body will change and the Higher vibratory rate will then neutralize any influence that the cabal had over your life). Once individuals make these changes in their diets and lifestyles, the combination of all this will act together (synergistically) to help raise their vibrations and consciousness, and then they will become much healthier and more powerful Light Workers with stronger immune systems.

The Volunteers Return

Within days of the million Volunteers being lifted up and if the concentration camps are activated throughout the U.S. (under the F.E.M.A. and REX 84 Martial Law), all of a sudden to the chagrin and shock of the cabal, the Volunteers will materialize back on Earth. Then, huge "Rainbow crystal cities" will suddenly spring up "overnight" throughout the country. These bubble- or domed-shaped cities, manifested by the Federation of Light, will be about one-half to one mile in diameter and will be referred to as "Sanctuaries of Protection." In addition to being the home base for the Volunteers, they will also be holistic healing centers. These bubble cities will be part of the Confederation's "consciousness technology" manifestation and will be used to vibrationally and physically prepare the one's who will be taken up in the next Wave. The cities will be temporary and will last only until the end of the Tribulation, when the total cleansing has been completed and when the final Wave of Evacuation has taken place. They will exist for about seven to eight years after the Secret Wave has occurred, so that every soul will have the opportunity to be salvaged through the Cosmic Law of Grace and be able to make their Spiritual Ascension to the Higher dimensional worlds. This is unlike the End Days of Atlantis where souls only had one opportunity to be rescued during the Emergency Evacuation that took place at that time.

Earthlings who come to these cities may be ones who have been rescued from the concentration camps by Teams of the Confederation or they may merely be drawn there by their Inner Guides. The walls of the cities will consist of powerful harmonic-energy that actually serves as ultimate security code protection. The individuals who will be able to (actually) pass right through the walls into the cities are those who possess positive intent and motive within their minds and consciousness. And, what they will feel, as they walk through these walls, will be a mild "tingling" sensation.

On the other hand with this ultimate "Cosmic Security System," anyone having negative or destructive intent and motives (like the Blackwater mercenaries or someone posing as a Light Worker trying to infiltrate it) will never be able to get past the wall. To them it will always be a solid wall of impenetrable material and, regardless of what they attempt to do; they will never be able to penetrate it. Any type of weapon used, whether firearms, missiles, lasers, or psychotronics, will merely bounce off the walls of these domes. The only possible exception might be if a nuclear missile was detonated, but with the Confederation closely monitoring every military installation on the planet, they will be able to neutralize any attempt long before the cabal could accomplish such an act.

Planetary Liberation Vehicles

The ET showed me a vision of an interesting type of vehicle that looked similar to a GM type recreational vehicle (RV) with large windows, a streamlined body, and curved corners. He continued to telepathically project these very compressed images into my mind at a very rapid rate, after which he moved on to giving me other types of information. Then, about a year later, as I was doing a channeled reading for a fellow Star Person and was discussing the upcoming Evacuation, the Higher Beings sent me a very intense vision of hundreds of these particular vehicles being "stacked up" one on top of another within a gigantic storage chamber (hanger) on a mother ship.

It was then explained to me that these were the "Reconnaissance Vehicles" (Planetary Liberation Vehicles) that the Being at Squaw Peak Park had showed me. They are also referred to as "planetary all-terrain-vehicles," because they are capable of operating on any type of Earth surface and can be driven on "impossible" terrain, that even the most rugged-type of Earth vehicles would not be able to get through. If the situation requires it, they also have the ability to navigate underwater in flood or hurricane conditions. (Note: In the comedy movie "Strips," Bill Murray drove a comparable type of vehicle, although it was not near as advanced as are these "Cosmic planetary liberation vehicles.") If necessary, the Returning Volunteers will use these vehicles to help rescue as many souls as possible from the "P.O.W. Camps of Earth" (if they have been activated). These vehicles will have a type of anti-gravity system and will even have flight capability, as well as numerous "consciousness technology" features, such as the power of invisibility. Similar (but not as advanced) anti-gravity cars were depicted in the movie "The Last Star Fighter," where the benevolent alien used a special shuttle-car and, again, in the T.V. show 'Knightrider" that had an advanced Earth computer system that helped overtake criminals.

Besides for the Planetary Liberation Vehicles (PLV's) that could be used to rescue large numbers of people from the concentration camps, some of us would be given "personal earth vehicles," that look like sports cars. These vehicles would be surrounded by a powerful energy force-field which totally protects them against Earth weapons. They too would be powered by a crystal which is telepathically attuned to the crystal pendants that the Volunteers would be wearing at all times and, also, is "telepathically linked" to the "consciousness holographic crystal computer" aboard the mother ships. (Tuella discussed this in depth.)

Prior to 1981, I had some very strong telepathic visions regarding these special crystal powered vehicles and I saw myself traveling around in a beautiful royal-blue sports car (like a cross between a Porsche and a Viper). I saw the pulsating crystal inside the engine compartment and knew that it was totally ecologically in harmony with the environment. I also knew that one day I would be driving this vehicle as a part of my Mission. At Christmas time (about a year later), I had a another strong telepathic vision in which I saw this beautiful blue colored car with a huge red ribbon around it, as if it was a "Christmas present" waiting for me to ultimately use one day, when I needed it. So, in 1981, when I was "officially" shown these larger land transports which would be used to rescue and transport people to freedom, it was a confirmation of the potential use of these types of vehicles during the upcoming planetary transition phase that is leading up to the Golden Age.

The PLVs were purposely made to outwardly look like Earth RVs, so they would appear more familiar (just like the Volunteers returning in their familiar-looking bodies). Never-the-less, this "familiarity link" (with the way things were prior to the total chaos of possible martial law and Divine Intervention) is very important later on so that the masses (who will have to be rescued) will recognize familiar people and vehicles. This "psychological familiarity factor" is something that must be utilized by those of us who will be acting as "Cosmic Liberation Teams" for planet Earth. This Liberation of an entire planet (using advanced "Consciousness Technology") will make the Liberation of Europe at the end of WW II look like "child's play" in comparison.

If needed, these Liberation Teams with obvious Sovereignty and power-fully, advanced-technological capabilities (far more than their captors have) will show up at these "POW camps." The enemy forces will not even be aware of these Liberation Teams as they approach for their vehicles will be powered for invisibility. Then, when the rescuers arrive, they will burst (molecularly merge) through the walls of the concentration camps and, then, physically (temporarily) paralyze the guards. They will ask the captives if they chose to be rescued; we would never force them to go with us, since under the Confederation's policy of "Non-Interference Laws for Planetary Cultures," we are not allowed to "force" or "manipulate" anyone against their free will (as the cabal has been doing for ages). Also, we will never withhold this help when it is needed the most.

One must believe that even the most unconscious person will willingly se-lect to go with these Liberation forces. For up to the point of rescue, these captives will have had there lives destroyed; they will have been rounded up without their consent and moved many miles away from their homes shackled in cattle cars; and they may have seen fellow prisoners tortured and killed, as well as other horrible inhumane treatment of all kinds. Obviously, their lives will never be the same.

Most souls will quickly step forward and accept our hand of friendship and chose SALVATION from the hands of the cabal. Then, we will instantane-ously neutralize and remove the microchip that was implanted in each prisoner and welcome them aboard the PLVs to be transported to the nearest domed city. Once they arrive at the Sanctuary, they will be "reprocessed." This will proceed according to consciousness and awareness levels, as well as how toxic their physical bodies are. (It was discussed earlier about how individuals' bodies will be very toxic, if they have been eating the typical American diet and how this toxicity will prevent them from being able to be physically beamed aboard the Merkabah Lightships.)

Individuals will recognize that they must (by their own free will, of course) put themselves through this holistic lifestyle "crash course" as fast as they can, so that their "harmonic-vibrational" levels can be raised. As they detoxify their bodies and become healthier, they will raise their vibrations above the 200 level mark on the vibrational chart and, ultimately, be able to Spiritually Ascend. Some of the therapies that they will experience during this purifying process are: Detox ionic footbaths (includes "blood-electro-purification"), colonics, and other advanced Earth and Galactic holistic techniques and "cutting-edge" health technology.

As a result of our actions to liberate those in the concentration camps, the cabal would consider us, and everyone associated with us, as outright criminals and would determine that we must be eliminated at all costs. But, very soon thereafter, "True Justice" will be served!

Denial & Prophecies

These dramatic, Earth-shaking events could be almost "too much" for the average, mundane soul to comprehend, let alone survive, under normal conditions. Even though every known religion has prophesized about these End Times, many people have not taken these warnings seriously because of the religious dogma and the fear that it generates. Because of this, they may not be prepared for such "world-shaking and mind-blowing" events. In the past, many people have lived in a state of "denial" and have believed that "things would just keep going on the way they have always have been." Many of these people were the ones who have accused those who "are prepared" of living in some paranoid or fantasy world. As these events dramatically unfold, in the "twinkling of an eye," some of these people will experience a huge initiation (and a Cosmic epiphany) and will no longer be able to continue their Denial.

Spiritual Boot Camp

When I was growing up and used to watch the original T.V. show of "Mission Impossible," I was sure that one day I would be involved in "similar" scenarios as part of the Liberation of this planet from the dark forces. I knew that these would be very interesting, exciting, and challenging real-life adventures that would involve us Volunteers in helping to set this planet free. I was also very much aware of many of the different aspects of the whole Divine Intervention scenario and that the Volunteers would regain their Higher powers and abilities (that we had prior to taking Earth embodiment) and we would have use of "consciousness technology" devices, such as these indestructible vehicles.

Volunteers have had to endure a great amount of spiritual testing during their assignments on the planet. Some, more than others, have had especially difficult experiences and may have even become "bewildered" at times due to the intensity and number of tests that their Higher Selves and the Spiritual Hierarchy has been putting them through. I refer to this period as "Spiritual Boot Camp." Volunteers, of their own free will, are pushed beyond what they think they can initially handle. It is important that they remember, while they are going through this experience, that "God never gives anyone more than they can handle" and that the degree of severity of the tests that they go through are based on their own capabilities and the level of responsibility that is required for their upcoming Missions. Volunteers must prove themselves beyond reproach, so that they will be fully prepared for their Missions. Additionally, since they will be given back their Higher abilities, powers, and the use of "consciousness technology," the Spiritual Hierarchy wants to be assured that they will in no way abuse their roles. And even though we have proven ourselves many times before, there is so much more at stake in this final "go round," that it is critical to test our abilities again. As we will be making many individual decisions that will influence large numbers of people, the Higher Beings have to be sure of how we will handle situations and, yet, stay "compassionately detached," at the same time. They want to be sure that we are not attached to the "emotional vortex" of negative Earth situations and that we will be able to transmute challenging circumstances by allowing the Divine Will and the Cosmic Law of Grace to be fully present and not block it in any way.

The End of the ET's Transmission

The ET, after telepathically transmitting all this compressed information, then turned away, walked off, and disappeared--as I continued to give my impromptu little lecture for a few minutes more. I have always wished that I could have had a chance to personally interact with him. But, I understand why this occurred as it did, and I know that this was how it was originally planned to happen by the Galactic Council. The important thing is all the information that I was given and how this was the "final" confirmation of what I was previously given when God merged with us in the Higher Council. After this occurred, everything was verified that I had been told and it is all manifesting as part of the Divine Plan.

I have also been warned (very intently) of the continual need for using great discernment, because of the tactics of the dark forces and what they might attempt to do to "fool the Elect" and deter us from our Missions; or to take away our faith and purpose; or to confuse and disempower us; etc. Yes, a great Spiritual Armageddon is being waged right now with the dark forces attempting to throw off the Divine Plan, the Divine Will, and the Divine Blueprint of God. We must all be strong and help enlighten others who may have "lost their way" or who have allowed themselves temporarily to become "victims" of the dark forces. Of course, we know that there really are no "victims" for everyone makes their own decisions as to whether they agree or disagree with the dark forces and their forms of manipulation.

Many have had to learn about this type of discernment and how to recapture their own free will. There have also been certain prominent Light Workers who were used by the dark forces to try to throw off the faith of others.

Fortunately, this "reign of terror" by the dark forces (cabal) will soon be over! Thank God!!! And, so it will be, that as the "Secret" Wave of Evacuation (First Contact) occurs and is followed by three major waves (exoduses) off the planet, then, Earth will experience a complete axis shift and total cleansing. Then, "A New Heaven and A New Earth" will manifest on a Higher dimensional level of Earth and the Golden Age of Peace will manifest upon Earth, as it now once more becomes an Official member of the Intergalactic Confederation of Worlds.

Exciting Last Minute Confirmation of Mass Planetary Divine Intervention

Just as we were completing the editing for this book and were ready to send the final manuscript to the publishers, a very exciting confirmation occurred that verified the reality of mass planetary Divine Intervention and Worldwide Evacuation. On December 13, 2008, I had a very special guest on my Internet Radio Show "Cosmic Connection." (This show is archived and can be found in the "schedule section" at Achieveradio.com.)

My guest was David Sereda, who is an author, UFO researcher, and film producer and director. David is very knowledgeable about many subjects, but, particularly, in regard to NASA's space shuttle UFO film footage. He is one of those rare individuals who is comfortable with either "left-brain" thinking (about advanced technical-scientific research and development projects) or "right-brain" thinking (New Age spiritual and metaphysical subjects). David's interests and endeavors have included: advanced technological research; professional photography (over 20 years); studies in world religion, science, physics, and paranormal psychology (over 25 years); and he has worked on a variety of environmental and humanitarian issues.

He is the author of <u>Evidence, the Case for NASA UFOs</u> and has produced the documentary film "Mona Lisa's Little Secret." One of his more well-known research projects, which he has documented very thoroughly on film, is known as the Space Shuttle STS-75 "Tether Incident" which occurred on February 25, 1996. This incident (of the 12 mile long tether breaking off of the shuttle) shows literally dozens, if not hundreds, of UFOs (or Higher dimensional spaceships) moving around (traveling in front of and behind) the tether.

The confirmation (which I mentioned above) occurred during my Internet show when David was talking about his own numerous experiences with extraterrestrials. He explained that he has also had many visitations and communications with Ashtar, especially, in recent years as he opened up more spiritually to the Higher realities. He stated that he had never (consciously) heard of Tuella until one night in 2007 when he had a very vivid "dream-vision" in which Ashtar and a woman, who looked like she was in her thirties, appeared to him. The woman identified herself as Tuella. (She was in her Higher Density space body, having left her Earth incarnation more than fifteen years ago.) During the "dream-vision," both Tuella and Ashtar specifically referred to the reality of the upcoming Worldwide Evacuation.

Next, David shared the following astounding experience that happened a few nights after he had the "dream-vision" about Tuella and Ashtar. David said that while he and his wife were sleeping:

Suddenly, I woke up as Tuella (Ashtar was not with her this time.) physically materialized right by our bed. She was dressed in a very beautiful, iridescent space outfit and was holding the book <u>Ashtar</u> in her hand. A few days prior to this experience, I had bought the book which I had placed on the nightstand beside me. Now, the book was missing from my nightstand and Lady Tuella was holding it in her hand.

Then, she specifically referred to a page in this book about the Worldwide Evacuation, which, interestingly enough, my wife Crystal and I had tried to find earlier. When Tuella and Ashtar appeared in my "dream-vision," they had mentioned this particular information. I believe that her appearance holding the book was to verify, not only the significance of her appearance, but also to confirm the plan of the Evacuation. (This was also a very significant

confirmation and **verification** of the authenticity of her work as a very clear and gifted Channel for Ashtar and his Command while she was alive on Earth.) She specifically stated to me that the page we had been trying to find earlier was "page 57." After that, she dematerialized. So, I immediately looked up "page 57" in the book, and, sure enough, there was the specific reference to the up-coming Evacuation.

Wow! What an incredible confirmation that was! And, what wonderful insight this provides that verifies the reality of mass planetary Divine Intervention and Worldwide Evacuation, which prompts all of us to **"Prepare for the Land-ings!"**

EPILOGUE

When I started writing this book, I was not aware of how much information I had compiled over the years. After I discovered the amount of materials that I had accumulated, I decided to create <u>The Divine Blueprint Series</u>. This series consists of six books that contain critical information about the upcoming Divine Intervention, the vast cover-up of UFOs and extraterrestrial contact, and how Volunteers can prepare for the coming times.

The second book of this series, <u>The Cover-Up on Human-Appearing ETs,</u> will document the facts of the cover-up of UFOs and extraterrestrials. It will show how a majority of those within the "UFO community," within the last 30 to 40 years, acted, both directly and indirectly, to mislead the public. It was not a lack of evidence that led to this bias against the Truth, rather it was due to a hidden agenda. This "conspiracy of silence" and bias was perpetuated by numerous well-known UFO investigators, who have had ties with the cabal.

The reader will discover how much of the actual historical events of the decades of the '50's and early '60's were suppressed and how those who spoke the Truth about these matters were ridiculed and their information distorted. This misinformation led to "prejudice" against the authentic pioneers and famous contactees of the "flying saucer movement." It also created false impressions of the benevolent and highly-evolved (spiritually, as well as physically) human-appearing ETs.

Fortunately, in the last few years, there are researchers who have become more open within the UFO community and have started re-examining the events and materials which have led them to very different conclusions. The author has conducted very thorough and in-depth research about this topic and will use this book to "set the record straight. "Much of the information that is in this next book is based on quotes from numerous UFO sources, such as George Adamski; out-of-print publications; old archives; personal library data; and informants. These informants include individuals from this planet who are now "speaking out," as well as Higher Beings from "off the planet" who have continued to connect with Earthlings and have brought important messages to share.

Due to the "Consciousness Awakening" that is happening on the planet, there is more and more of the Truth surfacing. So, until all is revealed and the Earth experiences the coming Divine Intervention, individuals should prepare themselves as best as possible. And, until then, ***"Keep your eyes on the Skies!"***

BIBLIOGRAPHY

Adamski, George and Leslie Desmond. <u>Flying Saucers Have Landed</u>, New York: The British Book Center, 1954.

Adamski, George. <u>Inside The Spaceships</u>, Vista, CA: The George Adamski Foundation, 1955.

Air Force Cadet Manual, <u>Introductory Space Science</u>, Volume II, Physics 370, U.S. Air Force Academy, Colorado Springs, CO.

Billings, Kurt. "Valuable Updates on Mind Control/Microchip," in *Psych Ops Newsletter*.

Billings, Kurt. "Learn about infiltration of the U.S. Public School Curriculum and how it was written by the same Institute that trained the Nazi doctors," in *Psych Ops Newsletter*.

Billings, Kurt. "Prisoners of Psych Ops" (Video).

Billings, Kurt. "The Nazi Curriculum Connection" (Audio).

Buckle, Eileen. <u>The Scoriton Mystery</u>, London, England: Neville Spearman, 1967.

Byrd, Admiral Richard Evelyn. <u>A Flight To The Land Beyond The North Pole Or The Missing Secret Diary of Admiral Richard Evelyn Byrd</u>, December 24, 1956.

Cathie, Bruce. <u>The Bridge To Infiniti</u>, Auckland, New Zealand: Quark Enterprises/Brookfield Press, 1984.

Cayce, Edgar. <u>Modern Prophet</u>, New York, NY: Random House Value Publishing, 1990.

Hurtak, J. J. Ph.D., <u>The Book of knowledge: The Keys of Enoch</u>, Ava, MO: The Academy For Future Science, 2000-2007.

Mars, Tex. <u>Project L.U.C.I.D.: The Beast 666 Universal Human Control System,</u> Austin, TX: Living Truth Publishers, 1996.

Montgomery, Ruth. <u>Strangers Among Us</u>, NY: Putnam Publishing Group, 1982.

Montgomery, Ruth. <u>Aliens Among Us</u>, NY: Fawcett Crest Books, 1993.

Paulsen, Norman. <u>The Christ Consciousness, The Pure Self Within You</u> (Originally titled: <u>Sunburst: The Return of the Ancients</u>), Salt Lake City, Utah: The Builders Publishing Co., 1994.

Poole, Patrick S. "Echelon: Part One: The NSA's Global Spying Network" in *NEXUS Magazine*, Aug./Sept., 1999. Web page: www.nexusmagazine.com.

Poole, Patrick S. "Echelon: Part Two: The NSA's Global Spying Network" in *NEXUS Magazine*, Oct./Nov., 1999. Web page: www.nexusmagazine.com.

Stanford, Ray. "Contact With A Flying Saucer", in *Fate Magazine*, Lakeville, MN.

Steiger, Brad & Francie Steiger. Star People, NY: Berkley Publishing Group, 1981.

Steiger, Brad. "Are You Really From Krypton?" *East West Journal Magazine*, Feb.1979.

Steiger, Brad. "Flying Saucers from the Middle Earth." *East West Journal Magazine*, Feb.1979 issue.

Stevens, Lt. Col. Wendelle C. UFO: Contact From Angels in Starships, Tucson, AZ: UFO Photo Archives, 1990. (Originally published by Bill & Rhoda Sherwood, Rochester UFO Study Group, Rochester, NY.

Tuella, Lady. Project: World Evacuation By The Ashtar Command. Salt Lake City, Utah: Guardian Action International, 1988.

Tuella, Lady. On Earth Assignment. Salt Lake City, Utah: Guardian Action International, 1988.

Tuella, Lady. *"Universal Network"* Newsletter.

"The Day the Earth Stood Still" (motion picture). Released on Sept. 28, 1951.

Wales, Jim. "In and Out of Saucers" in *The Interplanetary News*, Nov. 1965.

Williamson, George Hunt (aka: Brother Philip). In Secret Places of the Lion, NY: Destiny Books, 1983.

Zinsstag, Lou. UFO...George Adamski, Their Man on Earth. Tucson, AZ: UFO Photo Archives, 1990.

Zinsstag, Lou & Timothy Good. George Adamski, The Untold Story, England: Ceti Publications, 1983.

PERMISSIONS

The author gratefully acknowledges permission to reprint from the following sources:

Stevens, Lt. Col. Wendelle C. UFO, Contact from Angels in Starships. Tucson, AZ: UFO Photo Archives, 1990.

Tuella, Lady. Project: World Evacuation by the Ashtar Command. Salt Lake City, Utah: Guardian Action International, Ninth Edition, 1988.

HIGHLY RECOMMENDED WEB SITES

Learn more empowering information -

ChannelFortheMasters.com
Information about Michael Ellegion, his background, and experiences as a Channel for the Spiritual Hierarchy and Intergalactic Confederation. Many beautiful images of some of the Higher Beings that Michael channels for his clients, in the personal Transformational Channeling sessions. Includes complete list of the "NASA Star People Characteristics." Check out how many of the Star People Characteristics you have! Visit the "Channeled Material Section" for past and recent Channelings. Find out about workshops and events. Email Michael for your in-person or telephone Reading from the Masters at VortexNetwork@hotmail.com.

HealthGalleria.com
Cutting-edge holistic health products and tools for health and rejuvenation, including gorgeous custom-designed Rainbow Crystal Pendants - Aurora Atlantean Chakra Crystals, for activation, protection, and empowerment; The Aculight - acupuncture with light; Chi Balls - for Chi massage; The Chi Machine - opens meridians; Ionic-Detox Foot Bath Device with blood purifier and auric field strengthener; Km by Matol Botanical - #1 herbal elixir in the world; and much more.

UFOwest.com
Michael Ellegion and Aurora Light's backgrounds as UFO lecturers and contactees for the benevolent human-appearing ETs, listing some of the media interviews they have done throughout the years.

AmusingMuse.net
Aurora Light is a Muse and Health Intuitive who teaches private rejuvenation, diet, and lifestyle changes in personal transformational health and well-being sessions.

PreparefortheLandings.com
Individuals may use this website for downloading E-Book versions of this book and for ordering paperback copies.

PRG Press Release Million Fax on Washington

The Million Fax on Washington was launched to motivate the American people to send a clear collective statement to President Obama that the people "CAN handle the truth" and "DO have a right to know." Straightforward instructions and additional information is available at: www.faxonwashington.org. For further updates, PRG Executive Director Stephen Bassett may be contacted at: www.paradigmresearchgroup.org.

Here is a form letter you can use to mail, fax, and email President Barack Obama. Stephen Bassett suggests using all three methods for the greater amount of communication and, therefore, the greater chance that Obama will quickly respond. We want to send him more than a million of these form letters, so he will End the Truth Embargo about the UFO and ET Cover-ups. It has also been suggested that in addition to signing your name, you include an e-mail address, phone number, and even a mailing address in case Obama or his staff wants to contact you.

You may also contact Barack Obama at his website: change.gov. To make it simple for you, please feel free to copy and paste all or parts of this form letter into the comment section of his website.

The Honorable Barack Obama
President of the United States
Washington, DC

Dear Sir,

It is with great joy for my friends and me that you have been elected our 44th President of the U.S. We know that your "Mantra" has been to CHANGE the way things have been done, not only for the last eight years, but perhaps much longer than that regarding the subject of this most important letter to you.

I will attempt to be quite brief and to the point--and that is, the UFO & Extraterrestrial cover-up has gone on way too long. We feel, as do millions of fellow U.S. citizens, both civilians as well as many within the U.S. military, and also literally billions of citizens of every other country on the face of this planet, that it is time to END THE TRUTH EMBARGO on one of the most important cover-ups of all time--the reality that UFOs & Extraterrestrials have been visiting Earth for many ages. There is plenty of documented evidence that more than verifies the Truth of their existence.

We believe that it is time for all the people to know the truth about the world they inhabit. Having maintained the Truth Embargo has cost a fortune, undermined the social contract, and led to abuses of secrecy and power. Until this Truth Embargo is ended, there will be no public access to technologies derived from ET technologies at a time of mounting economic and environmental challenges.

You told us numerous times during your campaign how you wanted us to feel that you would be far more open to the needs of the American people, and that you would also listen to our needs and concerns. The following are several suggestions that we feel should be done to end this Truth Embargo of the extraterrestrial presence:

> 1. We believe it is time for you to demand and receive a full briefing by the military services and intelligence agencies regarding the extraterrestrial presence and related phenomena,

2. We request that you openly announce and support convening congressional hearings to take testimony from scores of former military and agency employees regarding extraterrestrial phenomena,

3. We request that you formally acknowledge and disclose to the American people the Extraterrestrial presence,

4. And, finally, we request that you release to the public domain, extraterrestrial derived technologies, secretly studied and reverse engineered for six decades, which is now essential to overcome the environmental, economic, and social challenges of our time.

Evidence shows that millions of citizens (including myself) all around the world have had UFO sightings--and yes, even physical contact with extraterrestrials. We can more than handle the END OF THE TRUTH EMBARGO on the Extraterrestrial presence!

Sincerely

Made in the USA